THE YOUNG DARWIN AND HIS CULTURAL CIRCLE

STUDIES IN THE HISTORY
OF MODERN SCIENCE

Editors:

ROBERT S. COHEN, *Boston University*

ERWIN N. HIEBERT, *Harvard University*

EVERETT I. MENDELSOHN, *Harvard University*

VOLUME 2

EDWARD MANIER

Department of Philosophy, University of Notre Dame

THE YOUNG DARWIN
AND HIS CULTURAL CIRCLE

*A study of influences which helped shape the language and logic
of the first drafts of the theory of natural selection*

D. REIDEL PUBLISHING COMPANY

DORDRECHT-HOLLAND / BOSTON-U.S.A.

Library of Congress Cataloging in Publication Data

Manier, Edward.
　　　The young Darwin and his cultural circle.

　　　(Studies in the history of modern science; v. 2)
　　　Bibliography: p.
　　　Includes index.
　　　1. Darwin, Charles Robert, 1809–1882.　2.　Naturalists—Eng-
land—Biography.　I.　Title.　II.　Series.
QH31.D2M28　　　575′.0092′4 [B]　　　77–25311
ISBN 90–277–0856–8
ISBN 90–277–0857–6 pbk.

Published by D. Reidel Publishing Company,
P.O. Box 17, Dordrecht, Holland

Sold and distributed in the U.S.A., Canada, and Mexico
by D. Reidel Publishing Company, Inc.
Lincoln Building, 160 Old Derby Street, Hingham,
Mass. 02043, U.S.A.

for
Michael, David and Maureen

TABLE OF CONTENTS

PART II. DARWIN'S NOTEBOOKS, MANUSCRIPTS, AND MARGINALIA: 1837–1839

PART III. CONCLUSIONS

LIST OF TABLES AND ILLUSTRATIONS

ACKNOWLEDGMENTS

This work was supported by grants from the National Endowment for the Humanities and the University of Notre Dame. It was begun in 1971–1972 while my family and I enjoyed the hospitality of St. Edmund's House, Cambridge University, and of Norman and Leslie Lewis, Finchingfield, Essex. Many friends and colleagues have provided stimulating and generous assistance: Ernan McMullin, Mary Hesse, Sydney Smith, Robert Young, Peter Gautrey, Michael Ghiselin, Paul Barrett, Everett Mendelsohn, John Greene, William Wimsatt, Michael Ruse, Gary Gutting, David Solomon, and Reidel's anonymous reviewer. Anthony Murphy and Daniel Rochowiak contributed to the arguments of Chapters Two and Eight, respectively. I owe a particular debt to my son, David, for many long discussions of the perspective and the arguments of the whole book.

P. J. Lawler, Edward Martin, Tom Hazy, and John Manier assisted in the compilation of the material for Tables I through VI. Mrs. Norma Davitt and Mrs. Beth Gadberry typed and retyped the manuscript with intelligent patience and good humor. The completion of the manuscript has been greatly facilitated by my association with the Center for the Study of Man in Contemporary Society, University of Notre Dame. Maureen Manier helped me read proof and prepare the index.

The book could not have been completed if I had not been the beneficiary of the love and patience of my children: Michael, David, Maureen, Edward, Jr., John, Daniel, and Jeremy. I will not try to express in words my gratitude to Dorothy Hickey, my wife.

Such errors of fact and interpretation as remain in the book are my responsibility.

7 April 1977   E. M.

William Paley, 1789

Dugald Stewart, 1811

Sir James Mackintosh, d. 1832

William Wordsworth, 1842

Some of the members of the cultural circle
Reproduced by courtesy of the National Portrait Gallery, London

CHAPTER ONE

INTRODUCTION

This book is an analysis of part of an important episode in the history of science. It deals with a short period in the life of Charles Darwin: the years 1837–1844 when he struggled with the first drafts of his "species theory." The primary textual basis of my inquiry is provided by two sets of notebooks which he kept during the interval 1837–1839, and which deal with the "transmutation of species" and "metaphysics . . . morals and speculations on expression." The notebooks point to additional manuscript material and to Darwin's marginal annotations of a number of the books he read at this same time. This collection of primary documents reveals the circle of philosophical, literary, religious, political, and ethical authors whose works were read and analyzed by the young Darwin. I call this group of authors his cultural circle. My first goal is the description and analysis of the various positions concerning the methodology of science, the place of mind in nature, ethics and social philosophy, and natural religion professed by members of this circle. The next step is the reconstruction of the circle's influence upon the young Darwin's effort to formulate and justify related aspects of his own scientific practice. I pay particular attention to the dialectical development of Darwin's standards for scientific explanation and the scientific uses of language, especially in his employment of the metaphors associated with the words 'selection' and 'struggle.' I argue that neither Darwin's methodology nor the meaning of his theory can be understood outside the context of his views concerning the evolution of man and his higher powers, including his moral sense and his sense of religious awe.

Given the size of the so-called Darwin industry, it is surprising that it has provided no systematic analysis of the general methodological standards or criteria which affected the structure and expression of the *first* formulations of the species theory. Such studies have been undertaken by Allegard and Hull for the period *after* 1859.[1] However, the years 1837–1844 are equally important, since there were important shifts in the membership of Darwin's reference groups between 1844 and 1859. It is well known that *The Origin of Species*, published in 1859, was seen to conflict with established views concerning the nature of man and the nature of human values. It is less well known that between 1837 and 1844 Darwin gave considerable thought and energy to the problem of the management or reduction of that conflict. During this interval he was interested in identifying the philosophy at the core of his own position, and in (privately) confronting it with all the major alternatives with which he had significant contact and which he understood. The period 1837–1844, therefore, provides an important opportunity to examine Darwin's exploration of his theory's philosophical and cultural roots and implications.

It has been widely assumed that Darwin had few, if any, philosophical or metaphysical views.[2] He lived and wrote in a period when scientific activity was increasingly professionalized and specialized, and when these tendencies were reinforced within the tightly knit structure of the English scientific community. By 1859, and in his later years, his self-image as a scientist was increasingly influenced by positivist views which denigrated metaphysical speculation. He contributed to the commonly received picture which places him firmly outside the battle which raged and still rages over the significance of his theory for the general understanding of man's place in nature. He confessed to his children that he had become something of a machine for processing facts and arguments. However, during the crucial years when he worked intensively to formulate his views on the "species question," he also devoted considerable energy and critical acumen to the assessment of the broader cultural implications of that question and his answer to it. He spent increasingly little time with these topics after 1839, and it is unlikely that he ever succeeded in effectively synthesizing his judgments concerning them. Nevertheless, they had a central impact upon the language, form and content of the theory of natural selection.

In July 1838, one year after he began keeping his *Notebooks* "On Transmutation of Species," Darwin began a parallel set of two additional *Notebooks* (keep concurrently with the last two of the four *Transmutation Notebooks*) under the title of "expression" or "Metaphysics on Morals and Speculation on Expression."[3] He also wrote a number of short manuscripts on subjects very similar to those treated in what I will call the *Metaphysical Notebooks*. He stored a number of these together under the disarming title, "Old and Useless Notes about the moral sense and some metaphysical points. . . ." Still other manuscripts from the period 1837–1839 are to be found in the Cambridge University Library, as are many of the annotated books from Darwin's personal library.

These Notebooks, manuscripts, and the marginal annotations of his personal library provide a fascinating, exceptionally well-documented picture of Darwin's intellectual development during the period 1837–1839. This period set the stage for the so-called "Essay of 1844," a particularly full and careful exposition of the theory of the transmutation of species, which served as a model for *The Origin of Species*, published fifteen years later. During the earlier period, Darwin's exuberant, ambitious, multifaceted concern for the elaboration of his theory and all its implications was at a peak. The Notebooks, manuscripts and marginalia dating from this time are important because Darwin used them to elaborate a strategy for avoiding unnecessary public controversy over some of the more radical aspects of his position, e.g., his tendencies to materialism and determinism.[4] These early materials require a re-examination of the philosophical guise of the published work. They contain frank comments concerning religious, metaphysical and ethical subjects which did not meet Darwin's standards of public professional propriety, but which are essential for the accurate interpretation of his published work and much of his correspondence. The early stages of Darwin's authorship had a compelling effect upon the structure and the content of those which followed. The young Darwin was a powerfully original and creative scientist, sensitive to methodological, metaphysical and moral issues. He did not aim at philosophical standards of clarity, consistency and rigor, however, and when it was appropriate to exploit rhetorical skill for his purposes, he did so.

The tension between his sense of the pedagogical power that came with the discovery, verification, and publication of an original and comprehensive scientific theory, and his awareness of the increasingly positivist temper of mid-nineteenth-century science is graphically illustrated by his continued use of *metaphor* in the elaboration of his theory. In the published work, the status of metaphor was left ambiguous. He implied that metaphors were merely convenient and brief expressions which could be eliminated. But he never eliminated them and continued inventing new ones for use in his later publications. Each of his metaphors trailed clouds of ambiguity. 'Struggle' had three different meanings, which "graded into" each other, but which also could seem opposed. 'Selection' referred to a process far more discriminating and farseeing than any comparable human activity, and yet not really conscious or intelligent — and certainly not divine. In *The Origin*, he thought it incorrect to speak of chance as the cause of anything, such language merely cloaked our ignorance of the real causes. Yet he also rejected LaPlacean determinism and biological mechanism, arguing that 'chance' and 'accident' had a strict and legitimate meaning, referring to events as resulting from the intersection of two distinct, irreducibly independent lines of causality. Even the word 'law' retained a number of distinct and ambiguously related uses: (1) the positivist sense of invariable succession, (2) the more realist and rationalist sense of an *a priori* statement of possibilities, and (3) the more colloquial sense of a social rule, open to moral appraisal.

The succinct management of ambiguous themes can be the source, not of confusion and choas, but of real leverage in the process of scientific discovery; Unless the process of discovery is analogous to creation *ex nihilo*, a new theory will retain continuity with the old. But it may combine old and new themes with a freshness which courts the appearance of paradox. The figurative expressions used in Darwin's published work were more enthusiastically and less cautiously employed in the earliest drafts of his theory. The aim of this study is not to replace the resultant ambiguities with a simple, literal account. It is rather to locate Darwin's most inventive expressions in the context of his first cultural circle, those authors who influenced him and many of whom, in return, he hoped to influence.

R. M. Young, in one of a series of provocative essays dealing with the nineteenth century debate concerning man's place in nature, holds a similar view concerning Darwin's management of the ambiguities of his position.[5] Young emphasizes the contrast between Darwin's "anthropomorphic, voluntarist descriptions of natural selection," and the Cartesian ideal of mechanical explanation. The latter ideal required scientists to banish "purposes, intentions, and anthropomorphic expressions from scientific explanations," and to limit the basic vocabulary of science to terms referring to matter, motion, and number. Comparing Darwin's actual performance with such austere criteria, Young concludes that the central argument of *The Origin of Species* was really more effective in eliciting faith in the philosophical principle of the uniformity of nature than in providing an "acceptable mechanism for evolutionary change."[6] This view is less heretical than it first appears, since such mainstream figures as G. G. Simpson typically credit Darwin with establishing the *fact* of evolution, and reserve the clarification of the mechanism of natural selection for post-mendelian developments in mathematical population genetics.[7] Nevertheless, Young's conclusion is unnecessarily misleading.

Young does an admirable job of blurring the dubious distinction between Darwin's "strictly scientific" views and their rather colloquial expression in *The Origin*. It is true, as Young claims, that Darwin's persistent use of ordinary language and its attendant imagery insured that his theory would be seen as a statement on metaphysics and morals, as well as a piece of scientific explanation. One can go further, as Young does, and claim that the explanatory, metaphysical and moral implications of Darwin's metaphors were interdependent and inseparable. This blending of scientific and metaphysical concerns is manifest in the earliest drafts of the theory and in the *Transmutation* and

Metaphysical Notebooks. It is also evident in the overlapping references to be found in the two sets of notebooks.

However, Young's thesis that the metaphor of natural selection is literally equivalent to the principle of uniformity or continuity in nature is surely mistaken. It implies that Darwin failed to articulate a scientific concept of natural selection and that history should reserve that accolade for someone else. I cannot accept this latter implication. To avoid it, I undertake a more thorough analysis of Darwin's metaphorical expressions and his use of explanatory models. In the remainder of this chapter, I analyze the metaphors Darwin built around the words 'selection' and 'struggle,' his use of the notion of an insular economy as a scientific model, and his claim to have divided the exposition of his theory into two parts corresponding to what later authors have called the hypothetico-deductive model of scientific explanation.

1. THE METAPHOR OF NATURAL SELECTION

Darwin first noted the difficulties associated with the expression 'natural selection' in lines introduced into Chapter IV of the third edition of *The Origin of Species*. "Several writers have misapprehended or objected to the term Natural Selection."[8] His response left no doubt that he was adept in defense of his own rhetorical originality, but it raised other questions concerning the methodological structure of his argument. In the first instance, he adopted the positivist strategy for avoiding the personification of Nature.

I mean by Nature, only the aggregate action and product of many natural laws, and by laws the sequence of events as ascertained by us.

It was orthodox positivism to interpret 'nature' as an aggregate of laws understood as records of observed sequences of events. But Darwin also justified the expression 'natural selection' by allusions to "chemists speaking of the elective affinities of various elements," and "an author speaking of the attraction of gravity as ruling the movements of the planets." Contemporary positivists *rejected* these expressions as relics of a bygone "metaphysical stage" which should be surpassed by a more critical method.

There were graver difficulties associated with the hyperbolic personification of nature implicit in a passage from the fifth edition of *The Origin*.[9]

Man can act only on external and visible characters: Nature, if I may be allowed to personify the natural preservation or survival of the fittest, cares nothing for appearances, except insofar as they are useful to any being. She can act on every internal organ, on every shade of constitutional difference, on the whole machinery of life. Man selects only for his own good: Nature only for that of the being which she tends. Every selected character is fully exercised by her, as is implied by the fact of their selection.

This hyperbole was not first formulated in the fifth edition, but was a more explicit expression of a theme present in Chapter IV since its first publication in 1859: natural selection "silently and insensibly working, whenever and wherever opportunity offers, at the improvement of each organic being in relation to its organic and inorganic conditions of life."[10] This form of the metaphor implies that nature's powers of selection are so intricate and powerful that one can never be sure that a given organ does not have a selective value, since nature works in ways which may be "silent and insensible." Such expression *cannot* be defended by the canons of positivism, and it suggests a serious ambivalence in Darwin's views concerning the scientific uses of metaphor.

Earlier drafts of the theory do not alleviate this tension between positivism and anthropomorphism in the explication of 'nature.' To the contrary, the *Sketch of 1842* describes a selecting "being infinitely more sagacious than man (not an omniscient creator)" who would exert his selective power and foresight in the service of "certain ends" for thousands of years.[11] This deliberate and explicit personification of nature permitted references to "differences in the outer and innermost organization (of a living thing) quite imperceptible to man." Darwin's strong early interest in the "laws of corelation" had been temporarily stymied by his relatively rudimentary and anecdotal knowledge of embryology.[12] He needed a place-holding allusion which did not depend upon accurate scientific knowledge of the laws of embryology. The metaphor of the intelligent selector who perceived changes in "innermost" organization imperceptible to man, provided a measured dose of hyperbole and the required place-holder.

But this only sharpens the tension between Darwin's positivist and anthropomorphic references to 'selection.' The puzzle remains. Was Darwin's methodology consistent?

2. THE MODEL OF AN INSULAR ECONOMY AND THE STRUCTURE OF DARWIN'S ARGUMENT

The first volume of *Variation of Animals and Plants under Domestication* established Darwin's familiarity with the characterization of two broad phases or stages in the construction and validation of a scientific theory. These two stages are, first, an effort to render an hypothesis "probable" in relation to a range of things which we "positively know," and second, the testing of the hypothesis "by trying whether it explains several large and independent classes of facts."[13]

This same point is supported by the division of the *Essay of 1844* into two parts: Part I invoking the analogy of the production of domestic varieties by artificial selection and the circumstances leading to the production of wild varieties in order to establish the *possibility* of the theory, while Part II is said to examine "direct evidence in favour or against" the theory. Such texts suggest that Darwin employed what is now known as the hypothetico-deductive method.[14] However, my thesis is that these texts express a *mistaken self-image* less interesting and less cogent than his scientific practice in the earliest drafts of his theory.

The *Sketch of 1842* and the *Essay of 1844* each contained a long summary passage at the end of Part I. The two summaries exhibit substantial verbal similarities and their logical form is identical.[15] Each summary was cast in the form of a complex conditional proposition, an "If. . . , then. . . ." sentence within which a second major "If. . . , then. . . ." sentence was embedded, and which was in its turn comprised of the conjunction of four more conditions. The following symbolism is intended to enable the reader to visualize the form of the argument, and uses an arrow only to symbolize the colloquial English connective "If. . . , then. . . ."

$$(V \& H \& M \& U) \rightarrow [(S \& R \& A \& I) \rightarrow O]$$

The detail with which Darwin fleshed out this formalism may be expressed as follows (This expression involves some reconstruction, which the reader may want to check against Darwin's original language.)

IF: 1. Slight variations do occur in organic beings in a state of nature (V). And

2. Such variations tend to be hereditary (H). And

3.* Not all organisms leave fertile progeny (M). And

4. There is no law of nature limiting the possible amount of variation (U).

THEN:

IF: 5.* If there are any individuals with (unspecified) slight deviations of structure more favorable to the then existing conditions, and there is a natural means of selection tending to preserve them and tending to destroy any with deviations of an opposite nature (S) And

6.* If (unspecified) conditions prevail in some districts, and new races are formed in those districts (R). And

7.* If other (unspecified) conditions prevail, and these races are adapted in the most singular and admirable manner, to external nature and to other surrounding organisms (A). And

8.* If these races were of different constitutions (or if certain other (unspecified) conditions obtained), and were infertile one with another (I).

THEN:

9.   Such races would be species. (O)

The sentence (3*) 'Not all organisms leave fertile progeny,' is used in place of Darwin's own (3) 'Every organism maintains its place by an almost periodically recurrent struggle,' in order to provide for the separate consideration of the argument's literal content and its metaphorical amplification.[16] The sentences '5*,' '6*,' '7*,' and '8*,' are formed by replacing vague, place-holding references to "some few districts," etc., with an explicit indication that such conditions were left *unspecified*, and would require further illustration or investigation.

Given this schematic reconstruction of Darwin's summary of Part I, *the phenomena of the origin of species cannot be deduced from the premisses of Part I.* The reason is not the familiar point that it is impossible to predict the details of evolution. It is rather that Darwin did not present the premisses of Part I (dealing with variability, heredity, and the fact that some organisms do not leave fertile progeny) as implying a statement open either to verification or falsification. On the contrary, they implied a second extremely complex hypothesis, itself a conjunction of no fewer than four additional conditions necessary for the origin of species. Since each of these four propositions alluded to conditions left unspecified, the argument as a whole could not and can not be empirically tested until supplemented with additional detail. Moreover, *no* empirical evidence could count *against* the final thesis of Part I.

New races of being will — perhaps only rarely, and only in some few districts — be formed. Such races would be indistinguishable from species.

It is a logical commonplace that propositions of the form 'Some A is B.' cannot be empirically falsified. Consequently, the final thesis of Part I could not be refuted and so could not be subjected to effective debate, unless it were strengthened or modified in some way.

Darwin stopped short of the claim that "good reasons" had up to that point been advanced for believing that distinct species had descended from common parents.

I merely wish to show that the proposition is not so monstrous as it at first appears, and that if good reason can be advanced for believing the species have descended from common parents, the difficulty of imagining intermediate forms of structure (are) not sufficient to make one reject the theory.[17]

The reduction of a proposition's implausibility and the postponement of its rejection, although modest and even diffident as the stated goals of arguments as elaborate and detailed as those of Part I, are serious and important steps in a general strategy the first phase of which is to establish the "possibility" of the theory of descent.[18] The goals of Part I included showing that the theory of descent was "not so monstrous" as it first appeared (showing that the whole theory ought not to be rejected at once) and explaining how traits, e.g., instincts, apparently considered as counter-examples to the theory, could be acquired by natural selection. Both might be understood as part of a coherent effort to show that it was *possible* that the theory represented a naturally occurring process. How can such seemingly modest claims be appraised? How does one go about deciding whether an argument for the *possibility* of an empirical hypothesis is sound or not?

In the *Essay of 1844*, the third chapter of Part II dealt with the geographical distribution of organic beings in past and present times, and toward the end of the chapter, Darwin offered "an attempt to explain the foregoing laws of geographic distribution, on the theory of allied species having a common descent." He introduced that attempt by recalling "the circumstances most favourable for variation under domestication."[19] It is interesting, but hardly surprising, that this restatement exhibited decided changes in emphasis when compared with the explicit summary of Part I. First, there was greater emphasis upon the uniformitarian notion of a *persistent, gradual* change in the conditions of life, repeated through several generations. Second, *sexual reproduction* – as distinguished from asexual budding – was explicitly identified and emphasized as a crucial source of inter-generational variation. Finally, reference to the reproductive *isolation* of incipient varieties was clearly included among the premisses of the theory for the first time.

This chapter's "explanation" of the laws of geographical distribution rested heavily upon the particularly powerful model of an "insular economy."[20]

Let us now take the simplest natural case of an islet upheaved by the volcanic or subterranean forces in a deep sea, at such a distance from other lands that only a few organic beings at rare intervals were transported to it, whether borne by the sea (like the seeds of plants to coral reefs), or by hurricanes, or by floods, or on rafts, or in roots of large trees, or the germs of one plant or animal attached to or in the stomach of some other animal, or by the intervention (in most cases the most probable means) of other islands since sunk or destroyed.

This model provided a graphic illustration of the change from a "small mass of rock" to a diversified array of stations:

lowland and highland, moist woods and dry sandy spots, various soils, marshes, streams and pools: under water on the sea shore, instead of a rocky steeply shelfing coast, we shall have in some parts bays with mud, sandy beaches and rocky shoals. The formation of the island by itself must often slightly affect the surrounding climate.

This simplified the context for the description and analysis of the relations among organisms and groups of organisms. Since few other organisms would provide competition for the first arrivals on a rising island the new arrivals would enjoy increased access to "room" and "subsistence." After a few generations under new conditions, some species might obtain "an increase of food, or food of a more nourishing quality." Many of the variations which would occur would be of "no use to the plastic individuals," but occasionally some would allow an organism "better to fill up some office in the insular economy and to struggle against other species." The model of an "insular economy" functioned to structure and guide speculation concerning the different sorts of "check" or selection pressure which might limit the tendency to logarithmic growth of the island's new inhabitants.

The insular model directly resembled the single concrete instance whose discovery has always been identified as the turning point in Darwin's scientific development: the flora and fauna of the Galapagos Archipelago. It took on central significance as a result of his adoption of the geological view that most continents originated as separate islands which gradually increased in size. The geological history of Europe was characterized as a series of "oscillations of level," the continent rose and fell, dividing into islands preventing free immigration, then rising again — providing new stations and opportunities for out-migration, limited by "barriers, the means of transportal, and the pre-occupation of the land by other species." The geological history of any of the earth's five major land masses was seen as embodying the central theses of continuous change repeated over a long series of generations and effective geographical isolation of new forms under set conditions, providing "steady selection. . .with a fixed end in view." The biological theses concerning variation, heritability, and the checks to population growth were corelated with a geological model of continent formation for the first time in this chapter. The result was a complex biological-geological *model* which complemented and implemented the *metaphor* of the selector 'infinitely more sagacious than man.' The model did not fill in all the missing details about the nature of specific checks to population growth, but it did provide a map for the investigation of the effects of changes in the physical and biological conditions of life upon incipient varieties of organisms.

The Part II model of an insular economy took Darwin's argument beyond the stage of the myth or allegory of the "being infinitely more sagacious than man" to be found in Part I. However, the logical role of the arguments of Part II cannot be distinguished from that of the arguments of Part I in the way that Darwin claimed. In each case the arguments tended to establish the *possibility* of the theory, but in neither case did they decisively *test* it. Neither in Part I nor in Part II were the premises of the argument cast in law-like form. Those which are at odds with each other, e.g.,

An island would be a far more fertile source of new specific forms than a continent.

and

There is no necessity of modification in a species when it reaches a new and isolated country. It might retain its old form for an indefinite time.

were not supplemented with the explicit boundary conditions necessary if their use were not to appear arbitrary and *ad hoc*. Part II introduced generalizations from biogeography and geology which helped to organize and specify the Part I hypothesis for the investigation of an impressive range of "independent classes of facts," but its logical role cannot be further distinguished from that of Part I.

Darwin failed to provide for distinct uses for the key logical terms 'necessarily follow,' 'must have been the case by our theory,' 'might *a priori* have expected,' 'throw light upon,' and 'instead of being metaphorical becomes plain.' Instead of sharply discriminating the logical relationships suggested by these terms, Darwin employed them in ways and in contexts which were effectively indistinguishable.[21] This failure gave his representation of the theory a logical fuzziness which confused his effort to distinguish positive evidence "for and against the theory." The theory retained sufficient ambiguity, in Part II, so as to seem compatible with almost any evidence. Darwin employed the rhetoric of falsifiability, but never formulated the relation between his hypothesis and any bit of evidence in a way which put the former convincingly at risk.

However, it would be going much too far to say that Darwin's claim to have *explained* a large and independent class of facts came to nothing as a result of this confusion in his logical vocabulary. Part II extended the range of cogent illustrations of the Part I hypothesis in an impressive and suggestive fashion. As already has been noted, the arguments by which this extension was accomplished were basically identical in logical form to those of Part I. Part II dramatically increased the reader's sense of the empirical possibility of Darwin's hypothesis. But Darwin claimed to have subjected his theory to a definitive test. This methodological goal motivated his use of a logical vocabulary which he had not mastered. We may find the reasons for this in his interaction with his cultural circle in the years preceding 1844.

3. 'THE STRUGGLE FOR EXISTENCE'

After 1856, Darwin's comments concerning the metaphorical sense of the expression 'struggle for existence' were relatively straightforward. Robert Stauffer's discussion of the uses of the expression in the "big species book" is particularly useful.[22] Stauffer points out that in the original draft of the relevant section of that book, Darwin used the title 'War of Nature' rather than 'Struggle of Nature,' and that he chose Hobbes' 'all nature is a war' as his topic sentence. He considered but set aside Lyell's phrase, 'equilibrium in the number of species,' although he regarded it as "more correct," because he thought it expressed "far too much quiescence." The choice of 'struggle,' therefore, was a deliberate selection of a term whose meaning or meanings were intermediate between those of 'war' and 'equilibrium.' In the "big species book," Darwin stipulated that three "ideas primarily distinct but graduating into each other," were designated by the term 'struggle.' These ideas were

(1) "The dependency of one organic being on another . . . .
(2) the agency whether organic or inorganic of what may be called chance, as in the dispersal of seeds and eggs . . . ,
(3) what may be more strictly called a struggle, whether voluntary as in animals or involuntary as in plants."[23]

The key passage from the first edition of *The Origin* distinguished three senses of 'struggle' which reflect what may be "truly," "less properly," or only in a "far-fetched" sense be designated as a struggle.[24] Its scheme for the interpretation of the metaphor of 'struggle' is similar to that formulated in the "big species book," and it deserves very close analysis.

First, two organisms are "truly" said to struggle if there is some limited resource which each must utilize or suffer a reduction in life expectancy or a reduction in the number of fertile progeny left for the next generation. Imagine "two canine animals in a time of dearth" struggling to determine "which shall get food and live." The notion of "success in leaving progeny" was also explicitly associated with this first of the three meanings. Secondly, an organism is less properly said to struggle against some environmental factor (e.g., drought) if the agency of that factor may reduce either the life expectancy of the organism or the number of fertile progeny produced by the organism. Darwin thought it would be more proper to say that the organism was *dependent* upon a contrary environmental factor (e.g., moisture). The third notion is expressed when two organisms are said to struggle (albeit in a "far-fetched" sense) when the conditions of the (first) strict sense are combined with the rider that if either of the organisms monopolizes the scarce resource so as to reduce the other's life expectancy or the quantity of its fertile progeny past a critical level, it suffers a corresponding reduction in its own life expectancy or the number of its fertile progeny. In this sense, 'struggle' characterizes parasite-host (mistletoe-apple tree) and predator-prey relationships. Both the second and the third senses of 'struggle' outlined in *The Origin* correspond to the notion earlier expressed by 'dependence,' with the second referring to an organism's dependence upon the non-organic aspects of its environment (moisture, temperature) and the third to relationships of inter-dependence among various types of organisms — paradigmatically, parasites and their hosts or predators and their prey.

Later chapters explore the reasons for Darwin's choice of 'struggle' to represent the inter-connection of the three concepts of conflict, biological dependence, and chance. It should be noted at this point, however, that he did not state (and there is no reason to think) that the three meanings were opposed or contradictory. He said that the three senses "pass" or "graduate" into each other, and it is necessary to consider the possibility that each meaning influenced his understanding of the other two. The domain of events referred to by the terms 'war' or 'conflict,' for example, may be significantly redescribed if the same term ('struggle') is used to designate it and two other domains (those more commonly designed by 'dependence' and 'chance') as well. The result is not the expression of "too much quiescence," but rather an elaborate qualification of the "strict meaning" of 'struggle' within the context of Darwin's theory. Darwin's use of this metaphor may have been poetic as well as scientific. He was willing to risk the ambiguity resulting from the inter-connection of a variety of related but distinct meanings in a single, compressed metaphoric representation.

'Struggle for existence' may have had a great impact upon ethical and political thought, and even upon practical affairs, than any comparably succinct expression in the history of science.[25] Most contemporary students of Darwin think his use of the expression was unnecessary or mistaken. For example, G. G. Simpson flatly states that the "word 'struggle' led to most serious misunderstanding of the process of natural selection," since natural selection is "a peaceful process in which the concept of struggle is really irrelevant."[26] J. A. Rogers employs a distinction of "purely biological meaning" and "social context" to argue that Darwin's theory contained "unnecessary concepts derived from the theories of human population of Malthus and Spencer."[27] Rogers' distinction of biological meaning and social context begs the question this book explores.

4. DARWIN'S CULTURAL CIRCLE: 1837–1839

Historians of science may still be skeptical of the claim that Charles Darwin's philosophical reading significantly influenced his scientific activities. His autobiographical allusions to "metaphysical books" were typically diffident, implying that he read them only because he was "not able to work all day at science."[28] His moral and political sensibilities could be aroused on such highly charged subjects as slavery and war, and we know that he followed the reform of the franchise with some interest while on the *Beagle* voyage. Yet there is nothing in the early manuscripts to indicate that he took politics seriously. For all his interest in Malthus, there was no hint of his reaction to the Poor Law Amendment, the Corn Laws, nor even to the social conditions leading up to the "hungry 'forties." His published remarks on such philosophical topics as determinism and design were evasive and ambivalent.

Nevertheless, his background reading in philosophy, at least until 1839, was relatively full and varied. Although he did not undertake this reading with cautious attention to the details of philosophical systems, his reactions to the philosophical doctrines he encountered provide a fresh and important perspective from which to interpret his comments concerning the adequacy and the significance of the theory of the transmutation of species. In general, he aimed at a comprehensive understanding of his developing conviction that man had evolved from a non-human primate ancestor. He sought to elaborate the thesis that man's special or distinctive attributes (from the expression of emotion to the religious sense of the sublime and the moral sense) arose by insensible gradations from simpler traits to be found in animals (and even plants).

His interest was often expressed by elliptical allusions to the remarks of less well known contemporaries. Many of his comments indicated a continuing vacillation on issues (such as the meaning of 'law' or of 'causality') remarkably close to the core of his methodological self-image. The presence of ellipses and of vacillation in such texts poses a particular problem for the historian. I cannot accept the inference that since Darwin's expressions on these matters were ambiguous, they were unimportant and extraneous to his central scientific projects. Nor do I presume that such ambiguity *must* (or can) be resolved. Ellipsis and vacillation in the expression of the cultural significance of scientific work may be symptomatic of a deeper cultural or social tension, which should first be described and understood.

Darwin's intellectual community was not comprised of geologists and natural historians alone. Nor was the structure of this community complicated by the merely occasional appearance of a figure such as Malthus, who — although he wrote political economy — aimed to insist upon the biological limits of his own discipline. Darwin knew that his interpretation of such terms as 'law,' 'explain,' 'continuity,' and 'consciousness' would both effect and be affected by "metaphysical" beliefs (both his own and those of his community) concerning materialism, theism, and the nature of morality — or, to put it most broadly, concerning man's place in nature. No single philosophical system dominated discussion of these issues in Darwin's intellectual circle in the thirties and early forties. It was a time of flux and of undigested eclecticism — a time when old notions concerning God and human responsibility were being subjected to fundamental criticism and reformulation. It is impossible to develop an accurate account of Darwin's self-image as an inquiring scientist unless one understands that his self-image changed and developed as a result of the changing social role of science and of a changing philosophical understanding of the nature of scientific discourse. Darwin's *understanding of his own role* and of the *basic meaning of his theory* were, in part, *functions of the influence* exerted by key members of his cultural circle.

Even a casual inspection of the list of individuals or groups mentioned five or more times in Darwin's Notebooks and early manuscripts indicates a pervasive and fundamental concern for the interaction of his new theory with alternative competing concepts developed in widely differing fields. The most important aspect of his awareness of these distinct approaches was his explicit examination of their implications for and within diverse philosophical perspectives, including those of David Hume, Dugald Stewart, August Comte, William Whewell, J. F. W. Herschel, Sir James Mackintosh, David Hartley,

Harriet Martineau, and Benjamin Smart. The range of philosophical options in epistemology, metaphysics, and morals represented by this group was so extensive and so disparate that it nearly overwhelmed his synthetic and critical abilities. The almost unmanageable ambiguity of his scientific language can be traced to the fact that he was the captive of no single school of philosophy or scientific methodology. If Comte made him appropriately suspicious that the so-called "theory of chances" might only be a cover for ignorance, Malthus and Quetelet demonstrated the utility of statistical analysis for the interpretation of demographic and social phenomena, and Paley provided an Aristotelian model for integrating the concepts of chance and teleological order.

The manner in which he represented his theory was remarkably effective and the *representation* of the theory — metaphors, allegories, and all — was a crucial and absolutely central aspect of Darwin's *scientific* accomplishment. Such notable historians as C. C. Gillispie are wrong in dismissing that representation as unnecessary baggage cluttering a simple scientific thesis. Darwin's *representation* of his theory is the key to its scientific and its cultural interpretation.

In all, he cited or mentioned 450 individuals in his *Notebooks* and early manuscripts. Of these, only 10 percent, exactly 45 individuals, were mentioned more than five times. J. F. W. Herschel was mentioned only four times, but since Darwin's autobiographical memoir identified Herschel's *Preliminary Discourse* as one of two books having the greatest influence on him (the other was von Humboldt's *Personal Narrative*), he seems to qualify as an honorary lifetime member.[29] Similar status should be accorded to William Paley, mentioned only twice in these materials, but like Herschel, so thoroughly assimilated in Darwin's undergraduate days that Darwin often employed the patterns of speech, the argumentative structures, and the basic concepts of both men as if they were his own. Other infrequently cited individuals who will be treated in this book as members of Darwin's cultural circle include the poet William Wordsworth, whose long *Excursion* Darwin boasted he had read twice through during the two years of his life under special consideration here.[30] Benjamin Smart, a relatively obscure author and elocution teacher, of whom Darwin said that his *New School of Metaphysics* had given his views on language *exactly*, receives relatively full discussion. One of the earliest English Hegelians, James Ferrier, is included because it is apparent that Darwin did *not* understand the central thesis of his articles on the philosophy of consciousness when they appeared in *Blackwood's Magazine*.

The Scottish zoologists John Barclay and John Fleming are discussed

together with the successful physician-author John Abercrombie, because of
their importance for locating Darwin in the context of the controversies
concerning mechanism and vitalism in the philosophy of zoology during the
1820's. Abercrombie's book is one of the most heavily annotated in Darwin's
personal library, and Abercrombie served as a foil for the development of
Darwin's views on materialism and determinism. Darwin's marginal annotations of Sir James Mackintosh's *History of Ethics* and William Whewell's three
volume *The History of the Inductive Sciences* are also important.

Darwin referred to "my father" 39 times in all, citing Dr. Robert W.
Darwin's opinions most frequently (35 times) in the *Metaphysical Notebooks*
and *Manuscripts*. His cousin William Darwin Fox introduced him to the joys
of bug-collecting. His brother-in-law, Hensleigh Wedgwood, deserves even
fuller analysis than he receives in this book as a member of Darwin's cultural
circle. It is likely that Darwin read Mackintosh's history of ethics at Hensleigh
Wedgwood's suggestion, for Mackintosh was the latter's father-in-law, and
Charles Darwin had met Mackintosh before the latter's death in 1832, at
Maer, the Wedgwood estate. Later mention is made of a paper included with
the Darwin manuscripts, but which I believe to have been written by Hensleigh
Wedgwood and then annotated by Charles Darwin. The identification of
Hensleigh Wedgwood as the second member of that unique manuscript
dialogue is based upon a careful comparison of the two styles of handwriting
which occur in the manuscript, and upon the philosophical position taken by
the party to the dialogue whose views were written down by a hand clearly
not that of Charles Darwin himself. The dualistic views taken by the second
party to the dialogue were repeated in Hensleigh Wedgwood's *On the Development of the Understanding.*[31]

In these Notebooks and early manuscripts Darwin mentions the views of
his sister Caroline, his brother Erasmus, his grandfather Erasmus, and his wife
Emma, at least 19 separate times. Comments about the Darwin children
might also be added to the list. The Darwin-Wedgwood family circle would
provide an interesting study in domestic dialectic: the skeptical materialism
of Darwin's brother, father, and grandfather, confronting the orthodox piety
of his wife and the strongly argued metaphysical dualism of *her* brother.

If all the individuals who are mentioned or cited in Darwin's Notebooks
and early manuscripts are counted as members of his cognitive circle for the
time in question, then 10 percent of their number account for 650 of a total
of 1389 references (or 47 percent of the total number). As Table II indicates,
at least 33 percent of the members of this smaller group were neither biologists nor geologists; and 13 percent of them were identified by the *DNB* or

the *Encyclopedia Britannica* as philosophers. Twenty-nine percent of the smaller, more influential group were not British. France, Germany, Switzerland, the Scandinavian countries and the United States provided these members.

TABLE I

The Most Frequently Cited Authors in Darwin's Notebooks and Early Manuscripts*

		Dates of birth & death	Field	No. of total citations	"OUN," "M"&"N"
1.	Charles Lyell	1797–1875	Geologist	42	3
2.	Robert Darwin	1766–1848	Physician	39	35
3.	William Yarrell	1784–1856	Zoologist	36	2
4.	Richard Owen	1804–1892	Naturalist	34	0
5.	John Gould	1804–1881	Ornithologist	28	0
6.	J.-B. de M. Lamarck	1744–1829	Biologist	27	5
7.	Andrew Smith	1797–1872	Army physician (zoologist)	27	2
8.	William S. McLeay	1792–1865	Zoologist	26	0
9.	William Darwin Fox		Amateur entomologist	24	0
10.	John Hunter	1728–1793	Anatomist & surgeon	22	0
11.	Darwin Family			19	
12.	Thomas C. Eyton	1809–1880	Naturalist	17	2
13.	Sir James Mackintosh	1765–1832	Barrister	16	16
14.	William Herbert	1778–1846	Dean of Manchester (botanist)	16	0
15.	John S. Henslow	1796–1861	Botanist	14	0
16.	William Whewell	1794–1866	Master of Trinity (philosopher)	13	3
17.	Edward Blyth	1810–1873	Zoologist	13	0
18.	George Cuvier	1769–1832	Zoologist	11	0
19.	John Bachman	1790–1874	Naturalist (U.S.)	11	0
20.	Robert Brown	1778–1858	Botanist	11	0
21.	John MacCulloch, M.D.	1773–1835	Geologist (Natural theology)	11	11
22.	Lord Henry Moreton	1802–1853	Breeder of shorthorns	10	0
23.	Thomas R. Malthus	1766–1834	Political economist	10	5
24.	David Hume	1711–1776	Philosopher	9	7
25.	Thomas I. Mitchell	1792–1855	Explorer (Australia)	9	0
26.	Herbert Mayo	1796–1852	Physiologist	9	7
27.	Baron L. von Buch	1774–1853	Geologist, geographer	9	0
28.	H. H. Beck	1799–1863	Geologist	9	0

29.	John S. Sebright	1767–1846	Agriculturist (breeder)	9	1
30.	Hensleigh Wedgwood	1803–1891	Philologist	9	4
31.	August Comte	1798–1857	Philosopher (sociologist)	8	5
32.	Augustin de Candolle	1778–1841	Botanist	8	1
33.	C. J. Temminck	1778–1858	Zoologist	8	0
34.	Alcide d'Orbigny	1802–1857	Micropaleontologist	8	0
35.	David Don	1804–1841	Botanist	8	0
36.	C. G. Ehrenberg	1795–1876	Micropaleontologist	8	0
37.	John Fleming, D.D.	1785–1857	Naturalist	8	0
38.	Alexander v. Humboldt	1769–1859	Explorer	8	0
39.	Carl von Linne	1707–1778	Botanist, taxonomist	6	1
40.	Thomas Bell	1792–1880	Surgeon, zoologist	6	0
41.	David Hartley	1705–1757	Philosopher	6	6
42.	Sir Walter Scott	1771–1832	Novelist, poet	6	5
43.	Dugald Stewart	1753–1828	Philosopher	6	6
44.	Charles Bell	1774–1842	Surgeon, neurophysiologist	5	1
45.	J. K. Lavater	1741–1801	Physiognomist	5	5
46.	Joshua Reynolds	1723–1792	Portrait painter	5	5

* Based on the index of Darwin's notebooks "B," "C," "D," "E," "M," "N," the "Old and Useless Notes on Metaphysics" prepared by Paul Barrett, Michigan State University.

TABLE II

Disciplines Represented in Table I

Discipline	Sub-discipline	No. of individuals
Biology		24
	Botany	(6)
	Zoology	(4)
	Medicine	(5)
	Natural History	(1)
	Physiology	(5)
	Ornithology	(1)
	Entomology	(1)
Geology		6
	Paleontology	(2)
Philosophy		6
Explorer		2
Agriculture		2
Political Economy		1
Philology		1
Novelist-poet		1
Physiognomy		1
Painting		1
Total		45

TABLE III

Darwin's Cultural Circle (1837–1839)

| | No. of Citations | | | |
	Total	M & N	Author of book owned by C.D.	Cited in C.D.'s Autobiography
Charles Lyell	42	3	yes	yes
J.-B. de M. Lamarck	27	5	yes	yes
James Mackintosh	16	16	yes	yes
William Whewell	13	3	yes	yes
Thomas Malthus	10	5	yes	yes
Hensleigh Wedgwood	9	4	yes	yes
David Hume	9	7	no	no
August Comte	8	5	no	no
John Fleming	8	0	yes	no
Dugald Stewart	6	6	no	no
J. F. W. Herschel	4	2	yes	yes
William Abercrombie	3	0	yes	no
William Lawrence	2	0	yes	no
William Paley	2	2	no	yes
William Wordsworth	2	2	no	yes
John Barclay	1	0	yes	no
Benjamin Smart	1	1	no	no
James F. Ferrier	0	0	no	no

PART I

DARWIN'S CULTURAL CIRCLE: 1837–1839

CHAPTER TWO

CHARLES LYELL AND THE TRANSMUTATION OF THE EARTH

In order to justify my use of the term 'cultural circle,' I must deal with the awesome question, "What is culture and what part does science play in it?" In this book, I use the term 'culture' in a sense which gives priority to the cultural problems posed by science. I categorize these problems under four separate headings: method, "materialism," ethics, and the tension between the sacred and the secular. The first heading (*method*), collects those questions which have to do with the nature of science itself. What is a scientific law? What are the criteria of adequate scientific explanation? What are the canons of linguistic propriety in science? What sets the boundary between science and the remainder of life's personal and social experience?

"Materialism" has to do with such questions as whether or not man is free, and whether or not every one of his activities can be regarded as a determined function of his body. Darwin's theory directly addressed the question of man's natural origin, and led him to the materialistic thesis that "the brain secretes thought as liver secretes bile." He was also concerned to test the implications of his theory for the moral standards to be used in the appraisal of various forms of human society and individual human acts, and he speculated about the epitomization of these standards in accounts of what man finds beautiful, awe-inspiring, and sacred. The answer to the question, "Did Darwin take philosophical questions seriously?" is that he took his *theory* very seriously, and that — as a *young* man — he was concerned to probe *all* its implications and deal with *all* the difficulties it raised. He had, we might say, a serious philosophical interest in *one* scientific theory.

1. LYELL AND DARWIN: FRIENDS AND COLLEAGUES

Lyell and Darwin were in continuing conversation concerning on-going research; they exchanged scientific materials prior to their publication; and they belonged to the same professional societies (The Royal Geological Society) and social clubs (the Athenaeum). In the *Autobiography*, Darwin repeatedly refers to Lyell as his friend and identifies him as the individual with whom he was in closest communication concerning his scientific work.[1] As we will see, the influence (or exchange) between the two men included matters of scientific detail and substance as well as important points under at least three of the four headings I have identified as important in the constitution of Darwin's cultural circle. The influence on issues related to scientific method, "materialism," and the tension between the sacred and the secular will, I think, be obvious. Lyell's views had few, if any, direct implications for ethics, but he and Darwin were in general agreement concerning the ethics proper to scientific research itself.[2]

On Henslow's advice, Darwin took the first volume of the 1830 edition of the *Principles* with him when he left on the *Beagle*, and he enthusiastically received the remaining volumes when they were mailed to him during his long voyage.[3] *The Principles of Geology* set a model for scientific investigation and exposition in a field nearly indistinguishable from Darwin's own. Its explanation of the gradual transformation of the surface of the earth provided one of the most important theses embedded in Darwin's account of the transmutation of species. Its discussions of the age of the earth and the law-like processes leading to the extinction of species determined Darwin's question: ←
What laws determine the appearance of new species? In the early editions of the *Principles*, Lyell *asked* this question, but did not answer it. Darwin insisted upon the most general possible answer from the start, an answer which *denied* two of Lyell's most strongly held views:

(1)   Organic species really exist in nature and although their individual members may vary from the specific type, there is a natural limit to such variability which prevents the transmutation of one species into another.

(2)   Human nature uniquely occupies a moral realm completely distinct and separate from the law bound realm of physical nature. Man cannot be seen as the last in a progressive series of increasingly complex organic forms; reason and morality as found in man transcend anything to be found in lower forms.

Darwin read over the text of the *Elements of Geology* before its publication in 1838, and there are numerous references to Lyell's published and unpublished opinions throughout the *Transmutation Notebooks*.[4] Darwin thought the science of geology more indebted to Lyell than "to any other man who ever lived," and he was convinced "of the infinite superiority of Lyell's (geological) views over those advocated in any other work known to me."[5] Lyell took a strong critical role in their conversations: "He would advance all possible objections to my suggestion, and even after these were exhausted would long remain dubious." But the older man was heartily sympathetic to the scientific work of others, and his "delight in science was ardent." He religious views were so thoroughly liberal that Darwin was not

Portrait of Charles Lyell, c. 1853
Reproduced by courtesy of the National Portrait Gallery, London

sure whether they should be called beliefs or disbeliefs, but his basic theistic convictions were strong and apparently unwavering. His great foible, in Darwin's eyes, was a tendency to over-estimate the significance of his social rank.

The *Notebook* references to Lyell's opinion offer more information about the points where the two were in *agreement*, and only three are critical or negative in substance. In the earliest pages of *Notebook B* (1837), Darwin utilized Lyell's views concerning the transport of living specimens to oceanic islands to sketch the possibilities thus provided for transmutation of species.

"If species (1) may be derived from form (2) etc., – then (remembering Lyell's arguments of transportal) island near continents might have some species same as nearest land, which were late arrivals, others old ones (of which none of same kind had in interval arrived) might have grown altered. Hence the type would be of the continent, though species all different" (*B*, pp. 10, 11).

Equally important were Lyell's "profound views" concerning the effect of geological change on the earth's climate and on the forms of life supported in different regions at different times.

"Whole world formerly possessed a climate compared to S. America at present days, which S. America now does to North America & Europe. – S. America favourable to Tropical productions. The world formerly much more so, yet climate of same order as that of S. America. – (explained by profound views of Lyell)." (*Notebook E*, pp. 37–38).

The difficulties confronted by Lyell's effort to establish a theory of gradual geological change and Darwin's to explain the transmutation of species were broadly comparable. In each case, the incompleteness of the historical record played an important role, and Darwin cited the famous metaphor of "missing pages":

Lyell's excellent view of geology of each formation being merely a page torn out of a history & the geologist being obliged to fill up the gaps, – is possibly the same with the philosopher who has traced the structure of animals & plants." (*D*, p. 60).

The two theories were likely to prove comparably offensive to established positions in physico-theology (*C* 74), and Darwin welcomed an alliance with Lyell in the effort to overcome the "opposition of divines to (the) progress of knowledge" (*Ne* 19). The *Notebooks* never directly addressed their crucial differences concerning the natural development of human reason. Even at this early stage in his career, Darwin held that every human mental faculty originated from some comparable non-human form, and Lyell just as clearly and emphatically denied this. On this crucial point, Darwin mentioned only the one matter on which they could agree: that man was *not* an intruder in nature; or in Darwin's slightly biased phrase, "Man acts & is acted on by the organic and inorganic agents of this earth like every other animal" (*E* 65).

Darwin did admit to himself that "Lyell's *Principles* must be abstracted and answered" (*C* 39), and he was momentarily troubled about a possible sophism in his friend's claim that some species displayed a greater amount of intra-specific variation than that which distinguishes other species (*C* 53, and *B* 170). However, the *Notebooks* record only one direct and specific challenge to Lyell's opinions. Darwin disagreed with Lyell over the extent and nature of the variability to be observed in domestic species. From the close similarity of animal forms mummified 3000 years ago by the Egyptians and those of present times, Lyell had argued that the variability of such forms must be quite limited. Darwin replied that such domestic forms would have been maintained under unusually uniform and well-protected conditions throughout the years, and that the example was not adequate to sustain the point.

Lonsdale is ready to admit permanent small alterations in wild animals & thinks Lyell has overlooked argument that domesticated animals change a little with external influence, & if those changes permanent so would the change in animal be permanent. – It will be easy to prove persistent varieties in wild animals, but how to show species. – I fear argument must rest upon analogy & absence of variates in a wild state – it may be said argument will explain very close species in isld near continent, must we resort to quite different origin when species rather further. – Once grant good species as carrion crow & rook formed by descent or two of the willow wrens &c &c analogy will necessarily explain the rest (*C*, pp. 176–77).

2. LYELL'S LANGUAGE AND THE CULTURAL TENSION INDUCED BY HIS THEORY.

Susan Gliserman (1975), has provided a compelling account of "the exchange of affective meaning" from science to literature in the early Victorian period. Her use of the techniques of psychobiography was sensitive to the rhetorical strategies and emotional persuasions used by science writers (Peter Mark Roget, William Whewell and Charles Lyell), and poets (Tennyson's *In Memoriam*), alike. She concluded that the literary structure of the science writing she examined (including Lyell's *Principles*), was "no different" from poetry in attempting to "recreate and manage the affective, psychological ambivalences and conflicts" science posed for culture. Her foil was Paley's relatively haphazard citation, in his *Natural Theology* (1802), of isolated "contrivances" to be found in the human body and in other organic forms. Paley's theistic convictions neither utilized nor were threatened by interest in systematic and coherent scientific explanation. The God whose existence his arguments established was an impersonal abstraction, incapable of *caring* directly for each individual creature.

Roget's relatively robust fidelity to detailed accuracy in description and consistent generality in explanation led him to describe the organic world as a complicated network:

If for the sake of illustration, we must employ a metaphor, the natural distribution of animals would appear to be represented, not by a chain but by a complicated net-work where several parallel series are joined by transverse and oblique lines of connexion.[6]

However, Gliserman emphasized two aspects of Roget's physico-theology which, in her opinion, placed its language in the most stark contrast with Paley's cool formulas. On the one hand, Roget emphasized "the supportive connections in a feminized environment rather than in a personal relationship with a masculine, father God." 'Nature' was given a personified, feminine use which implied a "closely woven fabric of caring and trust." On the other hand, Roget insisted "on the 'chasm' between man and his identity with the lesser animals who die," arguing that there was no direct connection between matter and mind and that "disclaiming any close alliance with inferior creatures, he (man) proudly stands alone, towering far above them all."[7]

Psychological analysis does less justice to the philosophical subtleties involved in Whewell's *Bridgewater Treatise*.[8] It is not *quite* fair, for example, to state both that "Whewell denies the possibility of logical proof," and that he "prove(s) the existence and care of God in the fact that his choices produced an environment in which man can live."[9] Nevertheless, Gliserman's approach throws light on the critical reaction to Whewell by influential members of the scientific community. David Brewster (1834), for example, thought the opinions expressed in *Astronomy and General Physics considered with reference to Natural Theology* "injurious – they lead to idle speculation. They found our Natural Theology on a basis of small considerations...The Engineer who should erect a buttress to Mont Blanc would terrify the inhabitants of Chamouni."[10] Brewster reminded his readers that natural theology was thought to deal with "unimpeachable proofs of design in created things." Whewell's assimilation of every bit of scientific information to natural theology would make the latter discipline as subject to historical criticism as science itself.

Mr. Whewell...calls upon us to praise God for the complex and refined contrivance of a *luminiferous ether*, and assures us that if the world had no ether, all must be inert and dead!' we cannot avoid asking that what will be the fate of the Natural Theology which embraces such views, if, in the progress of knowledge, this revolving function shall be disproved, and this life-giving either be struck out of the material universe?[11]

Nor was Brewster willing to admit that the ether, if it existed, was positive evidence of design rather than the absence of design. Its tendency might be to *retard* the motion of the solar system and counteract its "mathematical stability," but this stability had been described as an essential element in God's intentions concerning the earth. Brewster gave *no* attention to the possible cogency of Whewell's suggestions that the category of purpose, design or final causality had ontological significance as a pure postulate of reason which would not intrude upon the details of *physical inquiry* if the proper critical (Kantian) perspective were maintained. Whewell's rhetoric was at least partly to blame. Its intent was to help his readers deal with negative and anxious feelings aroused by the perception that the world discovered by science was hostile or indifferent to human existence. According to Gliserman, it accomplished this by imaginative "rescues" of threatening information about the indefinite expanse of geological time and cosmic space. Book I of the *Treatise* protrayed a number of logically and physically possible worlds inimical to human existence and then pointed up the many ways in which man is intricately adapted to his actual environment. Book II took a comparable tack with findings in astronomy, first showing the reader an "other-centered reality which threatens him with personal extinction and cosmic chaos,"[12] and then reminding him that the very inclusion of this information within a framework of scientific law implied an "intelligent and conscious Diety, by whom these laws were originally contemplated, established and applied."[13] At this level he smoothly concluded that the creator of the world must also be the creator of man's intellectual powers, and so the *governor* of man's *conscience* and *religious feelings* (in Gliserman's words, Whewell's God was a *personal force* who offered *control* as well as *care* for the world).

Brewster, Lyell, and Darwin exhibited varying degrees of impatience and opposition to Whewell's elaborate philosophical puns on 'law' and his relatively complex ontology. They shared a community whose satisfactions began to replace their own emotional need for the approval of those outside the profession of science. As Darwin put it, "though I cared in the highest degree for the approbation of such men as Lyell and Hooker, who were my friends, I did not care much about the general public."[14] Lyell and Darwin found it difficult and even inappropriate to deal directly with the emotional ambivalence and conflict aroused by scientific theories which challenged the unique moral status of man or implied that the world and the cosmos were not centered on man. In different ways, they sought to isolate their scientific theories in secular realms of "relatively low emotional charge," realms where the standards of approbation would be firmly under the control of the rational ego. Nevertheless, their work retains indirect evidence of their own anxieties over unsolved problems of suffering, death, identity, and dependence, problems which lay at the root of both personal and social crises. For Darwin, this evidence consists in an explicit and continuing preoccupation with the metaphorical structure used to express the core of his theory. Lyell's expression was less poetic, and relied instead on solid forensic skills: he identified real individual opponents and used every weapon of wit and every shred of evidence against them.

A curious feature of Lyell's rhetoric is the similarity of the imagery he evokes in discussing the history of the earth, the history of organic species on earth, and the history of geological science as a form of rational inquiry. On his account, the realms of reason, life and matter are quite disparate; each has its own tempo and pattern, its own laws. Geological change, even though it observes the same laws throughout time, and even though it is gradual rather than cataclysmic, may so suddenly and drastically alter the delicate balance in the "stations" of living things that the history of living things exhibits unequal rates of change in equal periods of time.[15] The historical record of organic forms, with its inevitable pattern of the extinction of species and its unexplained novelties, exhibits *no* overall progressive trend and yet its latest phenomenon, man himself, transcends every preceding animal form, and his superiority depends "not on those faculties and attributes which he shares in common with the inferior animals, but on his reason by which he is distinguished from them."[16] Nevertheless, Lyell uses the same set of highly emotional terms: 'constant and violent struggle,' 'checks and counterchecks . . . to preserve the balance of power' and 'war' for all three realms, without regard for his own underlying distinctions of the histories of thought, organic form, and geological formations. The effect, which is subtle yet pervasive, is to make the history of geological formations seem more human *and* to make the history of reason seem more secular.

The intent of Lyell's review of the history of his discipline is to insist upon its secularization. His sketch of its "progress" shows a "constant and violent struggle between new opinions and ancient doctrines, sanctioned by the implicit faith of many generations, and supposed to rest on scriptural authority."[17] In 1751, the Faculty of Theology at the Sorbonne had called upon Buffon to recant the view that "the present mountains and valleys of the earth are due to secondary causes, and that the same causes will in time destroy all the continents, hills and valleys, and reproduce others like them," and Buffon had been obliged to declare, "I abandon everything in my book respecting the formation of the earth, and generally all which may be contrary to the narration of Moses."[18] Toward the end of the eighteenth century, the neptunian geology of Werner had somehow become allied with religious orthodoxy, and the effect was to excite a "party feeling" against the Huttonian doctrines which were subjected to "odious" charges of infidelity and atheism.[19] Lyell found this attack upon Hutton "injurious in the extreme," and placed himself in clear opposition to the president of the Royal Academy of Dublin who held that "*sound* geology *graduated* into religion, and was required to dispel certain systems of atheism and infidelity." Preoccupation with the origins of the earth inverted the "natural order of inquiry," which proceeded from the known to the unknown, and began by studying the most modern periods of the earth's history. The monuments of the past were to be deciphered by assuming that they were formed by the same system of physical laws observed to operate in the present. The vision of an *autonomous* science of geology was held out as a source of immense emotional satisfaction:

Thus, although we are mere sojourners on the surface of the planet, chained to a mere point in space, enduring but for a moment of time, the human mind is not only enabled to· number worlds beyond the unassisted ken of mortal eye, but to trace the events of indefinite ages before the creation of our race, and is not even withheld from penetrating into the dark secrets of the ocean, or the interior of the solid globe; free, like the spirit which the poet described as animating the universe

——*ire per omnes*
Terrasque tractusque maris, coelumque profundum.[20]

The relationship between the science of geology (or the knower) and the universe (the known) could be as intimate as that between the soul and the body it animates, if geology were *free* to follow the natural order of inquiry. Such freedom could overcome man's limitations as a sojourner chained to a mere point in space.

Lyell was neither an atheist nor an infidel, but his statement of belief in a creative intelligence was reserved for the conclusion of his third volume. In this respect, he adhered to the *critical* perspective more carefully than Whewell who was involved in an almost *continuous* effort to rescue science from those emotional connotations and implications which might encourage religious infidelity. Lyell was careful to note that the original schemes of the creative intelligence lay far outside the reach of our philosophical inquiries.

In whatever direction we pursue our researches, whether in time or space, we discover everywhere the clear proofs of a Creative Intelligence, and of His foresight, wisdom, and power...To assume that the evidence of the beginning or end of so vast a scheme lies within the reach of our philosophical inquiries, or even of our speculations, appears to us inconsistent with a just estimate of the relations which subsist between the finite powers of man and the attributes of an Infinite and Eternal Being.[21]

Equally important was his omission of all references to the divine role of *moral* governor. His brief closing statement made no allusion to providence, care, or any fiduciary relationship between the Intelligence and the world. Nor was there appeal to divine moral guidance nor to divine ratification for a particular moral system. The Creative Intelligence was all-knowing, all-powerful, and infinitely distant.

Lyell's estimate of Lamarck's depersonalization of nature was negative,

Nature, we are told, is not an intelligence, nor the Diety, but a delegated power – a mere instrument – a piece of mechanism acting by necessity – an order of things constituted by the Supreme Being, and subject to laws which are the expressions of his will.[22]

but his own account might have been described in identical language. The factual evidence he cited contradicted H. Davy's speculation that "in the successive groups of strata, from the oldest to the most recent, there is a progressive development of organic life, from the simplest to the most complicated forms."[23] Lyell's position was more Cartesian and mechanistic: man, particularly human reason, was *not* united with nature as the epitome of an ascending ladder of organic perfection; the appearance of reason represented a sharp break with everything that had gone before. And what had gone before exhibited no pattern of increasing perfection; the geological record was not analogous to the pattern of organic growth and development, since some of the most complicated organic forms appeared in some of the lowest strata. Moreover, the relation between the laws of geology and the delicate web which balanced organic species in their various stations made the eventual extinction of every species necessary and inevitable.[24] The "checks and counterchecks which nature has appointed to preserve the balance of power among species" (ii, 133) included a state of virtual war among them. Lyell cited Kirby and Spence to the effect that "in five generations one aphis may be the progenitor of 5,904,900,000 descendants; and it is supposed that in one year there may be twenty generations."[25] While Lyell evoked the imagery associated with 'war,' 'struggle,' 'check and countercheck,' and 'balance of power,' to describe the relations between living species and the organic and inorganic constituents of their stations, he did so unreflectively, it appears.

There is not, as there is in Darwin, an explicit discussion of the use of anthropomorphic metaphors in a scientific treatise. It is curious that of all Lyell's images, Darwin chose that of *equilibrium* to distinguish his own theory of the struggle among organisms from Lyell's.[26] Lyell apparently believed that the war of nature preserved some sort of equilibrium in the total number of organic species, but this was not a point which he tried to support in factual detail.[27] However, he held to an equilibrium of the variations around the type in each separate species, and he attacked Lamarck's speculations on this point. Darwin would have been preoccupied with his friend's denial that the "best authenticated examples of the extent to which species can be made to vary" supported the hypothesis of unlimited organic variability. Lyell claimed that the "balance of evidence" showed that the individual variation which occurred within the species could be exploited for a time by the selective activities of the horticulturist or the breeder, but that "the quantity of divergence diminishes from the first in a very rapid ratio."[28]

3. THE STRUCTURE OF LYELL'S THEORY

The *Principles* stated hypotheses which organized immense quantities of detail. In order to deal with those "cosmogonists" who appealed to non-geological causes to explain the great climatic changes which the fossil record implied had occurred in the northern hemisphere, Lyell formulated a strictly geological explanation which could account for the "summers" and "winters" of the "great years" (*Annus Magnus*) of geological time. The fossil record of the British Isles and Europe indicated the prevalence, in older strata, of marine shells of a size to be found only in the tropic zones. The available botanical evidence also confirmed the inference that since those strata had been deposited, there had been a great diminution of the temperature of the northern hemisphere together with a general subsidence of the level of the seas near Europe. Lyell's explanation of this avoided "catastrophes" of every sort, both those mentioned in scripture and those which would arise from such non-geological causes as the tipping of the earth's axis, or the gradual cooling of an originally molten earth. He labelled theories of the latter sort "cosmogonical," and thought them excessively speculative for use in geology. Nevertheless, his own explanation was also highly speculative.

"We shall now proceed to speculate on the vicissitudes of climate, which must attend those endless variations in the geographical features of our planet, which are contemplated in geology. In order to confine ourselves within the strict limits of analogy, we shall assume, 1st, That the proportion of dry land to sea continues always the same.

2dly, That the volume of the land rising above the level of the sea is a constant quantity; and not only that its mean, but that its extreme height, are only liable to trifling variations. 3dly, That both the mean and extreme depth of the sea are equal at every epoch; and, 4thly, It will be consistent, with due caution, to assume, that the grouping together of the land in great continents is a necessary part of the economy of nature; for it is possible, that the laws which govern the subterranean forces, and which act simultaneously along certain lines, cannot but produce, at every epoch, continuous mountain-chains; so that the subdivision of the whole land into innumerable islands may be precluded."[29]

This hypothesis was *geological* in that it required no assumptions concerning the cosmic processes involved in the formation or origin of the earth. It connected geological events (elevation and subsidence) with climatic events (variations in climate and average temperatures) which could transform the "stations" of living organisms, and so account for the extinction of some among the forms found in the fossil record. The conjunction of these four theses established a network corelating significant geological variables and suggesting means of resolving particularly troublesome geological problems. In another sense, these four theses were quite speculative and theoretical: direct evidence supporting their affirmation or denial was available only in principle, not in fact. Lyell was aware of the limits of his perspective as a geological observer, asking his reader to supplement *experience* by *imagining* what might be observed by an amphibious being, or a dusky subterranean sprite.[30]

He proceeded in the same fashion in organizing his arguments against the adequacy of Lamarck's views concerning the transmutation of organic species:

"It is almost necessary, indeed, to suppose, that varieties will differ...if we assume that there is a graduated scale of being, and assume that the following laws prevail in the economy of the animate creation: − first, that the organization of individuals is capable of being modified to a limited extent by the force of external causes; secondly, that these modifications are, to a certain extent, transmissible to their offspring; thirdly, that there are fixed limits beyond which the descendants from common parents can never deviate from a certain type; fourthly, that each species springs from one original stock, and can never be permanently confounded, by intermixing with the progeny of any other stock; fifthly, that each species shall endure for a considerable period of time. Now if we assume, for the present, these rules hypothetically, let us see what consequences may naturally be expected to result."[31]

When he turned to the "positive facts" which could be "adduced in the history of known species, to establish a great and permanent amount of change in the form, structure, or instinct of individuals descending from some common stock," Lyell found none which supported Lamarck's account.

Therefore, he drew the following conclusions.

"First, That there is a capacity in all species to accommodate themselves, to a certain extent, to a change of external circumstances, this extent varying greatly according to the species.

2dly. When the change of situation which they can endure is great, it is usually attended by some modifications of the form, colour, size, structure, or other particulars; but the mutations thus superinduced are governed by constant laws, and the capability of so varying forms part of the permanent specific character.

3dly. Some acquired peculiarities of form, structure, and instinct, are transmissible to the offspring; but these consist of such qualities and attributes only as are intimately related to the natural wants and propensities of the species.

4thly. The entire variation from the original type, which any given kind of change can produce, may usually be effected in a brief period of time, after which no farther deviation can be obtained by continuing to alter the circumstances, though ever so gradually, – indefinite divergence either in the way of improvement or deterioration, being prevented, and the least possible excess beyond the defined limits being fatal to the existence of the individual.

5thly. The intermixture of distinct species is guarded against by the aversion of the individuals composing them to sexual union, or by the sterility of the mule offspring. It does not appear that true hybrid races have ever been perpetuated for several generations, even by the assistance of man; for the cases usually cited related to the crossing of mules with individuals of pure species, and not to the intermixture of hybrid with hybrid.

6thly. From the above considerations, it appears that species have a real existence in nature, and that each was endowed, at the time of its creation with the attributes and organization by which it is now distinguished."[32]

The proposition that "there are fixed limits beyond which the descendants from common parents can never deviate," is equivalent to the denial of particular, "existential" claim, i.e., that in at least one case the variability of the descendants of common parents exceeds any given limit. No empirical evidence could completely warrant such a denial. Therefore, Lyell's rejection of Lamarck was on *less* firm ground, logically, than his theory of the *Annus Magnus*, for which decisive empirical support was available *in principle*. Nevertheless, Lyell's procedures seemed sound and *adequate*, if not decisive. He examined those instances in which variation beyond typical specific limits would seem *most likely* to occur, noting that the failure to observe even one such instance under the most favorable circumstances provided some *justification* for his fourth conclusion concerning organic species.

Important features of Lyell's geological theory were cast in the *same form* later used by Darwin in the summary arguments at the end of the first part of both the *Sketch of 1842* and the *Essay of 1844*. Each author postulated or assumed a set of four or more related propositions, the conjunction of which had consequences which could be compared with ("tested" against) observable phenomena. In at least one instance, the thesis of "unlimited" organic variability, Darwin asserted what Lyell denied. Lyell's denial of such variability seemed warranted by the preponderance of empirical evidence: no example of the transmutation of species was available. The *prima facie* case *against* the transmutation of species was established, and the burden of proof was Darwin's. He bore it by organizing his own position with the same clarity and in the same logical form employed so effectively by Lyell. But neither Lyell nor Darwin could represent his theses with quantitative precision, and neither theory generated successful predictions of events still in the future at the time of the prediction. Although he differed from his good friend and mentor on the essential point of the possibility of the transmutation of organic species, Darwin could take comfort in the fact that the denial of his theory was in no greater conformity to the stated scientific criteria of the age than was its affirmation. Herschel and Whewell, the most eminent arbiters of British science in the 'thirties and early 'forties, developed accounts of the nature of science and scientific criteria some of which were as much beyond Lyell's reach as Darwin's.

CHAPTER THREE

SCIENTIFIC LANGUAGE AND CHANGING STANDARDS OF EXPLANATION

1. DUGALD STEWART: A REALIST THEORY OF METAPHOR

Dugald Stewart held that the dispositions and attitudes necessary for the cultivated appreciation of beauty in art and nature also supplied the foundation of good sense necessary both "in scientific pursuits and in the conduct of life." Heavily influenced by Hume's skepticism, Stewart knew the importance of the disciplined cultivation of taste *and* reason.[1] With the other Scottish realists, he stressed that it was important to avoid being "misled by the spirit of system," and placed his faith in the "common use of language" as a reliable alternative standard. He rejected as a scholastic prejudice the thesis that the different significations of any one term must all be related to each other as the species of some common genus. His account of the "transitive" or "figurative" development of the usage of such terms as 'beautiful,' 'sublime,' and 'taste' itself, was an important anticipation of the application of the concept of *family resemblance* to the analysis of *language*.

I shall begin with supposing that the letters A, B, C, D, E, denote a series of objects; that A possesses some one quality in common with B; B a quality in common with C; C a quality in common with D; D a quality in common with E; – while, at the same time, no quality can be found which belongs in common to any *three* objects in the series. Is it not conceivable, that the affinity between A and B may produce a transference of the name of the first to the second; and that, in consequence of the other affinities which connect the remaining objects together, the same name may pass in succession from B to C; from C to D; and from D to E? In this manner, a common appellation will arise between A and E, although the two objects may, in their nature and properties, be so widely distant from each other, that no stretch of imagination can conceive how the thoughts were led from the former to the latter. The transitions, nevertheless, may have been all so easy and gradual, that, were they successfully detected by the fortunate ingenuity of a theorist, we should instantly recognize, not only the verisimilitude, but the truth of the conjecture; – in the same way as we admit, with the confidence of intuitive conviction, the certainty of the well-known etymological process which connects the Latin preposition *e* or *ex* with the English substantive *stranger*, the moment that the intermediate links of the chain are submitted to our examination.[2]

Stewart's philosophy of language emphasized the historical development of human language, "traced the natural procedure of the mind, in the use of artificial signs," and described the interaction of language and emotion with the changing features of man's physical and cultural environment.[3] Its first principle was that "the formation of an artificial language *presupposes* the use of natural signs" (emphasis added). These consisted in certain "expressions of the countenance, certain gestures of the body, and certain tones of voice."[4] These basic natural signs were a part of a "language of nature" whose more simple and essential elements quickly became intelligible to human infants. But the acquisition of this language could not be reduced to the principles of experience and association; Stewart considered it *instinctive*. An infant's understanding of the expressive features of the human countenance was based upon a natural propensity to "sympathetic imitation" or physical mimicry, and the successful mimicry of an emotion usually aroused the feelings of the emotion.[5] This original "language of nature" was rooted in "the constituent principles of human nature, or in the universal circumstances of the human race."[6]

Stewart displaced the vain and illusory search for the common essence denoted by 'beauty' by means of a cautious use of the method of conjectural linguistic history, and thereby provided a comprehensive view of the great *variety* of usage in human language.[7] The reconstruction of the history of an expression clarified both its earlier and later meanings, not settling upon any one of them as paradigmatic and regulative of the others, but clarifying the significance of their interaction. Those "critics and philosophers" who sought a univocal definition of 'beauty' had failed to recognize the significance of the *development* of language.

The *developmental* and *historical* themes of Stewart's philosophy of language are of the first importance for an accurate interpretation of Darwin's understanding of his own theory. The Scottish philosopher had woven the findings of the first linguistic historians and etymologists into a sophisticated and comprehensive account of man's aesthetic sensibility. This account was in no sense reductive; it *denied* that 'beauty' meant nothing more than 'pleasurable color,' or that 'taste' denoted nothing but a simple biological urge or appetite. It provided a philosophical framework within which human communication, expression, or language was seen as continuous with the naturally expressive character of the world itself. The root of Scottish realism lay in an emphatic denial of Hume's claim that nothing but the force of association could account for the connections between the basically self-contained and atomic units of reality. Both physical objects and lower organisms were *naturally expressive* of their *real relations* to other such objects. Hume and Stewart shared a sense of the insufficiency of the picture of man's place in nature which had been assembled by seventeenth- and eighteenth-century science. But Hume's critical reaction was ironic, and his arguments concentrated upon a subtle exhibition of the absurdities in the positions he opposed. In contrast, Stewart's constructive and synthetic efforts provided Darwin with needed confidence that an historical account of human development need entail neither epistemological skepticism (as Hume thought), nor the aesthetic and moral crudities of certain elements of the French Enlightenment. In Stewart's *Essays* the history of language illuminated the history of mind, tracing man's complex faculties to their simple origins without *reducing* the complex to the simple. Stewart's rejection of the late medieval heritage of essentialism enabled Darwin to approach both the mind-body problem and the semantic difficulties associated with his theory from a perspective untried by those who had preceded him in elaborating theories of biological evolution. Darwin gave no explicit attention, during this period, to the definition of 'species' (nor of any particular species name) within the context of his theory. But Stewart's account of the etymological development of such words as 'beauty' provided a philosophical background against which the explicit statement of such "essential" definitions was much less crucial than it had been. It provided, much as Morton Beckner's analysis of the role of polytypic predication in current biological taxonomy, for the linguistic representation of family resemblance in a series of objects when no quality is "common to any three objects in the series."[8]

Darwin's *only* uses of the terms 'metaphor' and 'metaphorical' in the *Notebooks* and the associated manuscripts occur in his notes on Stewart's essays "On the Sublime" and "On Taste."[9] His comments indicate that he understood Stewart's critique of essentialist predication: "D. Stewart does not attempt by one common principle to explain the various causes of those sensations, which we call metaphorically sublime, but. . .it is through a complicated series of associations that we apply to such emotions this same term."

Dugald Stewart's may well have been the strongest form of philosophic realism known to Darwin; certainly Stewart's was the richest and most imaginative theory of the interaction of language, opinion, and the changing human environment as a complex vehicle for conceptual change. While his interpretation of new theories of matter fell far short of the standard set by his own analysis of 'beautiful' and 'sublime,' he pointed the way toward an historical analysis of man's sense of aesthetic wonder which was at once naturalistic and attentive to the complexity and depth of human experience. He thereby set a standard which Darwin was willing to extend to every aspect of mind — including the moral sense and the experience of religious awe. The increasingly positivist climate of the' fifties and' sixties saw Darwin hedge his use of the metaphors of 'struggle' and 'selection' with the claim that they might be eliminated in favor of literal expressions, if brevity were of no concern. But during the crucial period when the transmutation theory was taking shape under Darwin's own pen, the realistic themes of Stewart's philosophy of language and expression provided a congenial context for the articulation of views which were at once naturalistic (or "materialistic", as Darwin would have said at the time) and non-reductionist (in the sense that Darwin was more inclined to read human mental qualities back into nature than to accept Cartesian criteria for the mechanistic explanation of the functions of animals and plants). Stewart's account of the semantic implications of man's "natural progress in the employment of speech" played a crucial role in Darwin's movement toward a comprehensive understanding of the thesis that man had evolved from a non-human primate ancestor.[10]

2. HISTORICAL RELATIVISM AND COMTE'S CRITIQUE OF THEOLOGY AND METAPHYSICS

Darwin's *Metaphysical Notebooks* and the associated manuscripts contain five explicit allusions to the philosophy of August Comte. David Brewster had (anonymously) reviewed the first two volumes of the *Cours de Philosophie Positive* for the July 1838 edition of the *Edinburgh Review*, and Darwin's notebook entry for 12 August 1838, makes an explicit reference to the difficulties he experienced in reading "Review of M. Comte Phil." at the Athenaeum Club. All of Darwin's explicit references to Comte occurred between August and October of that same year.[11]

The two volumes covered by the review dealt only with mathematics, astronomy, and physics. The third volume of the *Cours*, dealing with chemistry and biology, was published in 1838; the final three volumes, dealing with historical and systematic sociology, and with the general conclusions of the positive system, were published successively in 1839, 1841, and 1842. It is likely that Darwin had information about Comte's views beyond that he obtained from Brewster's 1838 review.

Brewster had reviewed Whewell's *History of the Inductive Sciences* during the preceding year, and although he found it necessary to warn his readers against Comte's atheism, he considered Comte the more reliable historian and critic of scientific method. His review unhesitatingly admitted the general accuracy of the famous *Law of Three Stages* considered by Comte as necessarily exhibited by the history of the sciences. This point was not lost on Darwin, as the following fragment from *M* indicates.

. . .as first caused by will of gods or god secondly that these are replaced by metaphysical abstractions, such as plastic virtue, etc. Very true, no doubt savage state of mind the Chileno says the mountains are as God made them next step plastic virture natures accounting for fossils & lastly the tracing facts to laws without any attempt to know their nature. Reviewer considers this profoundly true.[12]

Darwin agreed with Comte in drawing exactly that inference which Brewster had sought to warn his readers against."

Now it is not a little remarkable that the fixed laws of nature should be universally thought to be the will of a superior being, whose nature can only be rudely traced out. When one sees this, one suspects that our will may arise from as fixed laws of organization. M. Lecomte argues against all contrivance it is what my views tend to.

It is important to note that this tendency to reject "all contrivance" antedated Darwin's reading of Malthus by at least six weeks, and that it was based upon his ready acceptance of the *Law of Three Stages*.[13]

Brewster's review and the first three volumes of the *Cours* presented the following positivist theses of particular importance for the development of Darwin's methodology:

(1) "Terrible blows" had been dealt to the doctrine of final causality by the development of true celestial mechanics since the time of Newton. In particular, the French Newtonians (e.g., J. Bernoulli and Fontenelle) had purged the Newtonian system of its theological and metaphysical overtones to show that the "single general law of gravitation," "without any inquiry into its first of final cause" accounts for all the order of the phenomena studied by astronomy. Laplace's cosmogony provided a comparable account of the dimensions of the solar system and the planetary orbits, and there was reason to anticipate the further derivation of the diurnal rotations of the different planets. For Comte, this implied that "the pretended final cause will therefore be reduced in the present case . . . to this puerile remark that there are no stars (*sic*) inhabited in our solar system but those which are inhabitable." Brewster rejected the anti-theological implications which Comte drew from his positivist critique of the history of astronomy.

The loftiest doctrines of natural theology appeal to us with more irrestible force when science carries us back to the Great First Cause, and points out to us, in the atmosphere of the sun, all the elements of planetary worlds so mysteriously commingled. In considering our own globe as having its origin in a gaseous zone, thrown off by the rapidity of the solar rotation, and as consolidated by cooling from the chaos of its elements, we confirm rather than oppose the Mosaic cosmogony, whether allegorically or literally interpreted.[14]

Far from thinking that science, properly understood, carried us back to the "gorgeous fabric" of the "Divine architect," Comte argued that,

This irrational and barren admiration is hurtful to science, by habituating us to suppose that all organic acts are effected as perfectly as we can imagine, thus repressing the expansion of our biological speculations, and inducing us to admire complexities which are evidently injurious: and it is in direct opposition to religious aims, as it assigns human wisdom as the rule and even the limit of the divine. . . . Though we cannot imagine radically new organisms, we can, as I showed in my suggestion about the use of scientific fictions, conceive of organizations which should differ distinctly from any that are known to us, and which should be incontestably superior to them in certain determinate respects.[15]

(2) In the positive stage of its historical development, a science renounces inquiry into the origin and destination of the universe, as well as into the causes of phenomena. While he granted that "facts cannot be observed without the guidance of some theory" and that without the introduction of hypotheses "all discovery of natural laws would be impossible in cases of any degree of complexity," Comte argued for a program of linguistic and speculative austerity.[16] He sought to eliminate animistic and anthropomorphic fictions in science by replacing such terms as 'cause,' 'nature,' 'will,' and even 'attraction' and 'elective affinity' with law-like statements of observable sequences of events, and by reformulating the criteria of scientific explanation in terms restricted to the logical connections between more or less general facts.

(3) In the *Cours*, Comte set it forth as an axiom that "all science has prediction for its object," a point which he thought distinguished science from mere erudition, "which relates the events of the past, without any regard to the future." However, he admitted that the complexity of biological phenomena allowed for little if any prediction in the current stage of development of that science.[17]

Darwin's reaction to the predictivist axiom exhibited a mixture of näivete and insight. On the one hand, he made particularly uncompromising use of the predictivist theme in his scathing commentary on Macculloch's *Proofs and Illustrations of the Attributes of God*, insisting that the appeal to the divine plan or the will of the deity provided "no explanation" of the morphological relations among the great classes. "It has not the character of a physical law (& is therefore utterly useless. – it foretells nothing) . . . ."[18] On the other hand, the term 'prediction' occurred only twice throughout the set of six notebooks together with the associated manuscripts. Each of these occurrences is in the same text, and that text admits two functions for law: prediction and the retrospective illumination of such otherwise "scattered facts" as those associated with the embryological "law of monstrosity."[19]

Comte had also argued that both prediction and man's ability to voluntarily modify chemical and biological phenomena established the opposition of positive science to all theological philosophy by showing that the events of the world are not ruled by a supernatural or providential will, but by natural law.

(4) Understanding and verification of the *Law of Three Stages* required its combination with the *Classification of Sciences* (Mathematics, Astronomy, Physics, Chemistry, Biology, and Sociology) which Comte also set forth. No one of the sciences could give an adequate conception of the positive method, since the phenomena of the various sciences were heterogeneous and the methodic procedure of each varied accordingly. For example, the extreme numerical variability and complexity of the phenomena of biology made them "inaccessible to the calculus"; and "all idea of fixed numbers" was "wholly out of the question" in physiology.[20]

(5) Comte's influence upon Darwin cannot be understood apart from his (Comte's) critical view of the role of hypothesis, conjecture, and even metaphorical expression in the language of science. Comte's "Fundamental Theory of Hypotheses" can best be understood in the dual context of his effort to emancipate natural philosophy from theological and metaphysical influence, and of his conviction that none of his predecessors, not even Newton in elaborating the theory of gravitation, had analysed the "conditions of positivity" with the thoroughness necessary to undertake the reform of science, scientific education, and ultimately, of society itself, which the positive philosophy demanded. The Newtonian theory of gravitation had encountered legitimate opposition because of its expression in a *metaphysical language* suggestive of the occult qualities which Descartes had sought to eliminate from physics. The term 'attraction' was particularly misleading in its suggestion of a personal force which could operate over various distances with equal ease. 'Gravitation,' in contrast, was unobjectionable: "It expresses a simple fact, without any reference to the nature or cause of this universal action. It affords the only explanation which positive science admits; that is, the connection between certain less known facts and other better known facts."[21]

Comte regarded the employment of hypotheses or conjectures as necessary for the discovery of the natural laws of phenomena of any degree of complexity, but he sought to ascertain definite conditions and limits for their positive use. He suggested that these conditions could all be included under the umbrella requirement of *verification*. A verifiable hypothesis was one whose suitability (truth or utility) could be appraised "at once," by "experiment and reasoning" under "favourable" circumstances. Since Comte recognized the heterogeneity of the phenomena studied by the diverse sciences and inferred corresponding modifications of their methods and procedures, he saw that verification could *not* conform to uniform and invariable standards of precision. The precision with which a hypothesis might be verified would be a function of "what we can learn of the corresponding phenomena," and might vary with the complexity of these phenomena.[22] Nevertheless, some conditions of verification could be applied categorically to all disciplines and to all the stages of their development. Admissible hypotheses were those which could be expressed in terms of the law-like connection of phenomena and which eschewed all references to *agency*, whether to the *nature* of the agents or to the *mode* of their *productive* activity.[23] Unless some atemporal condition of this sort were admitted, it would be impossible effectively to distinguish the three stages of historical development and to insure the superiority of the last, positive stage.

This reasoning led to Comte's denial of the utility for science of the "fantastic notions about fluids and imaginary ethers" which had been introduced into the analysis of the phenomena of heat, light, electricity, and magnetism. He sought to show that the way in which these hypothetical entities were *defined* was sufficient to deny them a place in "real science" or science with an adequate understanding of its own positivity. These fluids and ethers could not be detected by any experimental process then known or in prospect: they were "invisible, intangible, and even imponderable." Their invention represented the fictional tendency basic to the metaphysical stage of inquiry: the multiplication of properties to correspond to the phenomena to be explained and the subsequent attribution of a separate substantial existence to those properties. Comte asked, "What does it matter whether we call these abstractions souls or fluids?" He concluded that "the question of their existence is not a subject for judgment: it can be no more denied than affirmed: our reason has no grasp of them at all. . ."[24]. Abstinence from such conceptions might render the combination of scientific ideas "extremely difficult" for the generation educated under "prevalent habits of thought," but the use of a "fictitious instrument" presented the constant risk of falling into the delusion of its reality. Comte concluded that the next generation of scientists ought to be trained to attend directly to the relations of phenomena without the introduction of artifices which lacked explanatory value, which cleared away no difficulties, but created new ones which obscured "scientific realities."[25]

However, there were also currents of historical relativism and pragmatism in Comte's philosophy of science. For instance, he set forth an affirmative view of the historical role of the Cartesian theory of vortices. The creation and early use of the vortex hypothesis introduced the idea of mechanism where Kepler had imagined only "soul and genii." The value of the hypothesis of vortices could be seen as a function of its location in an historical sequence leading from Kepler to Newton. In relation to Kepler's mysticism, the vortices had the positive value of stimulating the search for specific mechanisms. After Newton's celestial mechanics, however, allusions to vortices were needless, and as soon as hypotheses were "needless" in the scientific effort to connect phenomena and a diminishing number of "general facts," these same hypotheses became "pernicious."[26] Comte sought to combine an historical law of scientific progress with a complex account of the relations of dependence and independence of the various sciences and of the various disciplines within the individual sciences. The law of progress exhibited *hypothetical necessity*: no other science could have attained the level of positivity if this had not been first achieved for astronomy; but it also allowed some *undetermined relativism*; each science — and each discipline within a science — had developed at its own pace and with its own variant of the positive method. Consequently the status of any particular scientific hypothesis would have to be determined by reference to the alternative available at a given stage in the development of a particular discipline.

As phenomena became increasingly complex, as they did with the great variety of biological phenomena, a correspondingly greater number of investigative methods became available for their analysis. Heavily influenced by de Blainville and the development of the comparative method in French biology, Comte anticipated that the basic laws of life and physiology would have a comparative form. His recommendation of the invention of hypothetical organisms to facilitate the expression of laws of comparative physiology suggests an enthusiasm for conjecture very much at odds with Brewster's account of his condemnation of all hypotheses.[27]

Comte's discussion of Lamarck raised particularly interesting questions for the implications of a positivist critique of the body of biological knowledge available in 1838. He assumed that all competent investigators would agree that the use of the natural method had led to a hierarchic classification of animal species, and that the hierarchy had the following properties, which he characterised as "three great laws":

First, that the animal species present a perpetually increasing complexity, both as to the diversity, the multiplicity, and the speciality of their organic elements, and as to the composition and augmenting variety of their organs and systems of organs. Secondly:

that this order corresponds precisely, in a dynamical view, with a life more complex and more active, composed of functions more numerous, more varied, and better defined. Thirdly: that the living being thus becomes, as a necessary consequence, more and more susceptible of modification, at the same time that he exercises an action on the external world, continually more profound and more extensive.[28]

Lamarck's evolutionary hypothesis implied that the whole zoological series had become "in fact and in speculation, perfectly analogous to the development of an individual; at least in its ascending period." Comte thought that the analogy between individual development and the hierarchical classification of organisms provided a particularly clear and profound conception of the latter, and this aspect of Lamarck's position was preferable to Cuvier's creationism.

Comte differed from Lamarck, however, on the equally profound issue of the relationships of organisms and their environment. Lamarck's theory was based on "two ill-described principles." Comte had no quarrel with the second, the "tendency of direct and individual modifications to become fixed in races by hereditary transmission." It was the first, "the aptitude of any organism (and especially an animal organism) to be modified to a conformity to the exterior circumstances in which it is placed," which Comte could not accept. He thought Lamarck's account of the relationship between an organism and its environment made the former completely plastic, so that the *environment* could *produce all* the *organism's characteristics*, "as if the organism could be supposed capable of modification, *ad infinitum*, by the influence of the medium, without having any proper and indestructible energy of its own." Moreover, Lamarck had implied that the different members of the organic series succeed each other by "imperceptible transitions" and that the series itself is "rigorously continuous." But "if we must admit the indefinite transformation of different species into each other, under the sufficiently-prolonged influence of circumstances sufficiently intense," it would be utterly impossible scientifically to define the fundamental notion of species. And without such definition, Comte held it would be impossible adequately to comprehend or represent the hierarchic classification of organisms.

The unstated conclusion to be inferred from Comte's criticism of Lamarck was that positive philosophy presented no methodological objections to any hypothesis or conjecture concerning the transmutation of organic species so long as it met two related conditions: (1) The relationship between organisms and their environment takes place within a framework determined, in part, by the properties of organisms themselves, (2) the series of organisms (reflected by the hierarchic classification) exhibits some *discontinuity*, even though there is no need "to limit *a priori*, in any way the small elementary intervals" which were the condition of such discontinuity.

3. HERSCHEL'S ANALYSIS OF 'LAW,' 'ANALOGY,' AND 'VERAE CAUSAE'

Although Darwin incorrectly referred to J.F.W. Herschel's *Preliminary Discourse on the Study of Natural Philosophy* in his autobiographical reminiscence of his student days at Cambridge, he spoke very highly of its effect on him, naming it one of the two most influential books he had ever read (the other was Humboldt's *Personal Narrative*).[29] The evidence of the *Autobiography*, taken together with allusions to the *Preliminary Discourse* in Darwin's Notebooks and the marginal annotations in his personal copy of it, indicate that Darwin studied the book carefully during his last undergraduate year at Cambridge, and then again during December and January of 1838–1839. The Notebook allusions to Herschel are not very frequent, and only two (at pages 49 and 60 of Notebook *N*) explicitly mention Herschel and involve points of substantial interest. One of these set forth Herschel's development of a Baconian variation of the principle of continuity, and the other dealt with law and causality.

Few philosophical issues came to as sharp focus for Darwin as did the meaning of causality and of natural law. In the context of his manuscript reflections on the mind-body problem and the meaning of materialism, Darwin wrote,

– The argument reduced itself to what is cause & effect: it merely is /invariable/ priority of one to other: no not only thus, for if day was first, we should not think night an effect. ((Cause and effect has relation to forces & mentally because effort is felt)).[30]

Although the text came down rather clearly on Herschel's side, denying that causality could be reduced to "invariable relations of succession or resemblance" as Thomas Brown held, it did not reflect a comprehensive understanding of Herschel's position. Neither did the other manuscript references to Herschel, nor the marginalia in Darwin's copy of the *Preliminary Discourse*, which, with the exception of one very small factual entry, were confined to vertical marginal lines setting off certain passages. Although the few passages which were marked are of philosophic interest, the markings do not justify any inference concerning Darwin's reaction to the material he was reading, except that he may have read the marked passages with care, or that he may have re-read them on later occasions. On the other hand, there are parallels between the logical structure of the transmutation theory as Darwin set it forth in manuscripts of 1842 and 1844 and the methodology advocated by the *Preliminary Discourse*. Consequently, there is good reason to think that a reconstruction of Herschel's views would throw light on Darwin's implicit philosophy of science.[31]

Darwin's *Notebook* discussion of causality stressed the subjective aspect of "felt effort" in effecting changes "depending on our own will." In the same vein, Herschel maintained the Lockean view that "the only act of causation of which we have an immediate consciousness" is in the exercise of our capacity to move our own limbs. Herschel also considered regularity, periodicity, or any degree of order among phenomena, insufficient to elicit the notion of causality or give us a clue as to the identity of a cause.[32] The notions of cause and law included the idea of contingency, and the basic laws of nature — when expressed in canonical form — were hypothetical: "If such a case arise, such a course shall be followed." But where Hume spoke of empirical regularity and the psychological force of habit, Herschel lent his considerable scientific prestige to an interpretation of 'law of nature' more like that of Leibniz. "Now, it is this provision, *a priori*, for contingencies, this contemplation of possible occurrences, and predisposal of what shall happen, that impresses us with the notion of a law and a cause.[33] The scientific analysis of nature would point to certain key phenomena, resistant to further analysis, which would open the greatest number of further enquiries and serve to "group and classify the greatest range of phenomena."[34] The most "direct action of causes" and the "most extensive and general enunciation of the laws of nature" were to be sought in such phenomena. However, once these were discovered, they "place in our power the explanation of all particular facts, and become grounds of reasoning, independent of particular trial: thus playing the same part in natural philosophy that axioms do in geometry."

The strong rationalist overtones of Herschel's interest in systems of laws setting forth the structure of possible courses of events were echoed in the argumentative strategy of Part I of Darwin's *Essay of 1844*. In order to establish the "possibility of my theory," Darwin set forth a system of laws under which the transmutation of species *could* happen. This emphasis upon the structure of coherent possibility provided a congenial context for metaphorical or hypothetical allusions to the activities of a "selector, infinitely more sagacious than man."

Herschel set exacting standards of adequacy for scientific explanation. He held that patterns of inquiry, or "separate branches of science," develop around phenomena whose analysis recurrently led to a common class of "ultimate facts," putatively expressing the "fixed qualities and powers" of things. The criteria of the "most general enunciation of the laws of nature," were: (1) the facts resist further analysis or decomposition; (2) the resultant expression of them suggests and illuminates the greatest number of enquiries; (3) the laws embody a nomenclature which facilitates the classification of the greatest range of phenomena;[35] (4) observed facts follow from the putative laws of nature as *necessary logical consequences*, and this, not vaguely and generally, but with all *possible precision in time, place, weight, and measure.*[36] If these standards are met, the laws have quasi-axiomatic status within the appropriate branch of science; i.e., they are "independent of particular trial" and determine the possible outcome of events which have not yet occurred, or which may never occur. In Herschel's terms, laws structure "contingencies," or "possible occurrences," so that their hypothetical expression must be conjoined with appropriate additional information before factual information can be deduced from them. For example, the laws of chemical combination must be conjoined with specific facts about the conditions under which two substances are brought together before an inference could be drawn about the nature of their reaction.[37]

Herschel admitted the method of *analogy* as an alternative to strict analysis. If the similarity of two classes of events was very close or striking, and if the causes or laws of one of them were well known, it would be difficult to deny the action of an analogous cause in the other. Causal hypotheses with strong analogical support could and even ought to be pursued in the face of such difficulties as: (1) the absence of additional hypotheses clarifying the causal mechanism involved; (2) difficulty in conceiving the existence of the putative cause in the circumstances to be explained; (3) *the artificiality or complexity of the causal hypothesis itself* (e.g., Ampere's theory of magnets); and (4) the generation of dilemmas or paradoxes when support is available for two or more incompatible causal hypotheses, e.g., the particulate and undulatory theories of light.[38]

Herschel's account of *verae causae* seemed more conservatively empiricist in tone, but it also allowed for significant theoretical invention (see 2', below). *Verae causae* ("meaning at present merely proximate causes") had to satisfy each of the following standards: (1) the existence of good inductive grounds for postulating their existence in nature; and (2) the possibility of experiments providing independent inductive evidence for laws setting forth their causal activity; (or 2') the *construction of suppositions about this causal activity which were not "contrary to our experience."*[39]

Portrait of J.F.W. Herschel, c. 1835; bust of William Whewell, 1851
Reproduced by courtesy of the National Portrait Gallery, London

Herschel's ultimate standard of the adequacy of any hypothesis was the possibility of its careful verification. He alluded to a number of different approaches to the task of verification, without pretending to any systematic classification or general discussion of them. The simplest of these was that a putative law would have to be shown to be universal in its application, "enabling us to extend our views beyond the circle of instances from which it was obtained." The *second* was the analogical extension of the domain of the law, so that we could predict what would happen in cases analogous to those originally contemplated.[40] The *third* attributed a stronger warrant to that hypothesis which not only furnished an explanation to all known facts, but which could lead to the *discovery* of such as were *previously* altogether *unknown*. The *fourth* and final means of verifying a causal conjecture, according to Herschel, was the discovery that the hypothesis successfully withstood an "antagonistic" endeavour to find exceptions to it, an endeavour which pushes its application to the most extreme cases, when the hypothesis is shown to be able to explain instances "which were at first considered hostile." Herschel gave this latter warrant the greatest value: "Evidence of this kind is irresistible, and compels assent with a weight which scarcely any other possesses."[41]

4. DARWIN'S CRITICISM OF WHEWELL'S TELEOLOGY

Darwin's reactions to William Whewell were mixed. The autobiographical allusions to the author of the Bridgewater Treatise *On Astronomy and General Physics* were polite and affirmative, but mild.[42] They met at Henslow's when Darwin was a Cambridge undergraduate, and walked back together to their rooms in Jesus and Trinity after Henslow's weekly open-house conversations. Whewell was accorded the left-handed compliment of being the second best converser on grave subjects (after the lawyer and historian of ethics, Sir James Mackintosh) to whom Darwin ever listened. But Darwin remembered praising his *History of the Inductive Sciences* to Owen, and maintaining in the face of Carlyle's scorn that Whewell's mathematical competence made him an effective judge of Goethe's views on light. Whewell was President of the Geological Society at the time of Darwin's admission and gave the customary anniversary addresses in 1838 and 1839.[43] Darwin's manuscript references to Whewell also indicate familiarity with the latter's *Bridgewater Treatise*, his *History of the Inductive Sciences*, and his preface to Mackintosh's history of ethics. Darwin's personal copy of the *History of the Inductive Sciences* was marked and annotated, particularly the sections dealing with biology and geology in the third volume. His list of "Books to be Read" includes the note, "From Herschel's Review, Quart. June 1841, I see I *must study* Whewell on Phil. of Science. – speculates on instinct."[44] But there is no other indication that Darwin read the *Philosophy of the Inductive Sciences*, and this work (first published in 1840) does not appear in the catalogue of books which he owned personally. However, he may have read Herschel's lengthy and generally sympathetic review, which covered both the *History* and the *Philosophy of the Inductive Sciences*.

The personal manuscript discussions of Whewell's positions include several which were vehemently negative.

Mayo (Philosoph. of Living) quotes Whewell as profound because he says length of days adapted to duration of sleep of man!!! Whole universe so adapted!!! + not man to Planets. – instance of arrogance!![45]

This passage, written within a fortnight of Darwin's reading of Brewster's review of Comte, reflected a growing antipathy for deistic or theistic uses of the notions of design and final causality, antipathy which was reiterated in the marginalia of Darwin's personal copy of Whewell's *History*, probably read during October–December 1838. The remarks about Whewell's preface to Mackintosh's history of ethics were also harsh.

Whewell gives Mackintosh's theory the remarks about contact with will is unintelligible to me. Conscience regulates feelings, as of cowardice. The whole appears to me rather rigmarole. He does not say anything about principles born in us. Great difference with my theory.[46]

Finally, there was the mild sarcasm of the suggestion that *induction* would support the *denial* of Whewell's views on the biological history of man.

Whewell thinks (p. 642) anniversary speech Feb. 1838 thinks gradation between man and animals small point in tracing history of man. – granted. – but if all other animals have been so formed, then man may be a miracle, but induction leads to other view.[47]

Two-thirds of Darwin's annotations of the *History* (28 of 43) occur in the sections of volume III which dealt with biology and geology. Most of the marked passages in the third volume related to the problem of "final causes in physiology." Whewell's study of the history of physiology, from Harvey's discovery of circulation to Sir Charles Bell's account of the distinct functions of the dorsal and ventral horns of the spinal cord, had convinced him that

those who have studied the structure of animals and plants, have had a conviction forced upon them, that the organs are constructed and combined in subservience to the life and functions of the whole. The parts have a purpose, as well as a law; – we can trace final causes, as well as laws of causation. This principle is peculiar to physiology; and it might naturally be expected that, in the progress of the science, it could come under special consideration.[48]

Darwin marked this passage more heavily than was his custom, pencilling in vertical lines and large question marks in both margins. The last sentence received three additional marginal lines and a separate '?' of its own; and Darwin wrote in the margin "mammae in man."

Darwin's ambivalence on the subject of teleology in biology was brought to a sharp focus by Whewell's account of the interesting position of E. Geoffroy St. Hilaire, and the contest between Geoffroy's "principle of unity of plan" and Cuvier's "principle of the conditions of existence of animals." Darwin's annotations indicate his flat rejection of Geoffroy's general position as it was described by Whewell. He marked as "clearly wrong" the passage where Geoffroy was characterized as holding that

the structure and functions of animals are to be studied by the guide of their analogy only; our attention is to be turned, not to the fitness of the organization for any end of life or action, but to its resemblance to other organizations by which it is gradually derived from the original type.

Geoffroy was portrayed as making no use of the concept of adaptation and as not taking into account the interaction of organisms with their environment. Darwin circled the reference to Cuvier's account of the "part which the animal *has to play* in nature," and drew a line to the marginal comment: "This qualified is correct. Owing to external contingencies and numbers of other allied species and not owing to mandate of God."[49] Whewell subsequently claimed "That the parts of the bodies of animals are made* in order to discharge their respective offices** is a conviction which we cannot believe to be otherwise than an irremovable principle of the philosophy of organization."[50] Darwin inserted the comments (at*) "born, altered", and (at**) "under changing circumstances," indicating an increasingly strong interest in distinguishing his own use of the teleological perspective from Whewell's. His comments on Whewell's claim that "The use of every organ has been discovered by starting from the assumption that it must have *some* use" made a full job, if a succinct one, of exhibiting the limited context within which he was willing to admit a role for the concept of final causality in his theory. First, Darwin lined out the occurrences of the word 'use' in the passage just quoted, and wrote in 'relation,' so that the sentence read: "The relation of every organ has been discovered by starting from the assumption that it must have *some* relation." And Darwin wrote in the margin, "In every science, one may trust that any fact has some relation, or use, to whole world. —" But just as he had earlier alluded to the apparent inutility of the rudimentary nipples in male primates as a marginal caution on Whewell's strong claims for the special role of reference to final causality in physiology, he here cited "Shrivelled wings of those non-flying coleoptera?" to indicate that his own approach could achieve a greater generality than one which assumed that every one of an organism's characteristics increased its adaptive relation to its environment.[51]

E. Geoffroy St. Hilaire had attempted to give a quasi-geometrical account of organic structure and function which eliminated teleological expressions completely. In contrast, Darwin sought to *naturalize* the notion of final causality, and to characterize it as just another relation among the facts available for scientific description and analysis. The parts of organisms were not "made" to fulfill their characteristic functions, they were simply "born," and in a changing environment the competition of other organisms placed a premium on those which enabled the organism to adapt to a place in the natural economy. Darwin did not reject Whewell's claims concerning the heuristic advantage which Harvey had made of the concept of design and its implications, but he did oppose those overtones of 'design' which erroneously suggested that *every* aspect of *every* organism had its *adaptive use*, and that there was no need to inquire into the natural origin of the adaptive modifications of organic form and function.

Whewell referred to Kant's account of the necessity of a regulative teleological principle in biology to show its importance even for a philosopher who denied the efficacy of the cosmological and teleological proofs of God's existence. But Darwin was not impressed, and marked the passage describing Kant's position, "All this reasoning is vitiated, when we look at animals, on my view."[52] Darwin probably objected to Kant's non-theistic employment of the teleological principle because it put the problem of teleology beyond analysis. Adaptation was not an inescapably general condition of organisms (or of a science of organisms) or if it was, 'adaptation' must have some meaning other than that which the philosophers offered. "When a man inherits a harelip, or a diseased liver, is this adaption. — . . . doubtless it is in one sense, but not in that in which these philosophers mean." Nor was adaptation to be regarded simply a necessary condition for the possibility of a certain kind of inquiry. It was a fact to be explained like other facts, and Darwin's annotations of Whewell's explication of Cuvier's *Principle of the Conditions of Existence of Animals* pointed the way to his explanation. Where Whewell wrote,

Nothing can exist if it does not combine all the conditions which render its existence possible,* the different parts of each being must be co-ordinated in such a manner to render the total being possible, not only in itself, but in its relations to those which surround it. . . .[53]

Darwin inserted (at*) "with innumerable other animals striving to increase," pointing to the Malthusian conditions which he now considered basic to the evolution of adaptation; and he underlined the last four words, *those which surround it*,' emphasizing the broad and relative sense in which he regarded adaptation, not as a characteristic of organisms as self-contained mechanisms, ("natural objects" in Kant's terms) but of organisms as situated in a *complex* and *changing* environment.

Whewell rejected E. Geoffroy St. Hilaire's announcement of the "termination of the age of Cuvier" and the "fading away from men's minds" of the belief in the immutability of species, on the grounds that it required the following "extremely arbitrary" assumptions:

A constant tendency to progressive improvement, to the attainment of higher powers and faculties than they possess; which tendency is again perpetually modified and controlled by the force of external circumstances. And in order to account for the simultaneous existence of animals in every stage of this imaginary progress, we must suppose that nature is compelled to be constantly producing those elementary beings, from which all animals are successively developed.[54]

Darwin's marginal note simply dismissed these, commenting "These are not assumptions, but consequences of my theory, and not all are necessary."

CHAPTER FOUR

MATERIALISM

Neither Darwin nor that sector of the British intellectual community which influenced him and which he sought to influence was able to approach the problem of materialism calmly or critically. The *Notebooks* reveal his sense of exhilaration in anticipating the revolutionary effect his theory would have on the established views concerning man's place in nature. But the subject of materialism elicited a more complex and confusing array of emotions on his part. He dreaded thinking of himself as a materialist, and at the same time deeply resented the social and cultural forces ("our arrogance, or admiration of ourselves") which insisted that man was superior to the merely material objects in nature, particularly when the insistence encroached upon his title, as a biologist, to the use of explanatory devices analogous to those employed by Newton.[1]

The cloudy and emotion laden use of the charge of materialism in early nineteenth-century England makes it necessary for the historian to exercise considerable caution in his own use of the same label. Whether in their self-descriptions or in their criticisms of others, the authors of this period were not to be trusted when writing "O you materialist!" Maurice Mandelbaum has proposed a useful typology for locating the different currents of thought which came under attack as materialist. He sees that the term was occasionally used as a label for all positions which (1) departed from orthodox views of God and God's relation to Nature. In a second nineteenth-century usage, 'materialism' was a label for the doctrine that (2) mental activity, or *thought*, is a *function* of bodily organs, usually the *brain*. Mill considered (2) the currently accepted definition of materialism, but its utility is limited by its compatability with idealism, as well as with positivist abstention from all metaphysical claims, whether idealist or materialist. If it is assumed that "unlike positivism, materialism is itself a metaphysical position," two more definitions of 'materialist,' can be distinguished.

(3) Anyone who accepts all of the following propositions: that there is an independently existing world; that human beings, like all other objects, are material entities; that the human mind does not exist as an entity distinct from the human body; and that there is no God (nor any other non-human being) whose mode of existence is not that of material entities.

(4) In the stricter sense materialists not only deny that there are entities which are not material; they also hold that whatever properties or forms of behavior particular material objects exhibit are ultimately explicable by means of general laws which apply equally to all of the manifestations of matter.

The fourth sense of 'materialist' depends on a commitment to reductionism — in the sense that "there should be one all-embracing and basic science of nature which would, in principle, be capable of explaining all aspects of the behavior of material entities by means of a single basic set of properties, regardless of how these entities are organized."[2]

1. AN EARLY ENGLISH HEGELIAN: JAMES F. FERRIER

Darwin made two bibliographical entries indicating that he had read, or intended to read, a "Paper on consciousness in Brutes & Animals in *Blackwoods Magazine*, June 1838." The *Wellesley Index* and the *Dictionary of National Biography* indicate that the author of the paper, which was the third in a series of seven, was James F. Ferrier, a pioneer of the English idealist movement, and the first to write understandingly of Schelling and Hegel in the English language. Ferrier's papers were actually entitled "An Introduction to the Philosophy of Consciousness," and their principal thesis was that while perception and rationality might be found in both brutes and man and investigated in each case by "purely physical" means, *consciousness* itself was unique to man.[3] Given the misleading version of Ferrier's title which Darwin entered into the *Notebooks*, it is difficult to imagine that he seriously came to grips with Ferrier's idealism. A number of Ferrier's themes were familiar enough. He ridiculed Dugald Stewart's brand of immaterialism, summing it up as a conjunction of the inconsistent theses that "Mind and matter . . . considered as objects of human study, are essentially different" and that "we are totally ignorant of the essence of either."[4]

His insistence upon the uniqueness of human consciousness and its inaccessibility to scientific investigation, however, led Ferrier to assign consideration of "laws and facts of passion, sensation, and reason" to "animal psychology." He was willing to concede the physicalism of Brown's *Physiology of the Mind* insofar as 'reason' ought to be understood, really could *only* be understood, in terms equally applicable to the actions of brutes.

"If by reason is meant (and nothing else can be meant by it) the power of adapting means to the production of ends, skill and success in scientific contrivances, or in the beautiful creations of art, then the exclusive appropriation of reason to man is at once negatived and put to shame by the facts which nature displays. For how far is human intelligence left behind in many things by the sagacity of brutes, and by the works which they accomplish?"[5]

Consciousness, however, properly understood, was a *purely self-constitutive, free act*, altogether outside the "dominion of the law of causality."[6] Ferrier insisted that only the absolute freedom of the self-creating ego was an appropriate subject of moral responsibility, and that all attributions of moral character to brutes or children were fallacious and without foundation. The self-constitution of the individual ego had to be understood as completely original and essentially non-replicable, since no person could teach another the true meaning and right application of the word "I". The self-constitution of the ego was essentially an act of negation; one in which the ego realized itself by refusing to identify itself with those sensations and passions which seemed to tie it to the causally necessary networks of the external universe. Ferrier saw in the birth of consciousness an initial self-realization which totally burst the harmony between the realm of freedom and the realm of nature.

There is no evidence that Darwin understood Ferrier's idealist insistence upon the self constitutive activity of the ego in a free, and essentially uncaused act of negation. Ironically, this did not prevent his gaining some support from Ferrier's shift of all *scientific* investigation of mental phenomena in the direction of animal psychology, or toward those traits of perception and reason which Ferrier considered men and brutes to hold in common.

2. SCOTCH ZOOLOGICAL PHILOSOPHY: BARCLAY, ABERCROMBIE, FLEMING

Darwin's concern for the broadest implications of the transmutation hypothesis involved him from the very beginning of the *Transmutation Notebooks* in reflections on man's place in nature. Considering the possibility that all man's actions, even his love of God, might be explained in terms of the organization and evolution of the human brain, he said of himself in apparent dismay, "oh you materialist!" and prescribed as a remedy, "Read Barclay on organization!" Barclay's sympathies were obviously on the side of those who "suppose a living internal principle distinct from the body, and likewise the cause of its organization," and against those who "ascribed the principal phenomena of life to organic structure." He regarded as "materialist," hypotheses explaining vital activity in terms of mechanical powers or chemical affinities. His objections to materialism were more philosophical than scientific.

"Even granting there is nothing in the universe but matter, yet where are the *kinds* that organize animals and plants? In the works of art . . . the mere materials have nothing to do with the organization."[7] (emphasis added)

On the scientific side, he appealed to Cuvier, Chaptal, and Thomson to argue that the pursuit of chemical and physical hypotheses of organization left a significant residuum of unexplained phenomena — the coordination of digestive, circulatory, respiratory, and excretory functions, and even (for Thomson) some "agent which characterises living bodies (but which) does not appear to act according to the principles of chemistry." The admission of these three authoritative figures that "even with a full complement of materials, and in just proportions he (the chemist) cannot reproduce any animal or vegetable substance that is once decomposed" provided an argument against materialism which remained unanswered in 1822. However, Barclay's debt to Cudworth's platonism remained the decisive consideration.

"Should we not say that, in our days at least, the structure appears to be rather super-added to the vital principle, than the vital principle superadded to . . . structure? Cudworth (assumes) a plastic nature . . . not a mere vis formatrix . . . but a vital incorporeal substance, acting under the directions of the deity, and endowed with a number of qualities sufficient to account for all the various phenomena which the ancients ascribed to their vegetative soul. . . ."[8]

Barclay's comprehensive discussion of the issues did not result in as strong an argument against materialist hypotheses as he might have wished. Inadvertently, he strengthened the case for a non-reductionist naturalism by failing to connect his Platonism with the investigation or the explanation of vital phenomena, and by admitting that the large majority of contemporary scientists had to be grouped under a heading which he could only label 'materialists.' In *his* hands, 'materialism' crudely and roughly signified no more than a *non-platonizing* approach to the tasks of scientific explanation. Darwin's personal copy of Barclay's *Inquiry* remained largely uncut and wholly unmarked.

   John Abercrombie's *Inquiries Concerning the Intellectual Powers and the Investigation of Truth* was a popular attempt (it went through eight editions) to apply the principles of Scottish philosophy, particularly as exemplified by Thomas Brown, to medical science. Abercrombie continued the tradition of Stewart and Brown in arguing that consciousness and sensation were distinct means of knowing one's own mental activities and of becoming aware of the physical world. He reiterated Brown's positivistic account of causality in terms of invariable succession, and he argued that the aim of science was simply "to observe the facts, and to trace what their relations or sequences are." However, he set out to show that materialism was opposed to the first principles of philosophical inquiry; not on the grounds that the issue between materialism and its denial was undecidable on factual grounds, but because of a number of negative analogies between properties of matter and those of mental activities. Darwin heavily annotated these arguments, and his comments were extensive and harsh. He marked the section on the application of the rules of philosophical investigation to medical science, "all trash," his ire being particularly aroused by Abercrombie's opposition to extensive use of the method of hypothesis on the grounds that only extensive observation could expose the latent fallacies which might result. Darwin drew a large 'X' through those remarks and wrote in the margin, "So much the better! Fee-hunting doctor."[9] He also exploited Abercrombie's desultory statement of the parallelism of moral and physical causality to clear away objections concerning the social consequences of psychological determinism. Abercrombie, in his dogged and unoriginal way, had done little more than insist that the human will was free, but not capricious, and that a uniform necessity could be traced in the operation of moral causes. Darwin took the cue to argue that although determinism might require a reformulation of the vocabulary used to describe moral responsibility, it need not undermine moral beliefs.

Darwin's copy of John Fleming's two volume *Philosophy of Zoology* was extensively annotated and read with general agreement, particularly with that section of the first volume which dealt with instinct and other "faculties of the mind." Fleming was a more heterodox figure than Barclay, and his free church proclivities led him in 1845 to resign the chair of natural philosophy at King's College Aberdeen for the chair of natural science at Free Church College at Edinburgh. He was flatly agnostic on the issue of materialism.[10] Unlike Lamarck, Fleming imputed both irritability and instinct to living things generally, including plants, but with Lamarck, he denied the faculty of sensation to vegetables, since they lacked nerves. Numerous annotations of the section on instinctive powers in Darwin's copy indicate his agreement with the view that "the intellectual powers of man differ, not in kind, but merely in degree, from those of brutes." Men and brutes both possessed the faculties of attention, memory, and imagination, and both were said to have ideas of time, power, truth, and duty. Darwin indicated dissent from the text only to raise counter-examples to Fleming's attempts to hedge on such points as the exhibition of curiosity by lower animals.

Fleming divided the instinctive powers into *appetites, desires, and affections*; and provided a detailed discussion of such *parental affections* as the provision of food, warmth, a nesting site, cleanliness, and protection from predators for young offspring; and of the *social affections* of respect for leadership and mutual support. Darwin marked examples of ducks covering eggs carefully to preserve their warmth and conceal them, and of warning cries of the sentinels of a herd or flock, as "difficult to account for." He marked without comment Fleming's *denial* of Stewart's claim that only man can form the general notion of happiness, and deliberate about the means of attaining it. [11]

Fleming's considerable prestige as a taxonomist and zoologist was all on the side of the continuity of all mental phenomena (with the single exception of the idea of God) in the chain of being linking animals and men, but he was equally insistent upon the "chasm" which divided the characteristics of inorganic and organic beings. He argued briefly for a "vital principle" distinct from the organization of living things, and claimed that "different operations of living beings ... can never be regarded as the effect of their peculiar organization." Characteristic limitations in the form and life cycle of organisms, together with the properties found in all living things: irritability (exhibited by phototropism in plants), instincts (for food, for adaptive modification — as in the differential growth of root structure in trees buffeted by the wind, and for healing or regeneration of injured parts), and a power of procreation were all attributed to the "vital principle."

Together with most, if not all, of the biologists which Darwin read during this period, Fleming was both a descriptive and an explanatory *vitalist* insofar as he not only attributed distinctive and irreducible properties to living things, he refused to accept the mechanical category of *organization* as providing an adequate explanation for them. [12] However, he experienced no difficulty in regarding mental phenomena as appropriate subjects for zoological investigation and, in opposition to Dugald Stewart, insisted upon strict continuity between brutes and man in this key respect. Anticipating the similar views of Benjamin Smart by nearly twenty years, Fleming drove the anti-metaphysical tendencies of the Scottish school to the conclusion that the supposed immateriality of mind was only a label for ignorance of the subject.

3. LANGUAGE AS "THE WAY OUT OF METAPHYSICS": BENJAMIN SMART

Between 1836 and 1839, Benjamin Smart, rhetorician and essayist, had composed a series of book length discussions of grammar, logic, and rhetoric, finally publishing them all under the title, *Beginnings of a New School of Metaphysics.*

Darwin specifically endorsed Smart's views concerning the origin of language, and its reciprocal effect on the development of reason.[13] On this point, Smart sought to avoid the extreme position represented by Horne Tooke, who made reason no more than an *effect* of language without recognizing its co-ordinate role in the *development* of language. Smart denied the philosophical tenability of any identification of the mind and the body, but he considered the "fundamental dogma" of the Scottish school, "that every man is led, by the constitution of his nature, to consider himself as something distinct from his body," to be equally contradictory and meaningless. He preferred "*man* thinks, feels, and reasons," since any investigation of mental phenomena which lost sight of man "such as he is in his whole nature" was sure to run into "egregious practical errors." He denied the possibility of resolving fundamental metaphysical disputes by any other device than Locke's plain, historical method, systematically turned to the study of words rather than ideas. He included among the questions where "neither side of the question admits of that sort of experimental or demonstrative proof which can compel assent in a mind inclined to think the other way": the "Being of a God, Materialism – Distinct Existence of Mind and Body in Man." Smart held that language was both the necessary effect of reason, and its necessary instrument, *evolving from originally expressive cries or natural signs*. As an artificial instrument, language developed gradually, becoming more complicated as the occasions of its use grew more numerous and refined. He agreed with Lord Monboddo that the first articulate sounds denoted whole sentences, not any one of the parts of speech, and that these sentences, in turn, were expressive of some appetite, desire, or inclination. The modification of the original natural words and of the first rude linguistic contrivances or artefacts occurred on the "spur" of the occasion, as a result of the practical demands of social life and a corresponding requirement of economy in expression which explained the tendency to express novel intentions by the combination of "old" words rather than by continually inventing new signs. The resultant complex expressions were not to be understood as if they corresponded, part for part, with correspondingly complex ideas. Smart rejected the correspondence view of language and thought for two reasons. First, his view of the origin of language required that both sentential forms and various parts of speech were dictated by the "necessities and conveniences" of social expression and *not* by an original effort of thought or mind considered independently of language. Parts of speech, therefore, did not correspond to originally distinct acts of mind, but reflected the diverse functions which originally natural words, or their artificial descendants, might have in complex combinations with other such words. Second, Smart's views of language were strongly colored by his own interest in rhetoric, and the inherent limitations of man's powers of communication and persuasion.

"As a rhetorical instrument, language is, in truth, much more used to explore the minds of those who are addressed, than to represent, by an expression of correspondent unity, the thought of the speaker; — rather to put other minds into a certain posture or train of thinking, than pretending to convey at once what the speaker thinks. ... It is only by expedients that mind can unfold itself to mind — language is made up of them; there is no such thing as an express and direct image of thought. Let a man's mind be penetrated with the clearest truth — let him burn to communicate the blessing to others; yet can he, in no way, at once lay bare, nor can their minds at once receive, the truth as he is conscious of it."[14]

His views on metaphor reflected this same sober, functional theory of language. He denied that metaphor was merely ornamental, and considered it part of the original texture of language and even insisted that *all* words were "tropes," or expressions *turned* from their first purpose and extended to others. In a mature language, however, he admitted that a word might become fixed in some acquired meaning.

Smart's final essay, which strongly influenced Darwin, was titled "A Way Out of Metaphysics." Smart's way out of such perplexities was "to consider what knowledge we really have under a word, and what we have not, and cannot have in our present state of being." Exploiting Stewart's repeated denials that neither matter nor mind could be known as they were essentially, and Brown's comparable insistence that all our causal knowledge was confined to the recognition of relationships of invariable succession among phenomena, Smart concluded, rhetorically but negatively, that "since we know nothing absolutely, either of matter or of mind, would it not have been wise, before making the distinction the ground of a science, to inquire whether it is a distinction which a philosopher is justified in making at all?" He drew the same conclusion from the Scottish criticism of the role of "ideas" in perception, arguing that this criticism left the presumed science of mind without a subject.[15] Only a single discipline, a single method, was available for settling questions concerning "all things which we believe or imagine to have existence distinctly from our notions of them, whether they come within the reach of our senses or not"; Smart called this discipline physics. He denied that this move confounded the Creator with the things created, but it quite clearly denied that theological knowledge could be based on anything but the inductive procedures of physical inquiry. Smart spoke with warmth of the emotional value of the theological images of "Guide, Friend, Father," comparing them favorably to the unembodied abstractions of both the atheist and the deist. He developed no particular account of theological language, however, and implied that the way out of metaphysics lay, *not* with a *definitive resolution* of metaphysical disputes, but in the *dissolution* of such disputes through the exhibition of their original ground in simple perceptual experience.

4. MATERIALISM: WILLIAM LAWRENCE AND THE POLITICS OF NEUROPHYSIOLOGY

The exaggerated legal and professional reaction to William Lawrence's lectures to the Royal College of Surgeons (1816–1819) was a symptom of contemporary British hostility to the unguarded application of physiological methods and categories to the explanation of human behavior. Anonymous pamphleteers and reviewers denounced Lawrence for making physiology "the road to materialism in metaphysics, to faction in politics, and to infidelity in religion." Lawrence was compelled to resign the Royal College chair of anatomy and surgery, in part because he rejected the view that "life, through the whole range of organized beings, consists in some principle of inherent activity superadded to the material structure," and was equally critical of the use in physiology of the thesis that "in man, who lives in a state of reflection as well as sensation, an immaterial and immortal soul is added to the living principle which he possesses in common with other animals."[16]

Lawrence's *Lectures on Physiology, Zoology, and the Natural History of Man* and his earlier *Introduction to Comparative Anatomy and Physiology* were published at a time when the Spa Fields Riots (1816) and the "Peterloo massacre" (1819) had set the scene for the repressive reaction of the Six Acts, which aimed, among other things, at the elimination of the radical press.[17] This climate did little to encourage Lawrence's critics to attend to the methodological subtleties behind his strong and clear statements concerning the political significance of science. At a time when England had just succeeded in overcoming the threat of domination by Napoleonic France, he was a strong advocate of the internationalism of the scientic community.

"Science, the partisan of no country, but the beneficent patroness of all, has liberally opened a temple where all may meet. She never inquires about the country or sect of those who seek admission: – she never allots a higher or a lower place from exaggerated national claims, or unfounded national antipathies. . . . The savage notion of a natural enemy should be banished from this sanctuary, where all, from whatever quarter, should be regarded as of one great family; and being engaged in pursuits calculated to increase the general sum of happiness, should never exercise intolerance towards each other, nor assume that right of arranging the motives and designs of others, which belongs only to the Being who can penetrate the recesses of the human heart."[18]

Nor did he promote the internationalism of science by isolating objective inquiry into nature's works from highly controversial points of political and moral principle. He emphasized the operation of the "fundamental law" of variety throughout creation, from the individual character of each leaf and flower to the distinctive countenance, gesture, feelings, thought and temper of each human being. He insisted that "this variety is the source of everything beautiful and interesting in the external world; the foundation of the whole moral fabric of the universe." Citing Locke and Jefferson on the spirit of toleration, he looked forward to the day when "attempts at enforcing uniformity of opinion will be deemed as irrational, and as little desirable, as to endeavour at producing sameness of face and stature." The moral fabric he sought to promote required "full freedom of opinion and belief" and the "destruction of all creeds and articles of faith."[19]

Lawrence rejected loose analogies between various "subtle" fluids, magnetic, electric, galvanic, and vital, and insisted that they were all equally open to doubt. Nevertheless, his basic aim was to remove the metaphysical obstacles to a full investigation of the physiological basis of mental activity.[20] He gave no attention to the possibility of the independent science of mind which Dugald Stewart and Thomas Brown sought to articulate. However, his methodological views were not reductionist. Like Lamarck, he was willing to enumerate the differences, not only between physical and vital *phenomena*, but even more fundamentally to insist on comparable differences between physical and vital *laws*. He held that the indiscriminate application of a poorly understood Newtonianism had *not* advanced the scientific interest of physiologists, who had been betrayed by it into "the error of seeking everywhere in the animal economy for attraction and impulse, and of subjecting all the functions to mathematical calculations," when the data were actually too uncertain and too variable to justify such precision. He insisted that there was no justification for the use of physical analogies in the explanation of vital phenomena.[21] His positivism, like Comte's, allowed considerable regulative significance to *prima facie* differences among different categories of phenomena; for example, the distinction of electrical and vital *phenomena* sufficed to assert the "*incommensurability*" of the *two fields of inquiry*. However, his English contemporaries were more in the mood to react to his distressing rejection of various theories of "vital principles" from van Helmont's to

Hunter's. The one-sided and polemical reaction to Lawrence's balanced methodological views may well have had extra-scientific roots. The orthodox establishment in England was hostile to the philosophical underpinnings of the French Revolution. The methodological skeleton of Lawrence's position was close to the views of the radical Priestley and of Lamarck and Laplace. In that historical setting, the uses of 'materialist' may have been determined by partisan social debate, more than by careful methodological analysis.

5. LAMARCK. "THIS MATERIALISM DOES NOT TEND TO ATHEISM"[22]

The entomologist William Kirby, in the introduction to his two-volume *Bridgewater Treatise* on the instincts and habits of animals, sharply criticized LaPlace and Lamarck for "their disregard of the word of God" and distinguished their naturalism from his conviction "that in order rightly to understand the voice of God in nature, we ought to enter her temple with the Bible in our hands." For Kirby, "Lamarck's great error" was materialism; "he seems to have no faith in anything but *body*, attributing everything to a physical, and scarcely anything to a metaphysical cause." Kirby warned against Lamarck's thesis that imponderable and uncontainable caloric and electric fluids were the source of vital activity in organisms without an organized nervous system. "Now, though heat, electricity, etc., are necessary to put the principle of life in motion, they evidently do not impart it. . . . Neither caloric nor electricity, though essential concomitants of life, form its essence." Second, he rejected Lamarck's version of Condillac's sensationalism, and his physicalist account of agency, even of acts of thought, in terms of the action and reaction of the brain, the nervous system, and particularly the "nervous fluid" and its motions.[23]

Finally, Kirby objected to Lamarck's general view of nature and to his particular form of deism. He criticized Lamarck's use of an ontology restricted to motion, space and time, order, and law as consisting "merely of abstract qualities, independent of any essence or being." He held that there were "inter-agents between God and the visible material world by which he acts upon it, and as it were takes hold of it"; these were "powers" which had a "real substance and being" and which could "act and operate, and impart a momentum." He was requiring a very finely tuned physico-theology, and the charge of materialism masked that deeper concern. Kirby was unable to decide whether Lamarck's God was excessively remote and indifferent or too immediately responsible for the shortcomings of the vital organization and action of animals, but either alternative was theologically unacceptable.

Lamarck's *Philosophie zoologique* was *ambiguous* on the subject of materialism. There was no doubt where Lamarck stood on the thesis "that human beings, like all other objects, are material entities; that the human mind does not exist as an entity distinct from the human body." Espousing the sensationalist interpretation of Locke's dictum concerning the understanding, "That there is nothing in the understanding which was not previously in sensation," Lamarck gave a strong physicalist account of intellectual activity.[24] However, Lamarck's standards of description and explanation were strongly *anti-reductionist*.

He identified no fewer than four breaks in the chain of being, which, if not unbridgeable, nevertheless represented real differences in kind:[25]

1. Inorganic bodies	Organic bodies
2. Plants	Animals
3. Animals lacking a nervous system (irritable but lacking feeling)	Animals with a nervous system (possessing sensation and feeling)
4. Unintelligent animals	Intelligent animals (capable of noticing their perceptions).[26]

An adequate interpretation of Lamarck must note both (1) his positive commitment to naturalistic patterns of explanation, and (2) his strong aversion for reductionist attempts to explain all vital activity in terms of some single structure or some one explanatory system.[27] He shared the common Enlightenment aspiration for harmonizing the realm of nature and the realm of morality and human value. But he opposed the reductive elimination of "higher" or more complex forms of organization or activity in favor of their simplest constituent elements and forces. Although his account *identified* sensation and emotion with physical activities ("the inner emotions of a sensitive animal consist in certain general agitations of all the free parts of the nervous fluid,") the wholistic context of this identification must be kept firmly in mind, if one intends to give Lamarck a fair hearing.[28]

Lamarck and Lawrence were not materialists in the fourth of the senses distinguished by Mandelbaum. Neither were they materialists in the sense implied by Cartesian mechanism. However, both were willing to apply the scientific method to the study of every aspect of man and human activity. Consequently, although they did not think that the laws of biology (or of thought) could be reduced to those of physics, they were *heterodox* in their willingness to classify man with other intelligent animals, or to apply to his brain and his "mental illnesses" the same investigative techniques applied to other experimental organisms. Whether this heterodoxy was frightening because of its association with the ideology of the French Revolution is the subject for another investigation. The important point at present is that in Darwin's cultural circle, the uses of 'materialism' were polemical and dogmatically negative. The word was rarely, if ever, used to refer to the strict methodological project which proposes to explain all properties and all behavior in terms of laws which apply equally to all physical objects. It was used most commonly to denote *heterodox* positions concerning man's place in nature, his relation to God, and his moral and political obligations.

6. SUMMARY

Darwin had little in common with that segment of his cultural circle most strongly opposed to materialism (Barclay, Abercrombie, Ferrier, and Wedgwood). On the other hand, neither he nor any member of the circle was a materialist in the fourth of the senses distinguished by Mandelbaum (p. 57).

However, if we may anticipate the findings of later chapters, we may conclude that Darwin and several members of his circle were materialists in Mandelbaum's third sense (p. 56). They did not recognize the human mind as an entity distinct from the human body, nor did they admit a deity whose mode of existence was not that of material entities. For Darwin, the concepts of force and of mind were alike in that each was formulated hypothetically, not given directly in experience; the distinction of sensation and introspection had no significance for the distinction of mind and body; and there were many analogies between supposedly distinctive mental activities (e.g., memory) and physiological functions (e.g., the repeated synthesis of bile by the liver). Darwin was willing to conclude that the brain secretes thought as the liver secretes bile and, as a young man, he would not have invoked positivist theses to limit the ontological significance of that conclusion.

CHAPTER FIVE

THEODICY AND THE LAWS OF POPULATION:
PALEY AND MALTHUS

The next chapter (Chapter 6) deals with two figures, Hume and Wordsworth, whose influence upon Darwin is impossible to document in satisfactory detail. In fact, the existence of influence in those two instances can only be *inferred* from the evidence of similarities in style, tone and theme. Nevertheless, a picture of Darwin's cultural ambience which omitted discussion of Hume or Wordsworth would be seriously deficient. The thesis that these three, Hume, Wordsworth, and Darwin, *shared* a complex critical sensibility which placed them *well outside the orthodox mainstream of the period* is one of the foundation stones of the reinterpretation of the significance of Darwin's theory which I am proposing in this monograph.

The two individuals to be considered in *this* chapter, William Paley and Thomas Malthus, were quite comfortably situated within, indeed they helped to construct, the established orthodoxy of English society and culture in the decade of the 1830's. The evidence that these men influenced the structure and content of Darwin's theory is definite. In fact, as I attempt to show in the third section of this Chapter, Malthus' influence is an exceptionally important topic for analysis of inter-disciplinary scientific communication. But it will be important for the reader to keep in mind that intellectual influence and the communication of ideas is *not* always grounded in consensus concerning the meaning of terms and the adequacy of evidence. *Influence*, in other words, not only *may be either positive or negative, it may take on any value along a continuous spectrum ranging from complete agreement to complete disagreement and polemical rejection.*

1. PALEY AND CAMBRIDGE THEOLOGY

Leslie Stephen's sardonic account of the position of Cambridge theology in eighteenth century thought suggested that Paley's efforts to develop an apologetic for Christian orthodoxy were basically misconceived, and that he usually implicitly sacrificed the ground he explicitly sought to defend.[1] As we will see, if "constructive deism" is defined, with Stephen, as the effort to "substitute for Christianity a pure body of abstract truths, reposing on metaphysical demonstration," then there is an important sense in which the quasi-mathematical arguments to be found in Paley's *Evidences of Christianity*, in spite of their orthodox intent, were deistic in substance as well as in rhetoric.[2]

In Darwin's day, contact with Paley's works was a matter of academic discipline and routine for Cambridge undergraduates preparing their B.A. examinations. The required works were Paley's *Moral and Political Philosophy* (1785) and his *A View of the Evidences of Christianity* (1794), and *not* the *Natural Theology* (1802). Darwin read both the *Evidences* and the *Natural Theology* with "as much delight" as he received from his generally enjoyable study of Euclid, and in each case the pleasure consisted in his susceptibility to the charm of "*long lines of argumentation*." It was the *Evidences* and the *Moral Philosophy*, however, and not the *Natural Theology*, which the pressure of the pending examination caused Darwin to study so thoroughly that he could have "written out the whole ... with perfect correctness."[3] The logical structure of the *Evidences* epitomized the dry, rational, yet pragmatic tone which permeated Paley's philosophy of religion.

Paley began by considering the "antecedent credibility of miracles" in the light of Hume's skeptical objections. Hume had argued that it was more likely that the human testimony for miracles was false than it was that miracles had occurred. Paley did not care to challenge Hume's empiricist criteria of belief, but sought to show that – even given those standards – *miracles were possible and not incredible*. He pointed out that Hume had covertly assumed that "either the course of nature is invariable, or that, if it be ever varied, variations will be frequent and general." Paley argued that the disjunction in question had not been shown to be truly exhaustive. Hume had not shown the *impossibility* of singular or unique interventions in the regular course of nature. Hume would have preferred to be understood to claim that human testimony could never raise an allegation of a miraculous interruption of natural laws from the level of merely logical possibility to that of empirical probability. But Paley concluded that Hume had not shown that miracles were impossible.[4]

He sought to use this *same form of argument* in presenting the succeeding theses which made up his position, arguing – for example – that the evidence did not rule out the claim that Christ's disciples were sincere in their reports of the details of his life.

Darwin's handwritten resume of Paley's position shows that he was sensitive to its logical structure, and that he was less credulous than he later imagined concerning some of its factual details. Darwin summarized:

The actual existence of Christ cannot be proved by evidence: but Sceptics must be reduced to this dilemma. Either Jesus did not exist or he actually lived but was not the son of God. Hence an impostor. – if impostor – would have preached a more popular doctrine."[5]

At some point, apparently as he wrote it, Darwin marked that passage with a large '?.' As he recalled so many years later, what "charmed" him about Paley was the man's Euclidean skill in developing long chains of argument. Fortuitously, Paley's task was similar in its logical requirements to Darwin's own. Each had to marshal evidence in support of a thesis which could not be proved directly by evidence. Each proceeded by pointing out that his opponents had failed to prove the *impossibility* of something they had dismissed as *improbable* (as Darwin found most of his contemporaries assuming that it was improbable that there was no natural limit to organic variation). Each was involved in some of the same difficulties resulting from the introduction of a scientific mode of reasoning into the reconstruction of an historical narrative. Darwin, for example, never directly addressed the difficulty involved in shifting from the claim that "we do not know of any ultimate limit to the extent of organic variation" to the firmer thesis "There is no law of nature limiting the amount of variation." The structure of this argument: " 'p' has not been proven impossible; therefore, 'p' is possible," was common to Paley and Darwin.

Paley also provided his readers with considerable analytic clarification of the concept of purpose in nature. His most succinct expression found purpose or plan in situations or systems exhibiting "variety obeying a rule, conducing to an effect, and commensurate with exigencies infinitely diversified."[6] Basic to his conception of design was the idea of a plurality of parts exhibiting the functional relationship necessary for the production of some one effect.[7]

Without identifying it as a necessary condition for the attribution of design to a complex organic system, Paley obviously considered it important that the distinctive relationship between its parts could *not* be explained simply in terms of physical laws. In a chapter dealing with "peculiar organizations" he alluded to the fact that the swim bladder of fish could not be interpreted as a natural consequence of life in the water; similarly, peculiar development of the woodpecker's tongue could not be understood as a result of forces at work in its environment.[8]

The repetition of some common pattern in a number of distinct but adaptive modifications was also sufficient to warrant the inference of an intelligent designer. Just as Arkwright's mill for spinning cotton had been modified for the spinning of wool, flax, and hemp, so the beaks of various birds, and even more generally, the bills of birds and the mouths of quadrupeds were examples of the pursuit of some one general plan. But this style of argument surely justified Stephen's ironic question as to whether or not Paley's God was only a little more clever than Arkwright and Watt.[9]

Finally, whatever his intent, Paley obviously failed to achieve a significant and fresh theoretical synthesis of the biological information relevant to the problems of natural theology and theodicy. He did not attempt an effort on the grand scale exemplified in Leibniz' critique of the conceptual foundations of physics and mathematics, and succinctly expressed in the Leibnizian principles of sufficient reason, perfection, and continuity. Paley admitted readily that

Throughout that order of nature, of which God is the author, what we find is a *system of beneficence*: we are seldom or never able to make out a perfect *system of optimism*. I mean, that there are few cases in which, if we permit ourselves to range in possibilities, we cannot suppose something more perfect, and more unobjectionable, than what we see.[10] (emphasis added)

This was close to the admission that there was *no one purpose in nature*. Paley did argue that a greater number of living things was maintained, given the variety of types and appetites (or, given some roughly hierarchical ensemble of organisms), than would be the case if the earth were inhabited by only a single species. He did not, however, identify the increase of the total quantity of life on earth as *the* purpose of the intelligent design which he found in organisms.[11] His attention was focussed on the great variety of "contrivances" to be found in nature, as the famous analogy of the watch suggested. His concerns were not those of the rationalistic tradition in natural theology: he looked for no unifying theoretical scheme in nature; he looked for no evidence that God's creation had achieved the greatest possible variety through the simplest possible means; he paid no attention to the principle of plenitude nor to the continuity of the great chain of being. Paley's concerns were *pastoral* rather than philosophical or metaphysical. God's power was so great as to make it impossible for man to plumb his purposes, yet His benevolence led Him to leave such evidence of His agency and wisdom as his natural creatures could receive. Thus Paley's answer to the question, "Why resort to contrivance, where power is omnipotent?" was simply that "It is only by the display of contrivance, that the existence, the agency, the wisdom of the Deity, could be testified to his rational creatures."[12] Paley's God was neither a Geometer nor an Optimizer; he was instead a master contriver. Paley thought *His* moral purposes could best be represented through the metaphor of a lottery — a fair lottery where the chances of birth, death, social station, happiness, and salvation were distributed without prescient bias.

Viewed from any rigorous philosophic perspective of the time (particularly Hume's) Paley's account of God's attributes (omnipotence and omniscience)

presented them as conditioned and relative.

'Omnipotence' 'omniscience,' 'infinite' power, 'infinite' knowledge, are *superlatives*, expressing our conception of these attributes in the strongest and most elevated terms which language supplies. We ascribe power to the Deity under the name of 'omnipotence' the strict and correct conclusion being, that a power which could create such a world as this is, must be beyond all comparison, greater than any which we experience in our-selves, than any which we observe in other visible agents; greater also than any which we can want, for our individual protection and preservation, in the Being upon whom we depend. It is a power, likewise, to which we are not authorized, by our observation or knowledge, to assign any limits of space or duration.[13]

L. Stephen concluded that Paley's God was "obviously a part, almost a material part, of the universe.... His God exists in time and space." The distinction between a being "infinitely more sagacious than man" and an "omniscient creator" was not one which Paley was interested in articulating, let along investigating.

On the other hand, as we have seen, Darwin not only articulated the distinction of a being "infinitely more sagacious than man" and "an omni-scient creator" in the *Sketch of 1842*, but it became the core of his metaphor of natural selection. The *Notebooks* make plain that he understood that he was departing from the English tradition in natural theology and the corres-ponding view of man's place in nature — that his account would destroy the "fabric" of that tradition.[14]

Darwin's procedure, in 1842, did not fit the positivist model proposed by Comte. His developing *self-image* was, in this respect, *delusive*. He did *not* take biology from its theological and metaphysical stages into Comte's posi-tive stage. Rather, he took concepts which Paley had used *apologetically* to *illustrate* religious belief, and without draining them of metaphysical (or extra-empirical) content, tried to employ them critically in the construction of a new scientific theory and its associated program of empirical investigation.

2. PALEY AND MALTHUS: A SHARED THEODICY

Little stress has been placed upon the interconnection of the views of Paley and Malthus, and yet there is clear evidence that their views blended in a common theodicy, or justification of God's action in creating a world in which evil and suffering were undeniably present. Both Paley and Malthus stressed the incomprehensibility of God's infinite power, and argued that even though it was "absolutely necessary that we should reason from nature up to nature's God", we should not presume to reason from God to nature.[15]

Each of them, in the tradition of English natural theology since Newton, sought to *reconcile* his religious beliefs and his scientific understanding of nature.

The polemical goals of Malthus and Paley, however, were distinct. Malthus did not seek to justify the claim that God might have intervened in nature in singular and miraculous ways; to the contrary, his work was undertaken to show that "imperious all pervading laws of nature" would ultimately frustrate any effort of the sort proposed by Condorcet and Godwin toward the egalitarian redistribution of primary resources, particularly food. Malthus, in other words, had no interest in "contrivance," but he had every interest in "law," and in the claim that the laws of nature were universal, necessary, and immutable.[16]

Although Paley's concerns had not led him to emphasize the universality and necessity of the laws of nature, this notion of law was an important element in the background of his theodicy. Relying on Malthus' first *Essay on the Principle of Population*, (1798), Paley wrote,

perhaps... no species... would not overrun... if it were permitted to multiply in perfect safety.... It is necessary, therefore, that the effects of such prolific faculties be curtailed. (These) may be necessary and useful... for the preventing of the loss of certain species from the universe: a misfortune which seems to be studiously guarded against. Though there may be the appearance of failure in some of the details of Nature's works, in her great purposes there never are. Her species never fail.... Compensation obtains throughout. Defencelessness and devastation are repaired by fecundity.[17]

He recognized the "appearance of chance" in the midst of design, taking as a model the classic Aristotelian example of the intersection of two separately planned itineraries.

The meeting, though accidental, was nevertheless hypothetically necessary (which is the only sort of necessity that is intelligible): for if the two journeys were commenced at the time, pursued in the direction, and with the speed in which and with which, they were in fact begun and performed, the meeting could not be avoided. There was not, therefore, the less necessity in it for its being by chance.[18]

Such concepts were not alien to Malthus (who later became one of the founders of the Statistical Society of London) nor to the model of the "great lottery of life," in which some unhappy individuals had "drawn a blank."[19]

Paley and Malthus were in agreement that such circumstances were for the best. Paley argued that a world which was both "furnished with advantages" and "beset with difficulties, wants, and inconveniences," was the "fittest to stimulate and exercise" the faculties of "free, rational and active natures," and so was their proper abode.[20] Malthus was more willing to flirt with theological paradox: "It seems highly probable that moral evil is absolutely necessary to the production of moral excellence," in order explicitly to align God's plan with the contemporary political and economic *status quo*.

> The middle regions of society seem to be best suited to intellectual improvement, but it is contrary to the analogy of all nature to expect that the whole of society can be a middle region. . . . It is not . . . improbable that as in the oak, the roots and branches could not be diminished very greatly without weakening the vigorous circulation of the sap in the stem, so in society the extreme parts could not be diminished beyond a certain degree without lessening that animated exertion throughout the middle parts, which is the very cause that they are the most favourable to the growth of intellect. If no man could hope to rise or fear to fall, in society, if industry did not bring with it its reward and idleness, its punishment, the middle parts would not certainly be what they now are.[21]

Paley's moral theology finally pushed this position to its logical conclusion. It was better that some events "rise up by chance, or, more properly speaking, with the appearance of chance, than according to any observable rule whatever." In particular, this was true of the distribution throughout humanity of talents, dispositions, and the constitutions upon which such attributes depended. Paley placed the *ultimate moral sanction* in the revealed certainty of *eternal reward or punishment* which would rectify any "disorder" in the temporal consequence of human behavior.[22] Since eternal happiness or damnation rode on the conduct of each human life, and since the conditions of life varied so markedly from individual to individual, God's justice was better vindicated if the distribution of these conditions were a matter of chance.

As Hume's *Philo* had already pointed out, however, such beliefs about the actual state of affairs might be *compatible* with a theistic position held for other reasons, but these beliefs about the world *justified no inferences* stronger than "there is some order in the world" and "man can be happy in it."

3. MALTHUS AND DARWIN: DIMENSIONS AND VALENCES OF SCIENTIFIC INFLUENCE

Darwin's relationship to Malthus has held considerable interest for historians of science, and their comments revolve around two related but distinguishable puzzles concerning the nature of Malthus' influence.[23] The first of these puzzles has to do with Darwin's agreement with A. R. Wallace that he had first established selection as the principle of change on the basis of his study of the practice of breeders of domestic animals and plants, and that the Malthusian law of population had then shown him how the principle of selection might operate in nature.

You are right, that I came to the conclusion that selection was the principle of change from the study of domesticated productions; and then, reading Malthus, I saw at once how to apply this principle.[24]

The *Autobiography* suggests a more significant role for his reading of *The Essay on Population*, implying that he "got a theory by which to work" only after he "happened to read for amusement Malthus on *Population*."[25] The *Autobiography* dates the first reading of Malthus as "October, 1838," but Sir Gavin de Beer, M. J. Rowlands and B. M. Skramovsky have located pages excised from *Transmutation Notebook D* which establish a slightly earlier date, September 28th, 1838. The difference may be significant, since it establishes that *Notebook D* had not been completely finished before its author read Malthus.

28th We ought to be far from wondering if changes in number of species from small changes in nature of locality. Even the energetic language of Decandolle does not convey the warring of the species as inference from Malthus. /Increase of brutes must be prevented solely by positive checks, excepting that famine may stop desire./ – in nature production does not increase, whilst no check prevail, but the positive check of famine & consequently death. /I do not doubt every one till he thinks deeply has assumed that increase of animals exactly proportionate to the number that can live./
   Population is increased at geometrical ratio in FAR SHORTER time than 25 years – yet until the one sentence of Malthus no one clearly perceived the great check amongst men. /Then in spring, like food used for other purposes as wheat for making brandy. – Even a *few* years plenty makes population in man increase & an *ordinary* crop causes a dearth./ Take Europe on an average every species must have same number killed year with year by parasites, by cold, &c. – even one species of hawk decreasing must affect instantaneously all the rest. /The final cause of all this wedging, must be to sort out proper structure, & adapt it to change/ – to do that for form, which Malthus shows is the final effect of this populousness on the energy of man. One may say there is a force like a hundred thousand wedges trying to force every kind of adapted structure into the gaps in the economy of nature or rather forming gaps by thrusting out weaker ones."[26]

Sandra Herbert's analysis of the notebook comments written before September 28th, 1838, suggests that prior to that time Darwin did not have a sufficiently clear notion of artificial selection to guide an explicit search for a comparable principle at work in non-domesticated organisms. To the contrary, she thinks that "the discovery of natural selection made the domestic analogy much more clear to Darwin than it had been before."[27] She emphasizes that although it is Lyell who might have been most closely associated with the phrase 'struggle for existence,'

In the universal struggle for existence, the right of the strongest eventually prevails; and the strength and durability of a race depends mainly on its prolificness, in which hybrids are acknowledged to be deficient.[28]

Lyell's conflation of the concepts of inter-specific and intra-specific competition *misled* Darwin.[29] Her conclusion is that "Malthus, by showing what terrible pruning was exercised on the individuals of one species, impelled Darwin to apply what he knew about the struggle at the species level to the individual level." Herbert, however, cites *no* evidence which shows how Darwin might have moved from Malthus' law of population (which does imply that not all fertilized eggs will survive the process of development and maturation and produce fertilized eggs in their turn) to a principle of selection or pruning (that the chances of producing fertilized eggs are *biased* in favor of adaptive variations distributed among individual members of the species). Malthus made *no* effort to link human fecundity with "fitness" of any sort. Darwin's copy of volume 1 of the 6th edition of the *Essay on Population* contains a list of page numbers written in by hand on one of the otherwise blank pages at the end of the book. This was his usual practice in recording the most significant loci in books he read and owned. Of the nine listed pages, he singled out four for special mention:

3 Malthus, & Franklin saw the law of increase in animals & plants clearly
23 increase of population may be prevented by some very powerful and obvious checks
343 Force of life in each country in increase ratio to Fecundity (Doubleday)
517 On doubling in U. States in 25 yrs.[30]

Darwin wrote in the margin on page 343, "This is much the same as to say well-fed are less fecund. give note after Doubleday." Thomas Doubleday had argued that the relationship between abundant food and fecundity was *inverse*, so that "in a nation highly and generally affluent and luxurious, population will decrease and decay."[31] On the pages in question, Malthus cited Muret's evidence that

the country where children escape the best from the dangers of infancy, and where the mean life, in whatever way the calculation is made, is higher than in any other, (is) that in which the fecundity is the smallest. . . .

together with the Swiss author's speculation that

Is not it that, in order to maintain in all places the proper equilibrium of population, God has wisely ordered things in such a manner as that the force of life in each country should be in the inverse ratio of its fecundity?[32]

However, the Doubleday-Muret thesis does *not* suggest Darwin's view: in a given population, the better adapted organism has greater chances of leaving fertile progeny.

Darwin *attributed* to Malthus the discovery of the "final effect" or "final cause" of "innumerable eggs" ("this populousness").[33] However, the view that "there is a force like a hundred thousand wedges trying to force every kind of *adapted* structure into the *gaps* in the œconomy of nature or rather *forming gaps by thrusting out weaker ones*" (emphasis added) was Darwin's own. The rhetorical effect of the September 28th entry in *Notebook D*, therefore, slightly exaggerated the influence of Malthus. Such exaggeration was not uncommon at the time, and J. R. Poynter argues that it is an error to think of Malthus as the "father" of the Poor Law Amendment of 1834, as is commonly done: "its immediate sponsors were Malthusians of the second generation, decidedly heretical if still respectful sons." Malthus was a controversial and well known author, who nevertheless "seldom maintained consistency throughout a long and complex thesis."[34] In the idiom of the times, therefore, to call one's views "Malthusian," as Darwin did, was an easy means of alluding to the conjunction of the "law of increase in animals & plants" with "some very powerful and obvious checks" which could prevent such increase. In the absence of explicit textual evidence, it seems unwise to attribute other influence upon Darwin to Malthus. In particular, the concept of "pruning" or "selection" does *not* appear to have come to Darwin *via* the 6th edition of the *Essay on Population*.

However, Herbert is obviously correct in pointing out that the Malthusian "checks" to population operated *within* a single species and that Malthus' accumulation of data concerning the human species lent that point both empirical and rhetorical force. If Lyell conflated the notions of species and individual and spoke only of an *inter-specific* struggle for existence, Malthus provided Darwin a new reason for *looking for* evidence of an *intra-specific* struggle. Herbert may also be correct in stating that Darwin's concept of artificial selection was not well-developed prior to the time he read Malthus, and that he used what he learned from reading *An Essay on the Principle of Population* to sharpen his subsequent investigations of the practices of breeders of domesticated plants and animals. The problem remaining, however, is the concise, accurate expression of the *nature* of the influence Malthus had on Darwin. On this point, neither Herbert nor Vorzimmer is much help.

The basis for an all prevading struggle for existence had certainly been *well-laid* by Malthus — and Darwin *picked it up* immediately.[35] (Emphasis added.)

Malthus must be ranked as *contributor* rather than *catalyst* to Darwin's new understanding, after September 28, 1838, of the explanatory possibilities of the idea of struggle in nature.[36] (Emphasis added.)

Serious problems are concealed by the over-use of such metaphors to describe relations of influence in the history of ideas. In what follows in this Chapter and later in Chapter 11, I will use the more prosaic tools and vocabulary of conceptual analysis to compare the matrices of data, theory, and metatheoretical criteria which structured the work of Malthus and Darwin. Such analysis is necessary for any clear account of relationships of scientific influence, but it is well to remember that it may not be sufficient. For example, Malthus' *reputation*, or that aspect of it most familiar to Darwin, may have been as decisive a part of the influence as anything Malthus actually wrote. Reputations, of course, are also subject to historical investigation, but the present study cannot pause for a full examination of the beliefs about Malthus held by various members of Darwin's cultural circle.

The second puzzle revolves around the question which Gertrude Himmelfarb correctly identified as the issue which gives the Malthus—Darwin relationship its special interest. "This is the circumstance that a purely economic and political tract should have inspired a purely scientific theory."[37] That is, no one has seriously attempted to decide between the opposed interpretations of this matter suggested by Himmelfarb on the one hand and J.D. Bernal on the other. Bernal distinguished that science "required for the working productive forces" of a society, and that science which was needed, "in conjunction with philosophy and religion, to buttress the current social system." He claimed that Darwin's theory of natural selection and the struggle for existence were simply a "reflection of the free competition of the full capitalist era."[38] On the contrary, Himmelfarb asserted that Malthus' theory was itself biological in its origins — so that Darwin just happened to find properly biological propositions in a "purely economic and political tract."

Perhaps, as Himmelfarb suggests, Malthus was no more than a medium for the clear perception of an idea whose origin and best evidence were to be found elsewhere. This suggestion, however, has considerable significance for the effort to understand the nature of scientific communication, to appropriately delineate the historical boundaries of scientific disciplines or research fronts, and to appraise the impact of social conditions upon the various aspects of scientific activity.[39] An examination of the role of "carriers" in the

history of science could provide important evidence for the continuing sociological and philosophical reassessment of the conditions and circumstances of
scientific rationality and objectivity.

No one measure of "compactness" or degree of consensus is characteristic
of science at various points in its history nor of different scientific disciplines
at the same time in history. Consequently, there is no predetermined standard
to apply to the Malthus–Darwin exchange in order to decide whether it was
intradisciplinary, inter-disciplinary, or an instance of the "reflection" of an
economic system and its ideology into Darwin's conceptual structure. Kuhn
and others have suggested that scientific communities are distinguished by the
relatively complete consensus among their members concerning the major
dimensions of a so-called disciplinary matrix, but there is no guide for the
formulation of empirical indices of such consensus. The absence of such an
important tool weakens any program for identifying shifting standards of
rationality in the history of science. Such tools will be necessary if any such
approach is to achieve any satisfactory degree of replicability when applied to
difficult cases by historians of science.[40]

Consider the following "minimum evidential base," a body of data which
both Darwin and Malthus could affirm, and whose significance Malthus' *Essay*
called to Darwin's attention:

1. Generally, the number of *seeds* produced (eggs laid, young per
    litter, litters/breeding life) by an organism (or pair) is *greater than*
    the number required for *replacement*.
2. In some circumstances (spring "blooms," population "explosions"
    resulting from sudden changes in environment, e.g., migration
    into new favorable territory), populations of organisms exhibit
    very *large surges* in size.
3. Typically, and in the long run, the numerical size of organic
    populations remains constant. If r = the rate of change of the
    numerical size of a population, in the most general case, $r = 0$.

The famous "ratios" of geometric and arithmetic series express a mathematical thesis affirmed by both men. There is nothing distinctive of political
economy or of human demography in any of this.

However, the major theses and conclusions of the *Essay*, those which were
most distinctively and originally Malthus' own, *were economic* and *political*.
These included his predictions about the effects of poor relief upon the price
of food, upon the human birth rate, and upon the moral character of those
who received the dole and became subject to the poor laws.[41] These proposi-

tions applied only to the behavior of human beings; they were not general laws describing (or predicting) the behavior of all organisms. Moreover, Malthus' own normative or moral biases concerning the way men *ought* to act were inextricably involved with his predictions concerning the way they *would* act. In his view, a social system of stratified classes with "self-love" the "main-spring of the great machine" was the inevitable result of the laws of nature.

He simply juxtaposed his views concerning A. Smith's "generous system of perfect liberty" and his opinions about the Condorcet–Godwin brand of socialism, without analysing the ethical roots of the dispute.

The concepts of self-love, benevolence, and sympathy had an important role in the major controversies of English ethical thought in the eighteenth century. Malthus and Paley were *uncritical* exponents of the "selfish system"; and each seemed unaware of a serious alternative to such a position.[42] Since Malthus assumed that human behavior is and ought to be rooted in self-love, and only self-love, the most probable effects of the dole upon human reproductive behavior seemed obvious.

Malthus did seek to base his theory upon suppositions concerning reproductive behavior and the limits to population growth which had a wider application among organisms. His account of the population "bloom" among the emigrants to the New World provided a striking analogy to those chance plant and animal emigrants to oceanic islands so important to Darwin's theory. *A Summary View of the Principle of Population*, published in 1830, began with a recitation of the geometric increase in the number of seeds gained from succeeding generations of carefully cultivated plants.[43]

This acceptably general biological proposition does not explain (give the "reasons" for), or warrant the inference that the *chances* of leaving fertile offspring are *biased* according to the heritable characteristics of the members of a breeding population. Malthus' biological evidence was not evidence of *competition*. In fact, Malthus provided nothing but ancedotal evidence about the behavior of any non-human organism. He never mentioned the quasi-competitive aspects of the growth and development of organisms, and of their relative adaptability to changing environments. He did provide a dramatic and widely familiar context for the interpretation of 'struggle for existence.' Given his basic assumptions concerning man's inability to convert all industrial productivity into food, and concerning the necessity with which human populations would inexorably and repeatedly double in size, he sketched a view of social life in which the spring of "self-love" was necessary for success (narrowly understood as entrance into and continued membership in the middle class). Within this world view, he understood the struggle for the means of subsistence as a *brake* or retardant upon change, the cause of a recurrent economic cycle of peak demand, overproduction, falling demand, unemployment, misery, vice, and death.[44]

Much of the misunderstanding of the social and cultural implications of Darwin's theory is rooted in the failure of Darwin's readers to note (and Darwin's failure to insist upon) the distinction of his use of 'struggle for existence' and Malthus' use of any comparable term. For Darwin, 'struggle' ('struggle$_D$') meant 'an effort to overcome a difficulty (through relations of dependence, chance variation, *or* competition).' For Malthus, 'struggle' ('struggle$_M$') meant 'a zero-sum competition for a *scarce* resource (subject to the law of diminishing returns).'

Darwin rarely, if ever, *used* 'struggle$_M$,' however much it may have *influenced* him. His *narrowest* use of 'struggle' was not so limited in application, since he *never* argued that food (or food plus "moral restraint") was *the* limiting factor in the growth of organic populations. In the *Essay of 1844*, Part I, he used the words 'struggle,' 'war,' 'wedge,' and 'weigh in the balance' almost synonymously to refer to the relative success of differing organisms in overcoming a relevant set of environmental obstacles to survival and reproduction. 'Struggle' in this Darwinian context was not just a struggle for food or a struggle for space; it was not just the kind of competition where two organisms would directly contest for the use of the same commodity. General hardiness, resistance to disease, drought, extremes of temperature, would be as relevant to this competition as success in obtaining food.[45] In this simplest Darwinian context, to say that organisms "struggle for existence," is to say that they exhibit varying degrees of success in the effort to survive and leave fertile progeny, in some single, but complex, environment (I will label this sense of 'struggle,' 'struggle$_{D1}$').

Darwin also failed to share Malthus' premonition of an ultimately unchanging and unchangeable environment which would enforce a final equilibrium on organic populations. A key aspect of the Darwinian thesis concerning the variability of the environment was his understanding of its complexity and particularly of the role of other organisms (of the same and other species) as elements of the environment of any given organism. The success of the earliest and simplest living organisms helped produce a new environment in which the possibilities for more complex life cycles arose for the first time. Darwin always denied that his theory implied the necessity of progress in organic complexity or any other attribute ("In my theory there is no absolute tendency to progression, exception from favorable circumstances!").[46] Nevertheless, he recognized that the contextuating background of his theory suggested a connection between the tendency toward geometric rates of increase in population size (which Malthus affirmed) and a certain kind of organic progress (which Malthus implicitly denied). His account of this matter was not articulated in much detail, but it amounted to the suggestion that while increasing organic complexity was not necessary on the terms of his theory, if it occurred, it could be expected that the resultant ecological systems would be more stable than those which contained only a few varieties of relatively simple organisms. It might be expected, on this view, that the success of any one group of organisms would create stable opportunities for other variant types.[47] Darwin's theory also provided a more significant role for the consequences of organic migration (or random relocation as a function of winds and ocean currents) and isolation. Malthus' assumption seemed to be that migration (and trade) offered no hope for the long range solution of the problem of human food consumption, and such factors did not complicate his understanding of 'struggle.' But for Darwin, the theoretical significance of the new opportunities resulting from organisms' colonization of virgin (and preferably semi-isolated) territory was immense. His hypotheses concerning the results of the chance colonization of "oceanic islands" served as his first working model for the natural process which could result in speciation. In this context, the 'struggle for existence' referred to differing rates of success in leaving fertile progeny in a range of distinct (whether simultaneous or successive) environments. This sense of 'struggle' (labeled 'struggle$_{D2}$') is easily distinguished from 'struggle$_M$' in that it is *compatible* with significant progress, and does not necessitate an eventually static equilibrium condition, or imply an unvarying "optimum population size." The concept of sexual selection was based on Darwin's recognition of the complexity of reproductive behavior. This set a decidedly non-Malthusian context for Darwin's formulation of the fundamental ethical significance of human social life. For Malthus the main spring of the social system was self-love; for Darwin, the basic rule of human social life was benevolent sympathy — an attitude for which he found appropriate sub-human analogues.[48] Within his own theoretical context, Darwin found that *organisms were dependent upon as well as competitive with each other*. Obviously, this opened up still other possibilities in the struggle for existence, and another properly Darwinian sense of 'struggle' ('struggle$_{D3}$') not to be found in Malthus.[49] The occurrence of such a number of uses of 'struggle' differing so markedly from that to be found in Malthus reopens the question as to the nature of Darwin's debt to Malthus. That debt is not adequately described in terms of Malthus' having provided "reasons" for Darwin's development of the concept. Nor is it satisfactory to suggest that Malthus provided no more than a *stimulus* for Darwin's thought. He partially articulated a concept which Darwin developed more fully by placing it in a much more general theoretical context (allowing for environmental variation, various forms of social organization, etc.). But his example was a striking one and his account of it was graphic and persuasive, providing a readily shared element in the background of all educated Englishmen of the time.

As a conceptual innovator and as an influential figure in English culture, Malthus was a political economist, first and foremost, a "devotee of the natural sciences" only as an afterthought. Consequently, I am inclined to think Bernal's view of the Mathus–Darwin relationship more generally correct than Himmelfarb's, but I hope I have indicated how complex a matter "reflection" of the free competition of the full capitalist era was in this instance. Darwin may well have chosen to use 'struggle' to overcome the quiescence suggested by Lyell's references to 'equilibrium' because the former term had a great currency in the political climate of the times. His use of the term, however, obviously overcame the limitations implied by Malthus' account of a static environment and finally inflexible social organization.

Even as an amateur, Malthus was not a very good biologist; he let his ethical preferences (for the principle of self-love as the main spring of society) determine his description of human reproductive behavior. Nevertheless, there was an interesting sense in which Darwin and Malthus shared a biological metaphor, the metaphorical vision of man as an animal. Malthus was a *biologizing political economist*, enthusiastically engaged in the discovery of natural and necessary biological limits to any program of political and social reform. The polemical Malthusian rhetoric, so devastating for the career of Godwinian socialism among English intellectuals in the first half of the nineteenth century, carried unmistakably biological overtones. The contradiction between man's animal urges, the unabating and unabateable passion between the sexes vs. the continuing requirement for food, set an insurmountable obstacle in the path of all radical social reform. (The piece-meal, gradual meliorism expounded in the later editions of the *Essay* did not obscure this basic fact from Malthus' contemporaries.) He saw man's alienation as the consequence of his biological, animal nature, and no political or economic institution could overcome this elemental flaw.

For reasons of his own, Darwin constantly flirted with the temptations of *anthropomorphic biology*. He continually sought to read human traits back into nature. The powerful metaphysical tensions generated by this effort, as well as his incomplete and ambiguous resolution of them, are clearly illustrated in his "metaphysical" notebooks.[50] The "materialism" espoused by Darwin in the crucial interval between 1837 and 1842 involved the postulate of a continuous chain of natural being. His later published work emphasized the thesis of insensibly slight gradations, "nature makes no leaps," to an extent which disconcerted his fellow evolutionists. One powerful motive for such emphasis was to block the intrusion of any metaphysical exceptions to the generality of his theory. Darwin's basic philosophic ambition was "to show hiatus in mind not saltus between man & brutes."[51]

This points to an even more fundamental metaphor held in common by Malthus and Darwin. Both subscribed to that powerful metaphor which characterized scientific laws as statements of objective fact. Both accepted the corollaries of this subscription, holding that man and animals were alike subject to one and the same law of population, one and the same struggle for existence. And (Darwin added) one and the same evolution under the law embracing all life, natural selection. Both were committed to *scientific realism* in sweeping and uncritical fashion. Both defined the course of moral honesty and courage in terms of a stoic facing of those facts which were made to seem important and inevitable by their theories. These similarities of underlying commitment determined a common idiom for the terms 'law,' 'life,' and 'man' which I believe to be another basic channel along which information flowed from Malthus to Darwin.

CHAPTER SIX

SKEPTICISM, ROMANTICISM, AND THE MORAL SENSE

Darwin formulated his transmutation theory in a complex and somewhat troubled frame of mind. While his views concerning theism (or deism) were never clearly formulated, he obviously agreed with Comte that biology should be advanced beyond its current "theological" stage. While he was able to say that his theory accorded with what we know of the law impressed on matter by the Creator,[1] that passage must be compared with the heavy skepticism expressed in his remarks on Macculloch's natural theology.[2]

N. B. The explanation of types of structure in classes — as resulting from the will of the deity, to create animals on certain plans, — is no explanation — it has not the character of a physical law & is therefore utterly useless. — it foretells nothing because we know nothing of the will of the Deity, how it acts & whether constant or inconstant like that of men. — the cause given we know not the effect.

When Darwin began, as he did in 1838, to utilize positivist themes in constructing his self-image as a scientist, he did so with the uneasy inconsistency of a transitional or marginal figure. Consequently, it is misleading to label him either a positivist or a deist.

1. HUME AND NATURAL RELIGION

Darwin mentioned David Hume frequently in the Notebooks and early manuscripts, and indicated an interest in at least six of his books and his correspondence with Rousseau. However, these references were almost all confined to succinct identifications of titles and topics. None of Hume's books were to be found in Darwin's personal library. The first full sentence comment by Darwin, dated August 24th, 1838, was so cryptic and muddled on the point of ideas "ordering muscles" to action that it raises doubts as to whether Darwin understood Hume's analysis of causality.

August 24th. As some *impressions* (Hume) become unconscious so some *ideas*, i.e., habits which must require ideas to order muscles to do the action.[3]

A later comment was similarly laconic.

I suspect the endless round of doubts & skepticism might be solved by considering the origin of reason, as gradually developed. See Hume on Sceptical Philosophy.[4]

Darwin praised *An Enquiry Concerning the Principles of Morals* for providing a "good abstract of Butler & arguments of beneficial tendency of affections," but this was in the midst of his analysis of Mackintosh's *History*.[5]

Given the lack of explicit indications of Hume's influence, one might be inclined to settle for the safe and limp conclusion that Hume's sections on "theory of knowledge and necessary connection" provided "methodological presuppositions that were important, indeed, in Darwin's century."[6] But this would understate the unmistakeable flavor of skeptical irony which permeates many of Darwin's comments concerning deism and the theory of special, divine creation of species.

Shall we then say that a pair, or a gravid female, of each of these three species of rhinoceros, were separately created with the deceptive appearance of true relationship, with the stamp of inutility on some parts, and of conversion in other parts, out of the inorganic elements of Java, Sumatra, and Malacca? Or have they descended, like our domestic races, from the same parent stock? For my own part, I could no more admit the former proposition than I could admit that the planets move in their courses, and that a stone falls to the ground, not through the intervention of the secondary and appointed law of gravity, but from the direct volition of the Creator.[7]

This passage, taken from a draft which Darwin directed his wife to publish in the event of his premature death, concludes with the customary deistic tag. But the phrases "a pair, or a gravid female" and "the stamp of inutility on some parts" carry an unmistakeably ironic tone.[8]

Cleanthes, the deist of the *Dialogues*, tried to side-step Philo's critique of the argument from design by insisting that *some* design was obvious in the world, yet the skeptical Philo was able to wring from him the concession that such design would *not* support inferences to the *infinity*, *perfection*, or *unity* of the designer. If Cleanthes was content at this point simply to repeat "design remains," the orthodox Demea was concerned that the reduction of deism to the uncontestable proposition that *there is some order in the world* rendered it "useless for the purposes of life." Philo hammered at this point with the metaphor of the "soul of the world animal," seeking to show that the evidence available to a careful observer did nothing whatsoever to establish the moral attributes of the designer. If one were prepared to concede, as Darwin did in the *Autobiography*, that on the whole there was more pleasure than pain in the experience of living things, Philo insisted that this would *support* no stronger inference than the even-handed "Nature is neither benevolent nor malicious." Cleanthes was unable, even when given the widest possible latitude for the presentation of relevant evidence for a completely natural theology, to support conclusions stronger than: *there is some order in*

*the world, and it is possible for a reasonably decent and tasteful man to be
reasonably happy in it.*

In the autobiographical memoir he wrote for his children, Darwin identified
his loss of taste for poetry and music as the most significant change — perhaps
the only significant change — in his character since the time, almost forty
years earlier, when he first formulated the theory of the transmutation of
species.[9] As a young man in his twenties he had received intense delight
and pleasure from his reading of Shakespeare, Milton, Gray, Wordsworth,
Coleridge, Byron, and Shelley. Yet with advancing years and increasing
preoccupation with science, and science alone, he found Shakespeare almost
nauseatingly dull, and he could no longer endure reading even a line of poetry.
He felt a tremendous sense of loss in this atrophy of aesthetic sensitivity. It
carried in its wake a "loss of happiness, possible injury to the intellect, and
more probably to the moral character, by enfeebling the emotional part" of
his nature. In the only passage of its kind in the *Autobiography*, Darwin
remarked that if he had his life to live over he would guard against such an
unwelcome transformation in spirit by making it a "rule to read some poetry
and listen to some music at least once every week."

His autobiographical reflections on his *religious* odyssey suggest no such
regret over his gradual acceptance of Huxley's label, 'agnostic.' What the
Autobiography failed to note, in spite of its charting of a drift away from
orthodoxy as early as the period 1837–1839, was Darwin's early enthusiasm
for Comte's positivism. Darwin was much less cautious about Comte's positivism than Huxley, particularly during the period under examination here.
The *Autobiography* ambiguously suggested that its author accepted a deistic
argument for the existence of God as the intelligent First Cause of the universe until some significant time after the publication of *The Origin of
Species*.[10] Then, he claimed, he settled into a final period of agnosticism only
after thinking through the implications of his theory for the evolution of man
and man's powers of understanding. The thought that man's fear of God
might have ancestral roots comparable to a young monkey's fear of snakes,
he remembered, finally destroyed his confidence that man's powers were
suited to theological labors.

The *Autobiography* thus suggested that religious issues were not allowed
to alter the course of a scientific inquiry during the time the transmutation
theory was being constructed and tested. But this self-image is inconsistent
with the contents of the early *Notebooks* and manuscripts. These materials
document a highly compressed, often dramatic analysis, dealing with all of
the themes which the *Autobiography* assigned to the period after 1859, all

except a positive effort to formulate any proof for the existence of God, even one so rudimentary as that to be found in the *Autobiography* itself.

2. WORDSWORTH'S EXCURSIVE QUEST

There is little in the *Notebooks*, largely completed before Darwin reached the age of 30, to reflect his enthusiasm for poetry. It was his "boast" that he had read Wordsworth's long poem, *The Excursion*, twice through during the busy years 1837–1839.[11] This most philosophical of Wordsworth's works would have repaid commentary at least as well as Mackintosh's *History of Ethics* and Abercrombie's *Discourse on Intellect*. But only one of the two brief *Notebook* allusions to Wordsworth can be counted as more than a listing. The evidence for Wordsworth's "influence" upon Darwin, consequently, is only circumstantial. Yet *The Excursion* provided powerful poetic expression for some of Darwin's deepest philosophical concerns and convictions. The contrasting voices of its major figures bore a striking resemblance to Darwin's conflicting and equivocal comments concerning the moral and metaphysical implications of his theory.

The title of Wordsworth's epic must have struck a resonant note for the young man recently disembarked from the five-year voyage of the *Beagle*. The dominant voice of the poem was that of the Wanderer, a former pedlar who found his wandering life provided such meaningful communion with nature and with the persons he met along the way that he continued his rambles in his later years. The voice of the Pastor, the clergyman charged with the spiritual care of a flock dispersed among the surrounding hills, responded to the Wanderer's quest

> for act and circumstance, that make
> the individual known and understood.[12]

with a series of observations which illuminated

> The universal forms
> Of human nature

Neither the Pastor nor the Wanderer succeeded entirely in assuaging the despair of the Solitary, a former devotee of the Enlightenment rendered cynical by the betrayal of the French Revolution and by the personal tragedy of early death of his wife and two children. Nor did the Wanderer and the Pastor, although they were the voices of hope in the poem, seek to demonstrate a theodicy for the Solitary. They did not claim to mitigate or even explain the depths of human suffering brought on by the natural and social tragedies following in the train of the chances of death, betrayal, and grinding poverty.

The argument of *The Excursion* gave full voice to the anguish brought on by human infidelity,[13] economic exploitation,[14] and by fatal natural coincidence.[15] Its resolution had a strongly bivocal theme:

> To a mysteriously united pair
> This place is consecrate; to Death and Life
> And to the best affections that proceed
> From their conjunction . . . . [16]

And

> Life, I repeat, is energy of love
> Divine or human; exercised in pain,
> In strife, in tribulation — [17]

It is fair to say of the poem that it did not aim so much at resolution as at defining the contextuating background of life's joys and sorrows. The Solitary was not won over by the perorations of the Wanderer, nor by the simple tales of the Pastor. At most, he admitted to a willingness to join them in another rambling excursion, another discussion of the meaning of suffering, another examination of the question

> Is man
> A child of hope? Do generations press
> On generations, without progress made?[18]

And, at the end of the long poem, the Pastor's wife says of the Wanderer himself,

> While he is speaking, I have power to see
> Even as he sees; but when his voice hath ceased,
> Then, with a sigh, sometimes I feel, as now,
> Than combinations so serene and bright
> Cannot be lasting in a world like ours,
> Whose highest beauty, beautiful as it is,
> Like that reflected in yon quiet pool,
> Seems but a fleeting sunbeam's gift, whose peace
> The sufferance only of a breath of air![19]

The excursion was a symbol of a *quest* Wordsworth meant to extol above all else. Its texture of intended destinations and chance encounters represented its author's convictions concerning the nature of moral truth:

The mind's repose
On evidence is not to be ensured
By act of naked reason. Moral truth
Is no mechanic structure, built by rule;
And which, once built, retains a stedfast shape
And undisturbed proportions; but a thing
Subject, you deem, to vital accidents;
And, like the water-lily, lives and thrives,
Whose root is fixed in stable earth, whose head
Floats on the tossing waves.[20]

Wordsworth, for all his foreboding over the natural and social ills brought on by the surge of technology at the turn of the nineteenth century, saw in science and its mastery of the elements a process by which man *could* participate in the ensoulment of nature itself.

Yet do I exult,
Casting reserve away, exult to see
An intellectual mastery exercised
O'er the blind elements; a purpose given,
A perseverance fed; almost a soul
Imparted — to brute matter, I rejoice,
Measuring the force of those gigantic powers
That, by the thinking mind, have been compelled
To serve the will of feeble-bodied Man.[21]

While he found *no hope in mere scientific enlightenment,*

How insecure, how baseless in itself
Is the Philosophy whose sway depends
On mere material instruments; — how weak
Those arts, and high inventions, if unpropped
By virtue.

he looked for the time when science itself might participate in the liberating quest, by *lending guidance to the mind's own excursion,* helping to build up the Being we are, thus taking science beyond itself.

Science then
Shall be a precious visitant; and then,
And only then, be worthy of her name:
For then her heart shall kindle; her dull eye,
Dull and inanimate, no more shall hang
Chained to its object in brute slavery;
But taught with patient interest to watch
The processes of things, and serve the cause

Of order and distinctness, not for this
Shall it forget that its most noble use,
Its most illustrious province, must be found
In furnishing clear guidance, a support
Not treacherous, to the mind's *excursive* power.
—So build we up the Being that we are;
Thus deeply drinking-in the soul of things,
We shall be wise perforce; and, while inspired
By Choice, and conscious that the Will is free,
Shall move unswerving, even as if impelled
By strict necessity, along the path
Of order and of good.[22]

Wordsworth's quest for the transcendent meaning of life might seem oddly combined with the empiricism so sternly professed by Darwin and his scientific contemporaries.

And that unless above himself he can
Erect himself, how poor a thing is Man![23]

The transcendence Wordsworth sought was *embedded in the cosmic sweep of nature and in the full story of human history.* The Wanderer had undergone a process of personal evolution, a process by which the appeal to fear and terror associated with the orthodox Scottish religion of his youth was gradually replaced by the calmer teaching of Nature herself.

In his heart,
Where Fear sate thus, a cherished visitant,
Was wanting yet the pure delight of love
By sound diffused, or by the breathing air;
Or by the silent looks of happy things,
Or flowing from the universal face
Of earth and sky. But he had felt the power
Of Nature, and already was prepared
By his intense conception, to receive
Deeply the lesson deep of love which he,
Whom Nature, by whatever means, has taught
To feel intensely, cannot but receive.[24]

Of the Wanderer, Wordsworth said, "in the mountains did he *feel* his faith," and "There his spirit shaped Her prospects, nor did he believe, — he *saw.* What wonder if his being thus became Sublime and comprehensive!"

What role did Wordsworth play in Darwin's personal excursion? It is plain that *The Excursion* did not match the religious vision of Milton's *Paradise Lost.* Wordsworth's was no saga of damnation and redemption; it was a tale in which the antipodes were "Despondency" and "Despondency Corrected."[25] Everyone was left some hope at the end of the excursion. No one was assured eternal happiness; no one was damned. On the whole, there was "ascent and progress."

> The vast Frame
> Of social nature changes evermore
> Her organs and her members, with decay
> Restless, and restless generation, powers
> And functions dying and produced at need, —
> And by this law the mighty whole subsists:
> With an ascent and progress in the main;
> Yet, Oh! how disproportioned to the hopes
> And expectations of self-flattering minds![26]

In his adulthood, the article of Christianity which Darwin *could not tolerate* was that of the *damnation* of infidels and unrepentant sinners. He found *that* a *damnable doctrine*. Wordsworth represented at least that departure from Milton's orthodoxy. Christ's blood was not a ransom paid to Satan. Contractual theology found no place in his account of the inarticulate charity of Nature.[27]

If Wordsworth's vision was not orthodox it just as certainly was not deistic. It had nothing in common with the platitudes of Paley, and less with the Malthusian hymns to the middle class. Nor would Wordsworth, with the authors of the *Bridgewater Treatises*, give thanks and faith to God because of the rational elegance of scientific representations of Nature. In all, if the author of *The Excursion* was a deist, with his exultation of affective communion with Nature and of the primacy of emotion and imagination for man's exploration of the world without and the world within, anyone but the most adamant atheist was a deist. To the extent that Darwin was under Wordsworth's spell, Paley, Malthus, Whewell would have seemed cold and incredible. If *their* fabric were to totter and fall, it would only be for the better.

In exploring Darwin's religious thought, it is necessary to attend to the structure of religious sensibility among a growing group of "sensitive and humane people who disbelieved in the reality of a Divine Purpose in human life as a whole."[28] Was Darwin responsive to their growing "fear that, with the arrival of the age of machines, society and even personal life were developing a soulless mechanical character?" Or was his preoccupation with opening a new and seemingly endless frontier of biological investigation so all-engrossing that he rejected every reference to man's *soul* as an instance of "arrogance"

or of some brand of sentimentalism lacking the hard seriousness of science?
Was he attentive to Wordsworth's sense that while

> Suffering is permanent, obscure and dark,
> And shares the nature of infinity,

there is nevertheless some justification for the human virtue of hope? The
young Darwin claimed "grandeur" for the view of life embodied in his theory
of the transmutation of species. What was the quality of the experience which
he distilled into the famous concluding passage of *The Origin*, and which was
first written for the Sketch of 1842?

He obviously did *not* regard his theory as a "life-less abstraction" with no
immediate implications for the understanding of human life.[29] He was far
from admitting that his transmutation theory could effect human life only
by improving the activities of those breeders of plants and animals whose
unscientific practice had supplied him with an all-important explanatory
analogy. Perhaps one could save the thesis that "information provided by the
strictly empirical sciences can be incorporated in the social life-world only
through its technical utilization" by stressing the technological roots of the
metaphor of natural selection. But certainly such considerations were not at
stake in Darwin's references to "simple grandeur," "fixed laws," and "endless
forms most beautiful and most wonderful."

The young Darwin had some interest in an immediate juxtaposition of
literature, art and science. Unfortunately, the *Notebooks* and manuscripts
contain only cryptic allusions to Wordsworth, Burke, Joshua Reynolds, and
the *Laocoon*. At the end of an "analysis of pleasures of scenery. –" written
in *Notebook M* a week or two before he read Brewster's review of Comte's
Cours de Philosophie Positive, Darwin discussed *imaginative* pleasures,

which correspond to those awakened during music. – connection with poetry, abun-
dance, fertility, rustic life, virtuous happiness: – recall scraps of poetry: – former
thoughts, & experienced people recall pictures & therefore imagining pleasure/ of imitation come into play. – the train of thoughts vary no doubt in different people, an
agriculturist in whose mind supply of food was evasive & ill-defined thought would
receive pleasure from thinking of the fertility. – I a geologist, have ill-defined notion of
land covered with ocean, former animals, slow force cracking surface, etc. truly poetical.
(V. Wordsworth about sciences being sufficiently habitual to become poetical.)/ the
botanist might so view plants & trees. – I am sure I remember my pleasure in Kensington
Gardens has often been greatly excited by looking at trees at (i.e., as) great compound
animals united by wonderful & mysterious manner. – There is much imagination in
every view. if one were admiring one in India, & a tiger stalked across the plains, how
one's feelings would be excited, & how the scenery would rise. Deer in Parks ditto.[30]

Wordsworth found science in its most noble office *only* when "her dull eye, dull and inanimate, no more shall hang chained to its object in brute slavery"; only when she was not seen as a mere purveyor of "material instruments," and only when she provided guidance and support for the imaginative liberation (the "*excursive* power") of the mind itself. He saw science serving the cause of order and distinctness, by watching the "processes of things" with "patient interest." But this was not her most illustrious province; science would be a "precious visitant" when she played some part in the larger human effort:

> —So build we up the Being that we are;
> Thus deeply drinking-in the soul of things.

As a human enterprise, science would thrive only in the context of a refined aesthetic sensibility, of a lofty and free imagination, and of devotion to moral truth. Darwin saw that "there is much imagination in every view," and that as a scientist he could experience a nearly poetic pleasure in the imaginative juxtaposition of ideas. Wordsworth, however, was not seeking to instruct scientists in the fashion of deriving a purer aesthetic satisfaction from their customary routines. Instead, he invited their participation in a larger excursion toward man's self-knowledge and moral development.

The impression that Darwin was *indifferent* to such romantic bias and its potentially *anti-scientific* implications, has probably triggered much of the extrascientific animus against his views. In this matter, Darwin's friends and supporters have sometimes damaged rather than aided his cause — by appearing to insist that his theory stands or falls with one's willingness to adopt the view that human life is and must be basically mechanical, loveless, and purposeless. As an older man, Darwin stated that a lifetime devoted to science had unwanted and alienating consequences; that it had made him a mere machine for grinding theories out of facts: not a self-congratulatory image to present to one's children in a final memoir. But that was the one aspect of his self-image Darwin would have changed, had he his life to live over.

How did the *young Darwin* see these issues? At the time that he was constructing his theory, did he exhibit any concern for Wordsworth's romantic critique of science? Was he concerned for "deeply drinking in the soul of things," for "furnishing clear guidance, a support not treacherous, to the mind's *excursive* power," as Wordsworth understood these phrases? Or was he simply imitating a mannerism of the decade in claiming a modish enthusiasm for Wordsworth, Coleridge, and Shelley?

There is no direct evidence to support any answer to such questions.

However sincere and profound Darwin's delight in poetry may have been, he kept no contemporaneous record of his reactions to that dimension of his reading. However, there are at least four themes, centering around the basic symbols of *love,* of a fundamental *struggle* within nature and within all natural objects, of *chance* and the deep significance of the unintended, haphazard occurrence; and of the significance, meaning, and justification of the human attitude of *hope* for the future, where I find notable consensus between Darwin's *Notebooks* and early manuscripts and Wordsworth's *The Excursion*. Taken together with the general trend of Darwin's methodological self image of this period (i.e., he was *not* a mechanist nor a reductionist; he was finally neither a positivist nor a predictivist), the evidence is that the young Darwin would have been sympathetic to the critique of science in *The Excursion*. His early *Notebooks* and manuscripts were an illustration of the scientist's participation in some part of the poet's quest for the meaning of life.

3. JAMES MACKINTOSH AND THE MORAL SENSE

Darwin's marginal comments on Sir James Mackintosh's *Dissertation on the Progress of Ethical Philosophy*, and his 2500 word manuscript "On the Moral Sense," (dated May 5th, 1839, Maer), located him in still another philosophical context: that of the widespread eighteenth century desire to equate or harmonize the moral with the physical world. On this point, Darwin's resolution was firmer than was typical of his response to philosophical issues. His growing positivist concern to avoid the anthropomorphic fallacy did *not* lead him to question the vestiges of natural law moral theory which he found in Mackintosh. To the contrary, he worked to correct Mackintosh's lapses from this view. Where Mackintosh wrote "it is equally certain that the word Ought introduces the mind into a new region, to which nothing physical corresponds," Darwin pencilled in the comment, "a pointer ought to stand."

Darwin was far from agreement with William Whewell on many philosophical issues, but his respect for his old Cambridge mentor ran deep. Whewell had written a preface to Mackintosh's history of ethics, and Darwin's fly-leaf notes in his personal copy contain the entry, "Whewell's Preface good abstract." Coincidentally, his *Autobiography* identified Mackintosh and Whewell as the two "best conversers on grave subjects" to whom he ever listened. Whewell identified one of the major problems of Mackintosh's ethical position:

Mackintosh . . . maintains that though the moral faculty is formed or educed by inter-course with the external world, it is a law of our nature; yet he allows that what this law prescribes, agrees with the rule, rightly understood, of bringing forth the greatest happi-ness. He was, therefore naturally called upon to account for this coincidence. If moral approval be a different sentiment from the estimation of general happiness, why does the moral sense of man invariably approve that which increases the happiness of his species?[32]

Darwin underlined this last sentence and wrote an exclamation point and a question mark in the margin.

Darwin's list of marked passages on the back fly-leaf of his personal copy of the *Dissertation* included the entry "The remarks on Butler contain the cream of Sir J's opinions." Joseph Butler (1692–1752), Bishop of Durham, marked an historic turning point for Mackintosh, who saw him as providing the definitive answer to Mandeville's thesis that the spring of action was private and egoistical self-interest. The "system of selfishness" was actually based on

A gross confusion of self, as it is a subject of feeling or thought, with self considered as the object of either. It is no more just to refer the private appetites to self-love because they commonly promote happiness, than it would be to refer them to self-hatred in those frequent cases where their gratification obstructs it.[33]

The basic drive for action was to be found in appetites or passions which sought "their own outward objects without regard to self." Mackintosh thought Butler might have gone farther to show that self-love is a *derived* and not an original principle of action. But Hartley's discussion of the laws of association had not been available to Butler, and Hartley was really the first to show that association could link thought with appetite, feeling, and emotion.[34]

Following Butler's revival of the dictum that "virtue consists in following nature" Mackintosh aimed at showing that moral science could have a firmer foundation in the "laws of sensibility, of emotion, of desire and aversion, of pleasure and pain, of happiness and misery; and on which arise the august and sacred landmarks that stand conspicuous along the frontier between Right and Wrong." Newtonian criteria were invoked to justify the derivation of "most of the principles of human action from the transfer of a small number of pleasures, perhaps organic, by the law of association to a vast variety of new objects." If association were a *vera causa*, Mackintosh could bypass Whewell's difficulties concerning the *derivation* of the idea of duty from the examination and explanation of physical facts.

Mackintosh opposed Thomas Brown's thesis that the "theory which derives the affections from association," was "a modification of the selfish system" on three counts. First, he was critical of Brown's confusion of the questions of the *origin* of the principles of human activity and of the *nature* of developed moral criteria. Like Dugald Stewart, Mackintosh read the science of his time as recognizing the complexity and variety of nature and abandoning Cartesian efforts to reduce *all* phenomena to one or two attributes. Mackintosh turned this consideration *against* those who had used it in *criticism* of Hartley and associationism.

Defects of the same sort may indeed be found in the parallel phrases of most if not all philosophers, and all of them proceed from the same source, – namely the erroneous but prevalent notion, that the law of association produces only such a close union of a thought and a feeling, as gives one the power of reviving the other; instead of the truth, that it forms them into a new compound, in which the properties of the component parts are no longer discoverable, and which may itself become a substantive principle to human nature. They supposed the condition, produced by its power, to resemble that of material substances in a state of mechanical diffusion; whereas in reality it may be better likened to a chemical combination of the same substances, from which a totally new product arises.[36]

Physics and chemistry provided many instances "where the most powerful agents and the most lasting bodies are the acknowledged results of the composition, sometimes of a few, often of many elements." The composite character of these powers or bodies did not make them less real, nor necessitate the confusion of their properties with those of the elements which constituted them. Analogously, "secondary" desires exhibited an "acquired relish" for something which had been indifferent or disagreeable; and the new pleasure was neither less real nor less "indestructible" for being acquired. As a law of mental chemistry, association did *not* imply that the properties of complex and derived mental states were simple aggregates of the properties of their primitive antecedents.

Mackintosh adopted Butler's effort to show that self-love was neither primitive nor a privileged acquisition, *but did not improve on Butler's basic failure to account for the social dimension of morality*. He placed benevolence, sympathy, the whole range of other-regarding passions and emotions, on a par with self-love as *acquired* mental states, but was unable to clarify the role of society in deriving the sympathetic emotions from those "primary pleasures, pains, even appetites which arise from no prior state of mind, and which, if explained at all, can be derived only from bodily organization."[37]

At this critical juncture in the argument, Mackintosh invoked the faculty of conscience, the very idea of which, he insisted, included its authority over all other principles of human action. Admitting that it was not possible to spell out the process by which conscience was developed or formed as a result of "more general laws," he sought to avoid the charge of circularity levied against Butler.

The most palpable defect of Butler's scheme is, that it affords no answer to the question, "What is the distinguishing quality common to all right actions?" If it were answered, "Their criterion is, that they are approved and commanded by conscience," the answerer would find that he was involved in a vicious circle; for conscience itself could be no otherwise defined than as the faculty which approves and commands right actions.[38]

Nevertheless, the thesis that the judgments of human conscience were both *universal*, *necessary*, and *immutable*, on the one hand, and, on the other, that this same faculty of conscience was derived or acquired as the result of the interaction of the laws of human nature and the demands of man's environment, carried a paradoxical flavor which Mackintosh could not dispel. His argument relied heavily on the metaphor of the "mental contiguity" of conscience to will and to all the other principles of human action.

Darwin saw a problem which Mackintosh only *claimed* to answer, "It may still be reasonably asked, why these useful qualities are morally approved, and how they become capable of being combined with those public and disinterested sentiments which principally constitute conscience?"[39] For Mackintosh, "The answer was, because they are entirely conversant with volitions and voluntary actions, and in that respect resemble the other constituents of conscience, with which they are thereby fitted to mingle and coalesce." Darwin marked this passage with a marginal line, and commented at the top of the page, "Nonsense . . . ." This rejection was intensified by Mackintosh's repeated statements about the autonomy of conscience. When Mackintosh wrote,

The question, why we do not morally approve the useful qualities of actions which are altogether involuntary, may now be shortly and satisfactorily answered: because conscience is in perpetual contact, as it were, with all the dispositions and actions of voluntary agents, and is by that means indissolubly associated with them exclusively. It has a direct action on the will, and a constant mental contiguity to it.

Darwin underlined the phrases 'as it were' and 'mental contiguity', and wrote 'Trash' in large letters in the margin. Darwin's dissatisfaction with this turn of the argument hinged on an ambiguity in the *Dissertation* and its Preface. Mackintosh thought that

It may be truly said, that if observation and experience did not clearly ascertain that beneficial tendency is the constant attendant and mark of all virtuous dispositions and actions, the same great truth would be revealed to us by the voice of conscience. The coincidence, instead of being arbitrary, arises necessarily from the laws of human nature, and the circumstances in which mankind are placed.[40]

Darwin thought this "poor" because he envisaged a framework within which the "laws of human nature" and the "circumstances in which mankind are placed" would have definite historical and biological significance. In his terms, the problem was to explain the datum of "moral conflict," both in man and in the higher animals, between the social instincts and the more immediate passions and appetites. Mackintosh had *not* solved the problem set by the "coincidence of morality with individual interest." Darwin had a surer insight into the importance of a social matrix for behavioral change, and his transmutation theory strictly presupposed the basic social relationship of sexual reproduction. Mackintosh arbitrarily stipulated both that conscience would approve separate objects which had a genuine utility for some part of the species, and that the coalescence of these separate acts of approval would "agree with the rules of the general happiness." Darwin had to wonder whether Mackintosh understood the basis of the interdependence of the "separate parts" of a species.[41]

Mackintosh's ethical theory opposed both selfish individualism and a purely utilitarian view of the general happiness as moral criterion. He found the Kantian insistence upon the "universality, immutability, and independence" of the judgments of conscience pointing toward a solution more acceptable than the unwantedly relativistic implications of the more genetic approach of Hume. But he failed to reconcile the Kantian themes of the autonomy of practical reason (or the medieval accounts of the authority or *imperium* of conscience) with their antitheses in Hartlean psychology. Actually he did little more than juxtapose these radically distinct approaches to a philosophical theory of morals, and secularize Butler's use of theology in redressing the balance of duty and interest.[42] Mackintosh sought to settle the question by an examination of the idea of conscience which showed that faculty to have a necessary authority over all other principles of action. Darwin detected this shift away from a descriptive approach and commented, "If so my theory goes. In child one sees pain and pleasure struggling."[43] The distance between the two men gradually increased with Mackintosh's repeated use of metaphors intended to justify the attribution of "universality, immutability, and independence" to the judgments of conscience. These metaphors were all variants of such as 'mental contiguity' and connoted a kind of psychological immediacy.

The moral sentiments in their mature state, are a class of feelings which have no other object but the mental dispositions which lead to voluntary action and the voluntary actions which flow from these dispositions.[44]

Darwin felt familiar ground slipping away, and entered the marginal comment, "How can cowardice, or avarice, or unfeelingness be said to be dispositions leading to action Yet conscience rebukes a man who allows another to drown without trying to save his life." For Mackintosh the immediacy of the moral sentiments to their objects implied that conscience "employs no means," and so it "never can be transferred to nearer objects, in the way in which he who first desires an object as a means of gratification, may come to seek it as his end."[45] In that form where its authority over the actions of men was truly universal, the dictates of conscience were also immutable.

Darwin was also skeptical of the grounds for Mackintosh's efforts to reconcile the doctrines of liberty and necessity. Mackintosh might claim that conscience had other laws than the causal connections traced by scientific reason, but his account of this difference did not challenge Darwin's growing conviction that the supposed freedom of the will was only the consequence of *an illusory foreshortening of attention*, or of the *range of critical analysis* of the motives for action.[46]

PART II

DARWIN'S NOTEBOOKS, MANUSCRIPTS, AND MARGINALIA: 1837–1839

PART II

INTRODUCTION

In Great Britain, in the nineteenth century, as in other modern societies then and now, perceptions of the legitimacy of moral, political and religious institutions were intertwined with beliefs concerning the methods and conclusions of the natural sciences. Established answers to the question, "What are the proper limits and methods of scientific inquiry?" were interlocked with the philosophical foundations of society and culture.[1] Consequently, a new scientific theory *could* challenge and even tumble the "whole fabric" upon which the self-understanding of the society was based. To think otherwise is to assume an unchanging line of demarcation between scientific language and other cultural uses of logic and language. When it came to scientific theories concerning the evolution of organisms and groups of organisms, including man and human society, no one among the young Darwin's elite cultural circle attempted to isolate science from cultural criticism or to deny the cultural significance of science itself.

Darwin's theory explicitly recast the relationship between science and the perennial effort to understand the place of man in human society, and of human society in nature. We have seen that he was relatively well-prepared for the consideration of the methodological and philosophical questions raised by his theory. The range, philosophical diversity, and cultural depth represented by his cultural circle is strong evidence of his willingness to challenge the orthodox ideology of the day. But more evidence is available. For this we turn to the examination of the *Notebooks*, manuscripts, and marginal annotations composed by the young Darwin during the crucial years from July 1837 to August 1839.

These materials are not the ideal subject for systematic analysis. Their brief diary-like style reflected the author's personal interests and concerns, and only rarely can they be read as *drafts* of prose which he intended to publish. They are highly telegraphic, with the flavor of private, extremely informal conversation. They reflect the personal sense of urgency of a man struggling to clarify his own position and assemble evidence in its support. Their mood and pace provide excellent evidence of Darwin's personal estimate of the metaphysical and ethical implications of his theory, but their use requires considerable caution. This is particularly true of the effort to construct Darwin's methodological canons by examining the relative frequency with which he used terms with logical (and other) connotations. For example, in Darwin's usage the term 'law' occurred with great frequency, but it took on a bewildering variety of (sometimes opposed) meanings: positivist, realist, and colloquial. The relative frequency of the terms included in Tables IV, V, and VI may suggest interesting features of Darwin's implicit methodology. Perhaps there is some significance in the fact that the terms 'probable' and 'analogy' occur frequently, while 'predict,' 'foretell,' 'deduce,' and 'induce' occur infrequently. However, the methodology to be employed in this part of the book does not essentially depend upon the evidence presented in Tables IV, V, and VI. Rather, these tables present a background against which to weigh my arguments concerning Darwin's methodology, his use of consciousness as a biological category, and his efforts to locate man's moral sentiments in those social instincts presumably shared by other "mammiferous animals."

TABLE IV

Occurrences of Key Methodological Words in Darwin's Notebooks and Early Manuscripts (Notebooks B, C, D, E, M, and N; "Old & Useless Notes on Metaphysics; Mss on Macculloch) Based on Paul Barrett's index.

	4 12 30 40 60 80 100 120 140 160	
'probable'		157
'law'		153
'analogy'		142
'cause'		125
'theory'		112
'argument'		98
'explain'		65
'necessary'		62
'possible'		50
'prove'		37
'chance'		35
'consequence'		31
'infer'		15
'struggle'		11
'induce'		10
'hypothesis'		8
'war'		7
'metaphor'		4
'deduce'		4
'foretell'		3
'predict'		2
'selection'		1*

Grammatical derivatives of a word were counted as occurrences of it, e.g., 'predict,' 'predicted,' 'prediction,' etc. The total number of words in the Notebooks and manuscripts tabulated here is approximately 70,000. *The only occurrence of 'selection' or any derivative of that word was a later insert on the cover of "D". "Toward close I first thought of selection owing to struggle."

TABLE V

Variations in Frequency of Methodological Terms
(by Manuscript)

Text		B & C	D & E	M & N	OUN	T	'42	'44
No. of words (1000's)		25.5	21.4	17.7	6.0	1.1	10.4	37.4
'probable'	Total	60	50	38	8	1		
	Freq./1000 wds.	2.4	2.3	2.2	1.3	0.9		
'law'		46	70	15	12	10	13	38
		1.8	3.3	0.9	2.0	9.1	1.3	1.0
'analogy'		72	30	27	11	2		
		2.8	1.4	1.5	1.8	1.8		
'cause'		42	32	36	10	5		
		1.7	1.5	2.0	1.7	4.6		
'theory'		30	49	17	12	7		
		1.2	2.3	1.0	2.0	6.4		
'argument'		42	26	20	9	1		
		1.7	1.2	1.1	1.5	0.9		
'explain'		25	11	12	13	4		
		1.0	0.5	0.7	2.2	3.6		
'necessary'		14	21	17	9	1		
		0.6	1.0	1.0	1.5	0.9		
'possible'		27	13	7	3	1		
		1.1	0.6	0.4	0.5	0.9		
'prove'		17	12	8	1	0		
		0.7	0.6	0.5	0.2	0.0		
'chance'		17	9	7	2	0		
		0.7	0.4	0.4	0.3	0		
'consequence'		9	7	10	3	1		
		0.4	0.3	0.6	0.5	0.9		
'infer'		4	8	1	1	1		
		0.2	0.4	0.1	0.2	0.9		
'induce'		3	3	1	0	0		
		0.1	0.1	0.1	0	0		
'hypothesis'		4	2	2	0	0		
		0.2	0.1	0.1	0	0		
'metaphor'		0	0	0	4	0		
		0	0	0	0.7	0		
'deduce'		1	1	1	1	0		
		0.04	0.05	0.06	0.2	0		
'foretell'	Total	1	1	0	0	1		
'predict'	Total	0	2	0	0	0		

TABLE VI

Frequency of Ethical Metaphors

Notebook or Manuscript	"B"	"C"	"D"	"E"	"M"	"N"	"OUN"	"T"	Total
'love'	0	3	2	0	5	6	16	0	32
'sympathy'	0	3	2	0	8	1	5	0	19
'check'	2	3	4	1	1	0	5	1	17
'struggle'	0	0	1	1	3	2	4	0	11
'war'	0	3	4	1	0	0	0	0	8
'benevolence'	0	0	0	0	0	2	3	0	5
'balance'	0	0	0	1	0	1	1	0	3
'wedge'	0	0	3	0	0	0	0	0	3

"OUN" refers to the "Old and Useless notes on the moral sense . . . ."
"T" refers to Darwin's manuscript reflections on Macoulloch's theodicy.

CHAPTER SEVEN

ASPECTS OF SCIENTIFIC EXPLANATION

1. ANALOGY AND METAPHOR

The term 'selection' occurs only once in the approximately 70,000 word assembly of *Notebooks* and manuscripts under scrutiny in this section. That occurrence has all the marks of a later insertion, "Toward close I first thought of selection owing to struggle." There is good reason to think that sometime in the last six months of 1838 Darwin had formulated the strategy of investigating the consequences of artificial selection by breeders and gardeners, and of emphasizing the natural analogues of this agricultural technology.[1] But the *Notebooks* and early manuscripts give no indication of a comparably early interest in the *verbal expression* − or indeed of any *representation* − of the key analogy between *artificial selection* and *natural selection*. These materials conspicuously *omit* anticipation of the allegory of the *selector infinitely more sagacious than man*. The themes of *war* and *struggle* in nature were also given little attention.

Given Darwin's interest in philosophical issues during this period, these omissions cannot be dismissed as the consequence of the author's indifference. On the evidence now available (a more complete edition of Darwin's early correspondence would be most welcome in this regard), it must be *tentatively* concluded that Darwin did not give the analogy between natural selection owing to a struggle for existence and the technological practices of breeders and gardeners any *verbal expression* until he began to prepare a draft of his theory, i.e., to concern himself with its presentation to a larger scientific and extra-scientific community. I would not deny the heuristic significance of these analogies for the design of inquiries preceding 1842. I would date Darwin's concern with the semantic details and overtones of these analogies with the first drafts of his theory, and not with his earlier working notebooks. As Darwin moved from his role as investigator and discoverer to the explicit and self-conscious status of an author who intended to publish, persuade, and teach, he found that his account or "story" took on overtones (even a "life" of its own), which, for all the caution and thoroughness of his scientific and extra-scientific investigations during the preceding five years, he had simply failed to anticipate. During those years he had given a surprising amount of attention to the philosophical issues which divided contemporary positivists and realists, empiricists and rationalists. He had given explicit consideration to a publication strategy for avoiding the charge of *materialism*. He had pondered the theological implications of his views, and examined their implications for theses of human responsibility and ethical behavior. He was aware, I believe, of the radical implications of his position — a framework or fabric much more extensive than the provincial and anthropomorphic theological orthodoxy of his day would "totter and fall" because of his views.

Nevertheless, his autodidactic elaboration of his position (in the interval 1837–1839) did not enable him to anticipate the swarm of additional problems that arose when he began to articulate it for publication to a wider and somewhat unknown audience. In that latter role, he began to use his gifts as a story-teller. Unfortunately, there is no indication that he continued to subject the full-blooded "story" to the same self-critical, philosophical scrutiny he so painstakingly devoted to its bare logical skeleton during the preceding five years. There is good reason to think that by 1844 Darwin's professional role was much more rigidly set than it had been until then. By 1844, he was a *natural historian*. Where he had been willing to challenge philosophers on their own ground, a *mask of diffidence* began to set firmly in place. After 1844, he left such matters to a distinct group of *experts*.

The *Notebook* and early manuscript materials provide some illumination of his views on analogy and metaphor. Although 'metaphor' occurred only four times in the 70,000 word sample compiled by Paul Barrett, 'analogy' (142) was one of the three most frequently used terms (along with 'probable' and 'law') having methodological connotations. 'Analogy,' of course, is ambiguous — with both biological and methodological meanings. But in Darwin's working vocabulary the biological and methodological uses of 'analogy' were so closely interconnected that he could claim that his *biological theory justified his methodological practice* — a really startling reversal.[2] Darwin argued that his theory transformed the biological use of 'affinity' and 'analogy,' taking such usage from the realm of metaphorical expression and enabling it to express intelligible fact.

such are my reasons for believing that specific forms are not immutable. The affinity of different groups, the unity of types of structure, the representative forms through which foetus passes, the metamorphosis of organs, the abortion of others, cease to be metaphorical expressions and become intelligible facts.[3]

This last formulation overstated his actual accomplishment. While he could appropriately claim to have explained the apparent "family likeness" to be found at various levels of the taxonomic hierarchy, his explanation *depended* upon the analogy between the "undescribable" likeness of the members of a human family and the likeness to be found among certain groups of animals — at least when the latter were arranged in a natural manner. Since 'family resemblance,' in the strictest and most narrow use of the term, expressed a concept which Darwin used but did not analyze, if his theory moved anything from the realm of metaphor to that of literal fact, it did *not* accomplish this for 'family resemblance.'

His uses of 'metaphor' all occurred in a single short manuscript dealing with Dugald Stewart's views on the figurative usage of 'sublime' and of 'taste,' primarily in aesthetic literature.[4] Stewart's theory and Darwin's semantic practice exhibit a strikingly similar ambivalence. As has been noted, Stewart anticipated Wittgenstein's commentary on the notion of family likeness.[5] One and the same name might be applied to a set of objects not distinguished by any set of properties which they all, and only they, exhibited. Instead, the common appellation signified only that if these objects were arranged in an appropriate *sequence*, it would be possible to exhibit close affinities between any two *adjacent* members in this properly ordered array. Comte's critique of Lamarck raised doubts about the propriety of insisting upon the *continuity* of the chain of organic being, given the resultant difficulties in formulating a scientifically acceptable definition of 'species.' Darwin could have effectively used Stewart's semantic discovery to answer Comte's criticism. But Stewart himself made little of his discovery in his inquiries into the *Philosophy of the Human Mind*. Nor is there any evidence that Darwin, although he was clearly aware of the principle and its meaning for Stewart's analyses of 'sublime' and 'taste,' thought to himself, 'Ah! Now I see how to solve the problem of scientifically adequate definition of 'species' in the context of my transmutation theory!"

There is more irony in the truth of the matter. Stewart, for all his orthodox efforts to preserve the distinction of mind and matter, provided an analysis of 'sublime' and 'taste' which showed Darwin how man's sense of aesthetic wonder could be adequately explained within a completely *naturalistic* context, how, in fact, that sense of aesthetic wonder might have evolved from rudimentary animal experiences. Darwin was willing to extend this same pattern to every aspect of mind, including man's moral sense and his experience of religious awe. Stewart's account of the evolution of language broadened Darwin's semantic practice and rendered it more subtle, without making it more rigorous, consistent, or precise. Stewart rendered a more decisive service by indirectly alleviating Darwin's concern for the adequacy of evolutionary explanations of distinctive human traits from antecedents in non-human, primate ancestors.

2. NATURAL HISTORY AND THE LAWS OF LIFE

In a remarkable text from *Notebook E*, written before 7 November 1838, Darwin revealed his confidence that the natural history of the transmutation of species would lead to the discovery of the physical cause of such change, and to the physical laws of the corelation of parts of living individuals.

Those discovering the formal laws of corelation of parts in individuals, will care little whether the individual be species or variety, but to discover physical laws of such corelations, & changes of individual organs, must know whether the individuals forms are permanent, all steps in series, their relation to the external world, & every possible contingent circumstance. The laws of variation of races may be important in understanding the laws of specific change. When the laws of change are known, then primary forms may be speculated on, & laws of life, the end of natural history will be approximated to. Treating of the formal laws of corelation of parts & organs, it may serve perfectly to specify types & limits of variation, & hence indicate gaps. By this means the laws probably would be generalized, & afterwards by the examination of the special cases, under which the individual stages in the series have been fixed, to study the physical causes.[6]

A number of different types of laws and causes were identified in this passage:

1. Formal laws of corelation of parts in individuals,
2. Physical laws of such corelations,
3. Laws of variation of races,
4. Laws of specific change,
5. Laws of change,
6. Laws of life,
7. Speculation on the primary forms,
8. Laws which probably would be generalized after laws of life were known,
9. Physical causes of the individual stages.

Comte's distinction of *fundamental* and *historical* laws may not have been known to Darwin, although it was developed in the volumes covered by the *Edinburgh Review* article which he read and to which he responded with such enthusiasm.

Comte's "fundamental" laws (e.g., the laws of physiology) were abstract and general, applicable to "all conceivable cases" and not restricted to the plant or the animal kingdoms. Comte saw natural historians in the modest role of *applying* these laws to "the actual history of existing beings." Botany and zoology were dismissed with the implication that they lacked the sort of abstract generality required for sciences which had real philosophic import. He made no comment concerning a possible role for natural history in the *discovery* of basic physiological laws.[7]

Darwin's emphasis was different. He identified speculation concerning the "primary forms" of life, the "laws of life," and the "laws of change of organic form," as among the *ends or goals of natural history*. His argument might be reconstructed as follows. Assume that the topic under investigation was "What laws stated the corelations of individual organs in a developing living thing?" To formulate such laws, Darwin argued that it would be necessary to locate the embryological sample in its geneological and geological context. The developmental process could not be characterized in law-like propositions unless it were known whether or not the process was to be found only in a small group of organisms or in highly unusual environmental situations. The laws of developmental physiology could *not* be formulated in the absence of an adequate account of the evolutionary history of the forms being studied, an account which had to include an analysis of the functional relationships between those forms and the details of the physical conditions of their individual life histories. In contrast to Comte's starkly simple assumption that natural history "applied" the laws of physiology, Darwin assumed a complex sequential communication between the natural historian and the student of the laws of life. The outline of his methodology began to emerge: a sketch of the organism's evolutionary history and the history of its environment was necessary for the formulation of the laws of the corelation of parts, which were in turn necessary for any general of law-like statements concerning the variation of races.

If there were in fact "laws of specific change" and "laws of variation of races" it would be impossible to express the former without reference to the latter. Knowledge of "laws of specific change" would make it possible to speculate on the "primary forms" of living things, the putatively small number of different ancestral forms from which all living things have descended. It was only in this evolutionary context that Darwin mentioned the "laws of life," presumably the basic laws of reproduction, growth, the "mental attributes," and so forth. Once the "end of natural history" was approximated in this fashion, a second movement of thought, utilizing this first approximation to the laws of life, could accomplish a more perfect and a more general statement of the formal laws of corelation of parts and organs, of the types and limits of variation, and of the "gaps" to be anticipated

ASPECTS OF SCIENTIFIC EXPLANATION

between various races or various species of the same ancestry. A *revised* evolutionary history would then set the stage for the final and more thorough study of the "physical causes" and conditions of the basic vital activities of reproduction, growth, and so forth.

Far from being merely applied physiology, natural history was portrayed as an indispensable element in the design of basic physiological inquiry. It was from this perspective that Darwin thought we need "no longer look at an organic being as a savage does at a ship or other great work of art, as a thing wholly beyond his comprehension, but as a production that has a history which we may search into."[8] It was only in this context that he spoke about the *generalization* of the laws of life.

Not only did the complexity of Darwin's on-going research program undermine Comte's distinction of fundamental laws of nature and their concrete historical applications, but it appeared to by-pass Herschel's important distinction of "empirical laws" and "laws of nature."[9]

Laws thus derived, by the direct process of including in mathematical formulae the results of a great or less number of measurements, are called "empirical laws." . . . Empirical laws in this state are evidently unverified inductions, and are to be received and reasoned on with the utmost reserve. No confidence can ever be placed in them beyond the limits of the data from which they are derived; and even within those limits they require a special and severe scrutiny to examine *how nearly* they do represent the observed facts. . . . When so carefully examined, they become, however, most valuable; and frequently, when afterwards verified theoretically by a deductive process (as will be explained in our next chapter), turn out to be rigorous laws of nature, and afford the noblest and most convincing supports of which theories themselves are susceptible. The finest instances of this kind are the great laws of the planetary motions deduced by Kepler, entirely from a comparison of observations with each other, with no assistance from theory.

Darwin located the notions of 'law' and of 'theory' in a much more problematic and heuristic context than Herschel's distinction would allow. For instance, in October of 1838, after he had read Malthus, Darwin wrote that

Thinking of effects of my theory, laws probably will be discovered of corelation of parts, from the laws of variation of one part affecting another. *I, from looking at all facts as inducing towards law of transmutation cannot see the deductions which are possible* (emphasis added).[10]

Thus there are solid grounds for disputing Darwin's later neat division of his method into distinct inductive and deductive phases.[11] It is a gross exaggeration to label the inferences of the second phase deductive. Even more important, *the distinction between that evidence which could count toward the "possibility" of his theory* (as outlined in part one of both the *Sketch* and the *Essay*) *and that which could count as "positive evidence" for or against it, was not one for which there is any argument in the Notebooks. It certainly did not mark the chronological path of his reflections or investigations as he wrote them down in the Transmutation Notebooks from 1837–1839. Nor do these Notebooks make anything of the distinction of "possibility" arguments and the "testing" of theories. On the contrary, the laws of geological and geographical distribution were among the very first to be considered in the Notebooks, as one might well expect from the extreme importance of the Beagle voyage to Darwin's grasp of their importance.*[12] Moreover, from the very start of the *Notebooks* Darwin was working with at least a rough outline of his theory, and employing the theory in a decidedly heuristic fashion to open up new areas of investigation and to determine new lines of inquiry.[13]

Astronomers might formerly have said that God ordered each planet to move in its particular destiny. In same manner God orders each animal created with certain form in certain country, but how much more simple and sublime power let attraction act according to certain law, such are inevitable consequences – let animal be created, then by the fixed laws of generation, such will be their successors. Let the powers of transportal be such, and so will be the forms of one country to another. – Let geological changes go at such a rate, so will be the number and distribution of the species!!

With belief of transmutation and geographical grouping we are led to endeavour to discover causes of changes, the manner of adaptation. . . . My theory would give zest to recent and fossil compative anatomy it would lead to study of instincts, heredity and mind heredity, whole metaphysics. It would lead to closest examination of hybridity, and generation, to what circumstances favour crossing and what prevents it causes of change in order to know what we have come from and to what we tend, this and direct examination of direct passages of structure in species might lead to laws of change, which would then be main object of study, to guide our speculations with respect to past and future. The grand question which every naturalist ought to have before him when dissecting a whale, or classifying a mite, a fungus or an infusorian is what are the laws of life?

Herschel made a clean contrast between "unverified inductions" and "rigorous laws of nature." Darwin's *Notebooks* revealed no procedure as purely empirical as Herschel's "direct process of including in mathematical formulae the results of a great or less number of measurements, called 'empirical laws,' " nor one as deductive as the *theoretical* verification of laws of nature. If there was ever a point in his actual research program where he proceeded on "pure Baconian principles," it is not possible to reconstruct it from the *Notebooks*, where *every* factual inquiry was initiated and understood within a general theoretical framework.

3. CHANCE, NECESSITY, AND DESIGN

'Chance' was one of the most puzzling terms in Darwin's lexicon. His published opinions on the topic fall into two opposed categories. On the one hand there are those passages where he takes the view that it is wholly incorrect to speak of chance as the cause of anything and insists that such language can only be understood to acknowledge our ignorance of the cause.[14] On the other hand there is at least one clear and lengthy passage where he quite clearly states that certain events may, in the strictest possible sense of the word, be termed 'accidental.'[15] Accidental events are those which result from the haphazard intersection of two or more lines of causality. Of the two positions, the first or "deterministic" view is expressed more frequently in the published works. However, the word 'chance' occurs throughout the early notebooks and manuscripts and it is not at all clear that the sort of "determinism" which Darwin espoused required the elimination of the concept of chance. To the contrary, that concept played a cogent, controlled, and central role in his theory from the start.

Therefore, his ambivalence concerning the word 'chance' requires careful scrutiny. Not surprisingly, the ambiguity of the term is linked to the ambiguity of 'cause': He insisted that each organic modification or variation must have its own distinct, precise and sufficient cause, which if it occurred a hundred times in a hundred comparable circumstances, would have a hundred identical effects.[16] In his view, the "understanding revolts" at the conclusion that either the birth of species or of the individual was the result of "blind chance." But it must be remembered that he was equally skeptical of the view that:

every slight variation of structure, the union of each pair in marriage, the dissemination of each seed, and other such events, have all been ordained for some special purpose.[17]

Helmholtz' critical comments on the psychophysical "design" of the eye, introduced in the last edition of *The Origin*, are crucial for the understanding of Darwin's view.

Natural selection will not produce absolute perfection, nor do we always meet, as far as we can judge, with this high standard under nature. The correction for the aberration of light is said by Muller not to be perfect even in that most perfect organ, the human eye. Helmholtz, whose judgment no one will dispute after describing in the strongest terms the wonderful powers of the human eye, adds these remarkable words: "that which we have discovered in the way of inexactness and imperfection in the optical machine and in the image on the retina, is as nothing in comparison with the incongruities which we have just come across in the domain of sensations. One might say that nature has taken delight in accumulating contradictions in order to remove all foundation from the theory of a pre-existing harmony between the external and internal worlds."[18]

Natural selection acted in the circumstances and on the variations that *happened* to be available at a given time. Hence the level of adaptation was always relative to the competitive pressure the organism actually met, and the resultant contrivances might be not only deficient but abhorrent to our ideas of fitness.[19] The notion of design that Darwin rejected was not one that might be equated with that of imperfect mechanical contrivance, arrived at by a process of trial and error. Rather, he rejected the hypothesis of a single, perfect and all-embracing theoretical design. He distinguished the problem of form in crystals and in organisms because organic form is determined by an "infinity of complex relations . . . due to causes far too intricate to be followed."[20] He did not accept the regulative ideal that this is the most intelligible of the possible worlds. He rejected the efforts of a continental sympathizer to account for taxonomic relationships as reflecting more or less efficient variations of a number of mechanically ideal archetypes.[21] Instead, he emphasized the brute fact of descent, whatever the consequences for neatness of system.

Darwin's position concerning chance, necessity and design was best captured, in his published works, in the allegory with which he concluded his work on *The Variation of Animals and Plants under Domestication*. The allegory describes a builder who constructs an edifice by carefully selecting fragments of rock from among the haphazard shapes to be found at the base of a precipice. The erection of the building was compared to an evolutionary sequence in that both involved materials (whether fragments of rock or organic variations) which resulted from causally determined and causally explainable sequences of events. But when the laws or causes resulting in the fragmentation of rocks at the base of a precipice are listed, it is clear that no single theoretical scheme could imply both that set of laws *and* the architect's design. Darwin held for a strictly analogous "decoupling" of the causes of organic variability on the one hand and the selective forces determining the chances of leaving fertile progeny on the other.

This allegory located Darwin's concepts of chance, necessity, and design in a basically Aristotelian framework. The real occurrence of chance events in nature told equally against an all-encompassing Laplacian determinism and an all-encompassing divine purpose.

The first use of 'chance' in the *Notebooks* was in the context of a genealogical explanation of the gaps in structure to be found between such great groups as the vertebrates and the articulata.

If we thus go very far back to look to the source of the mammalian type of organization, it is extremely improbable that any of the successors of his relations shall now exist. In same manner, if we take a man from any large family of 12 brothers and sisters in a state which does not increase it will be chances against any one of them having progeny living ten thousand years hence because at present day many are relatives, so that by tracing back the fathers would be reduced to small percentage therefore the chances are excessively great against any two of the 12 having progeny after that distant period.

Hence if this is true that the greater the groups the greater the gaps or solutions of continuous structure between them. For instance, there would be great gap between birds and mammalia, still greater between vertebrate and articulata, still greater between animals and plants.[22]

Chances are against any family leaving descendants after a period of 10,000 years, and would favor extinction for even large families over such a span. He was sure that even in a growing population not all the members would leave descendants after a sufficiently long period, but he was not sanguine about the possibility of assigning any generally applicable causal explanation for this phenomena.

"At present day in looking at two fine families one will have successors for centuries, the other will become extinct. Who can analyse causes, dislike to marriage, some delay, disease, effects of contagions and accidents, yet some causes are evident as, for instance, one man killing another. So is it with varying races of man then races may be overlooked many variations consequent on climate, etc. The whole races act toward each other and are acted on, just like two fine families no doubt a different set of causes must act in the two cases."[23]

Darwin was not concerned in *Notebook B* to assign or calculate a definite value for an organism's chances of leaving living descendants 200 or ten thousand years in the future. Those chances were small, and a correspondingly small fraction of a population would be represented by descendants so far into the future. This rough statistical inference served as an *explanation* of the great structural gaps between such large groups as the vertebrates and the arthropods or articulata. Assuming common parentage at some distant point in the past, the relatively high extinction rate would tend to eliminate intermediate forms and produce great gaps in what might have been a continuum if every organism at least replaced itself, generation after generation.

Not only was it *not necessary* for Darwin to calculate an organism's exact chances of leaving living descendants, *it was also not necessary*, in this context, for him to claim that the distribution of these chances was in any sense *non-random*. The bare qualitative assertions that the chances were low the extinction rate high, would account for the hierarchical pattern of phylo-genetic classification. The pyramidal hierarchy was a simple consequence of the fact that as one traced lineages back into the past, one encountered increasing numbers of organisms or types of organisms which had *not* con-tinued to replace themselves with living descendants, and had become extinct.

Since Darwin's "laws of chance" were *not* causal laws, he had more reason than Comte to insist upon the distinction of law and causality. However, he did not self-consciously construct a new philosophy of science reflecting this practice, and his comments generally indicate that he became uneasy about any technical use of the term 'chance.' His critical reaction to a suggestion of Henslow's that the colonization of the island of Keeling ought to be explained in terms of the *fitness* of the various families available for transport to the island marked the start of his ambivalence about the acceptability of statisti-cal explanation.

Henslow in talking of so many families on Keeling seemed to consider it owing to one of each being fitted for transport. May it not be explained by mere chance? Or is it like each great class of animals having its aquatic, aerial, etc., type. This of consequence because applicable to N. Hemisphere.[24]

Darwin's *Notebook* references to 'chance' occasionally verged on an aware-ness of the importance of statistical explanation as an alternative to various causal hypotheses, often with vitalist overtones, which might be offered to account for pertinent aspects of the geographical distribution of organisms.

There certainly appears attempt in each dominant structure to accommodate itself to as many situations as possible. Why should we have in open country a ground woodpecker. Do. parrot. A desert kingfisher. Mountain tringas. (?) Upland goose. Water chionis, water rat with land structures. Carrion eagles. This is but carrying on attempt at adaptation of each element.

May this not be explained on principle of animal having come to island where it could increase, but there were causes to induce great change. Like the buzzard which has changed into caracara at the Galapagos. Law of chance would cause this to have happened in all but less in water birds.[25]

Did each element or dominant structure attempt to adapt itself to as many situations as possible? To have accepted this proposition would have been to affirm a vitalistic form of the "so-called progressive tendency law." Generally, in *Notebook B*, Darwin made a serious effort to connect his use of such terms as 'dominant' and 'adaptation' with the various implications of his usage of 'chance.' The dominance of a particular group was not to be accounted for in terms of its inner organic characteristics, nor by meteorological, nor by geological phenomena alone — none of these, considered in isolation from the others, was acceptable. 'Chance', *in causal contexts, signalled that an irreducible plurality of otherwise distinct forces had intersected to produce the phenomenon in question.*

The number of genera on islands and on arctic shores evidently due to the chance of some ones of the different orders being able to survive or chance having transported them to new stations. When the new island splits and grows larger, species are formed of those genera, and hence by same chance few representative species. This must happen and then enquiry will explain representative system. Of these we see example in English and Irish Hare. Galapagos shrews and when big continent, many species belonging to its own genera.[26]

Darwin's image of his explanatory scheme attributed no causal force to chance itself. Birds were blown by gales; amphibians or small land animals were carried by sea currents or floating debris; plant seeds could be transported in any of these ways, and even by other organisms being transported in any of these ways. He did not speak of chance as a distinct causal agency, able to account for the transport of an organism incapable of migration in any of these familiar, if somewhat haphazard, ways. The point was that these ways *were haphazard*. It was less important to give an exact causal account of the migrations of specific organisms than it was to argue that such migrations were physically possible and that their broad patterns might be accounted for on statistical grounds: the chances of colonization *would fall off with distance* or with the average height of an isolating barrier; the chances of colonization would be greater for the members of an already numerous (or dominant group); and so on. Such an account did not attribute a mysterious causal agency to chance, but reflected such realities as the relatively large size of well-adapted or dominant populations, and the viability of certain seeds subjected to salt water for certain periods.

It is worth noting that the words 'war' or 'wars of organic being' were associated with 'chance' in several texts in *Notebook C*, written well in advance of Darwin's reading of Malthus in September of 1838.[27] The association of 'war' and 'chance' helped illuminate the conceptual structure of his theory. The diversification of a group resulting in its descendants occupying a number of different sorts of stations with differing physical conditions was not the consequence of some unfolding of a natural property of the group in itself. His criticism of the quinarians was directed against their thesis that organic taxonomy ought to have a geometrical rigor independent of the chance interaction of various types of organisms (with each other and their environments), under various physical conditions. Success in these wars of organic being could *not* be traced to variations which were *favorable* in some *absolute* sense; on the contrary, a variation must be understood to be *successful in relation* to some particular segment of the range of alternative variations, and in the context of the chances of life which happened to be available in the given physical circumstances or conditions. Such expressions as 'chance offspring' or 'round of chances' alluded to the complexity of the predicates used in Darwin's hypothesis, and implied that this complexity could not be reduced in the way that Newton had reduced the complexity of planetary motion by formulating a few generally applicable laws.

Darwin often spoke as if the term 'adaptation' might play a role in natural history comparable to that played by 'attraction' in theoretical astronomy. But the chances of victory in the wars of organic beings were not to be computed in the same straightforward fashion dictated by the inverse square law. He could not identify relatively simple one or two place predicates such as 'mass' or 'distance' to incorporate in a general equation for the calculation of specific values or degrees of adaptation. The trait which made one seal "victorious" over another in the complex social routine characterized as "combat" varied with the history of that particular population and of closely associated populations. In *Notebook E*, he specifically took note of the fact that an organic trait might be disadvantageous in one generation and advantageous in the next.

Case of Mexican greyhounds. Young being habituated instance such as hunter, or some one mention of influence on parent affecting offspring & as adaptation. However mysterious such is case. Therefore chance & unfavourable conditions to parent may become favourable to offspring. Australian dogs having mottled coloured puppies case of this. Tendency in manner of life to be mottled & hereditary tendency determines the puppies to be so.[28]

The concept of chance was connected with many of the basic methodological and metaphysical concerns in Darwin's intellectual community. The importance of statistical analysis in a wide range of subjects attracted sympathetic attention in Herschel's review of the work of Quetelet in 1850.[29] On the other hand, Comte's unremitting determinism, his flat rejection of Quetelet's approach, and his denunciation of the "theory of chances" as "offering our own ignorance as the natural measure of the degree of probability of our various opinions" were a clear indication that the methodological status of allusions to chance was by no means secure.[30] Darwin's publications reflected this indecisive state of affairs: *he used the statistical approach in spite of an inability to mention it without deprecating it as a facade which concealed our ignorance.* There was much less ambiguity, so far as Darwin and his circle were concerned, about the concept of progress. Not even the Bridgewater theologians cared to embrace Condorcet, Godwin, or Lamarck, and they generally denied the possibility of writing one type of general law, a law of progressive development linking *all* organisms and their changing natural environment. *Darwin defended the thesis that the relation of basic organic variability and environmental change was a random or chance affair by stressing the problematic character of evolutionary improvement and progress.* The facts of failure and extinction were not controversial; they supplied the rhetorical medium necessary for the implication that, in the theory of evolution, the concept of chance was not merely a cover for our ignorance, but that it would play a lasting role.

4. 'LAW' IN THE *NOTEBOOKS* AND EARLY MANUSCRIPTS

The word 'law' occurred more than 150 times in Darwin's *Notebooks* and early manuscripts, but these occurrences were not tightly controlled by any one explication of the term. Some were flavored with the metaphor of obedience, and others were strictly positivistic. Laws were said to "unite" matter, to "govern" both the inorganic and the organic worlds, and vital laws were said to "act definitely as chemical laws as long as certain contingencies were present." Herschel, in a passage of the *Preliminary Discourse* which Darwin read and marked, had noted the ambiguity of such uses of 'law.'[31] While Darwin did not always explicitly allude to the ambiguity of his own use of 'law,' his concurrent reading in Herschel and Comte (or David Brewster's review of Comte) certainly brought the significance of such ambiguity to his attention. David Brewster had stressed Comte's interest in general facts, e.g., "gravitation," along with his rejection of the task of deciding "what this attraction and that gravity are in themselves, or what are their causes" as "not within the domain of positive philosophy." After summarizing the details of the law of the "three different theoretical states," the reviewer translated Comte as follows,

finally, in the positive state the human mind, recognising the impossibility of obtaining absolute notions, renounced the attempt of enquiring into the origin and destination of the universe, and of detecting the intimate causes of phenomena, in order to set itself only to discover, by a judicious combination of reasoning and observation, their effective laws; that is their invariable relations of succession and similitude. The explanation of acts, then reduced to real terms, is henceforth but the connexion established between different individual phenomena and some general facts, the number of which becomes more and more diminished in the progress of science.[32]

Darwin's reaction to the methodological and metaphysical issues raised by Brewster's review of Comte was an uneasy and strained, if not inconsistent, compromise. He gave frequent lip service to the positivist program of eliminating animistic and anthropomorphic fictions in science by replacing such terms as 'cause,' 'nature,' and 'will,' with law-like characterizations of observable sequences of events.[33] It ought to be noted, however, that the term 'prediction' occurs only twice in these *Notebooks* and manuscripts. Both occurrences are in the same text; and that text admits two functions for law: prediction and the retrospective illumination of such otherwise "scattered facts" as those associated with the embryological "law of monstrosity."[34]

The "Old and useless Notes on Metaphysics" contain a manuscript whose special interest is its implication that Hensleigh Wedgwood weakened Darwin's convictions concerning both materialism and positivism by insisting upon a detailed analysis of the metaphors of attraction and elective affinity.[35] The vectorial character of gravitational and chemical forces rendered their analysis incomplete (for Wedgwood) in the absence of the identification of an originating causal source. As did Herschel in the *Preliminary Discourse*, Wedgwood claimed that the concept of *causality* was based upon a subjective awareness of our own capacity for originating "an opposition of forces" to balance or move an object. In his postscript to the manuscript, Darwin *accepted* Herschel's criticism of the reduction of causality to a relation of invariable succession.[36] Faced with the critical possibility that positivism was inadequate as an account of the conceptual foundations of physics and chemistry, Darwin had serious second thoughts about Comte's account of law. For Herschel, the notions of cause and effect, and the dependent notion of laws of nature, were not based upon the experience of regular succession or successful prediction, but instead upon the "contemplation of possible occurrences," the "provision, *a priori*, for contingencies," and the prospect of "change depending on our own will" in the succession of events.

In the last analysis, Darwin's own positions, both methodological and metaphysical, were seriously at odds with those of both Herschel and Comte. Methodologically, he was uneasy with the unequivocal determinism to be found in the writings of Herschel and Comte which were available to him during this period.[37] Nevertheless, of the two, it was *Comte* who was the more explicitly considerate of the difficulties associated with the precise quantification of biological data. Although there is some evidence that his views softened somewhat by the time he reviewed Quetelet's work in 1850, the Herschel Darwin knew in 1839 sternly required that observed facts follow from putative laws of nature as "necessary logical consequences, and this, not vaguely and generally, but with all possible precision in time, place, weight, and measure." Darwin was well aware that his own system provided *no deductions* which satisfied such demands, modelled as they were on the mathematical power of theoretical astronomy. Concern for Herschel's prestige as the monitor of scientific excellence in Great Britain at that time may have contributed to Darwin's relative de-emphasis of 'law' in the *Sketch of 1842* and the *Essay of 1844*. In any case, Darwin exhibited few qualms about his failure to construct a mathematical theory with precise deductive consequences of the sort which recommended Newton to the astronomers. On this point, his allegiance was to the relativistic implications of Comte's historicism.

Metaphysically, Darwin leaned the other way and favored Herschel's realism. He sought to explain man, living nature, and the fossil remains of the past as he found them, and not as they would be if forced into methodologically pre-determined categories. Where the issue over the meaning of causality was squarely joined between Comte and Herschel, Darwin clearly preferred Herschel's position:

the argument reduced itself to what is cause & effect: it merely is /invariable/ priority of one to other: no not only this, for if day was first, we should not think night an effect. /Cause and effect has relation to forces & mentally because effort is felt./ [38]

Darwin also accepted the realist's task of accounting for the metaphysical and moral implications of a scientific theory; before 1844, he never sought to diminish this task by suggesting that his theory was a convenient fiction, intended only to unify the phenomena. In a very perceptive note, commenting on his reading of a review of Coleridge, he identified his position as mediating between Kant and the empiricists on epistemological issues. [39]

CHAPTER EIGHT

'CONSCIOUSNESS' AS A BIOLOGICAL CATEGORY

Darwin's approach to psychological topics was neither reluctant nor tardy. Not only were the *Notebooks on Metaphysics and Morals* begun in July of 1838 specifically to deal with such subjects, but his work for the first two *Transmutation Notebooks* convinced him that the subject required special and independent consideration. The first of these passages expressed the recurrent theme that it would be *more* difficult to explain the origin of the first thinking being than to account for the appearance of "intellectual man."[1] His reference to the "*first* thinking being" was not one which he made much effort to elaborate, nor did he devote any explicit attention to the *origins* of consciousness. From the very earliest pages of the *Notebooks*, however, he included references to instincts, feelings, imaginings, and reasonings among those traits which differed in organisms of the same type and whose differences might be passed along to their offspring by inheritance. In these same passages he emphasized the fact that man did not constitute an exception to the general hypothesis of descent.[2]

A little later, he stressed the analogies to be found in human and animal passions, expression, signals, and voice.

Animals have voice so has man. Not *saltus* but *hiatus*; hence if sickness death, unequal life. – stimulated by same passions, brought into the world same way, animals expression of countenance. They may convey much thus. Man has expression. – animals signals, (rabbit stamping ground), man signals. – animals understand the language. They know the cry of pain as well as we. –[3]

These passages emphasize Darwin's early recognition that the general validity of the hypothesis of descent required its applicability to man as well as to any other organism. Since comparative anatomy and systematics had classed man with the mammals, the admission of an *unbridgeable* gap within that great class would give his hypothesis the same *ad hoc* status to which he referred in rejecting creationism and other accounts less general than his own. The motto 'not *saltus* but *hiatus*' anticipated the later '*natura non facit saltum.*' There is adequate evidence in the *Notebooks* to conclude that one of the first problems Darwin set for evolutionary anthropology was the demonstration of this motto. Toward the end of *Notebook M*, he wrote, "To show hiatus in mind not saltus between man and brutes."[4] In *Notebook N* he asserted the continuity of vital and mental phenomena in man and the simplest algae (*conferva*).[5] Invoking Herschel's authority, Darwin asserted that life and will and mind — as these occurred in men and animals — varied only in degree, on the grounds that this thesis would prove "a fertile source of physical discovery."

1. DETERMINISM

The Charles Darwin manuscripts at University Library, Cambridge, include a packet of manuscript sheets of various sizes, written at various times, which Darwin himself had collected together and stored with the title "Old & *useless* notes about the moral sense & some metaphysical points written about the year 1837 and earlier." Dr. Sydney Smith thinks the notes were collected and titled by Charles Darwin himself in 1856 and that the disparaging estimate of their utility indicated only the absence of material used in preparing the manuscript version of *The Origin of Species*. One of these manuscripts, dated 6 September 1838, was composed of two letter sheets folded in half to make eight pages.[6] Darwin wrote on four alternate pages, except that overleaf of page one, he entered three footnotes, marked to correspond to sections of the text.

This manuscript is of particular interest for its discussion of the problem of human freedom. In it, Darwin copied out his own marginal notes from the corresponding pages of the eighth edition of *Inquiries concerning the Intellectual Powers and the Investigation of Truth*, by John Abercrombie, M.D.[7] These notes sketch a strategy for dealing with consciousness as a biological category, and provide a valuable introduction to a number of other related manuscripts in which Darwin puzzled over the meaning of "every word expressing a mental quality (desire, etc., etc.)." They coalesce the concepts of free will and of chance and imply that there is something illusory in the *former*. Darwin began developing this line of thought in the early pages of *Notebook M*.

Therefore properly no free will. We may easily fancy there is, as we fancy there is such a thing as chance. Chance governs the descent of a farthing, free will determines our throwing it up. Equally true the two statements.

I verily believe free will & chance are synonymous. Shake ten thousand grains of sand together & one will be uppermost so in thoughts one will rise according to law.[8]

The *Transmutation Notebook* discussions of the chances of organisms' transport to an island or of leaving progeny ten thousand years hence were generally without reservation or ambiguity. Unequivocal references to the "law of chance" and to Quetelet and the statistical society also occurred, but such references were not to be found in the *Metaphysical Notebooks*.[9] An important factor in this shift was the influence of Comte. Comte's positivism required rejection of the explanatory value of the concept of *will*. He sought to concentrate scientific interest upon laws, and to dispute the significance of the metaphysician's interests in natures, powers, and mental faculties as well as the theologian's concerns about the will of God. Darwin remarked on this sympathetically, and extended it to a speculation of his own about the possibility that "our will may arise from as fixed laws of organization."[10] He spelled this out in discussing the conditions of moral conversion.

To the argument that man autonomously put himself in the way of such contingencies, (e.g., "hearing the Bible"), Darwin replied that the knowledge that it would be "good for him" to do so was determined by education and heredity. The appearance of freedom and autonomy could and ought to be explained either by a deterministic account of the force of passion, or by a phenomenon basically analogous to chance. 'Chance' in this context was interpreted as the *coincident involvement of a complex set of weak and opposed passions*. "Free will," on this view, is a misnomer reflecting man's incomplete and mistaken impressions concerning his own motives.

Later in this same manuscript, Darwin surveyed the changes at other points in the semantic web which would result from the elimination of 'free will.' His remarks were suggestive of his concern for the use of a consistent vocabulary in describing man as a social mammal who had evolved from mammalian ancestors belonging to a different species. He was aware that his rejection of the concept of free will would raise doubts about the concept of moral responsibility. His first move in attempting to assuage such doubts was to suggest a corelation of the notions of good and evil with those of health and sickness. If wickedness were like disease, problems concerning responsibility and autonomy would not arise. However, we punish the wicked and reward the good, and he saw how dubious punishment became if wickedness were rooted in disease and not in personal guilt. However, other animals attack the weak and sickly as we punish the wicked. He held that the justification of man's behavior in punishing others could only consist in the deterrent effects of punishment and not at all in its retributive dimension. We "ought" to pity the wicked, rather than be disgusted with them; moreover, we ought to "assist and educate" them by "putting contingencies" in their way to aid their "motive power."

2. REFUTATIONS OF DUALISM

As we have seen, Darwin read and annotated the eighth edition of Abercrombie's *Inquiries* sometimes before 8 September 1838. His reaction was decidedly skeptical; e.g., he marked the introduction to the section dealing with the application of the rules of philosophical investigation to medical science, "All trash." However, he also wrote inside the back cover, "It requires much attention." His marginal comments on the problem of materialism are equally important.

His first reaction was to mark with a marginal line Abercrombie's reiteration of Brown's thesis on causality:

When we speak, therefore, of physical causes, in regard to any of the phenomena of nature, we mean nothing more than the fact of a certain uniform connexion which has been observed between events.[11]

The transparent intent of Abercrombie's electicism was to isolate and protect key deistic themes from scientific criticism, while attempting to provide a sympathetic account of scientific method. For Darwin, on the other hand, the laws of gravity, of the crystalline arrangement of particles, and of the attractive forces of chemical elements and compounds, provided knowledge both of material things and of the principles of their organization. Chemical laws corelated "the kind of attraction" exerted with the "nature of the element(s)" involved, and he thought it reasonable to search for comparable laws corelating "kind of thought with form of brain."

To the dualist argument that the actions of the mind were not known directly or objectively by the external senses, as were the events of the physical world, Darwin countered that the *attractive forces* postulated by physics and chemistry were equally unavailable to direct observation. He sought to document an analogy between mental and physiological processes by pointing to the similarity of memory and examples of repetitive production of an identical substance by a given organ (e.g., semen by testes or bile by the liver), and by claiming that the goal-oriented complexity of the development of an adult organism from a simple egg cell was similar to the goal-oriented intentionality found in human experience.

At least as early as the spring of 1838, Darwin thought he might deserve the label *materialist* because of the position he took concerning the heredity of thought, "or desires more properly." Breeders of animals, particularly of dogs, made successful crosses in order to strengthen certain instincts, and he inferred that the animals' tendency to behave in certain ways was inherited, or that these instincts were inherited.[12] Next he argued that analogy would suggest that the inheritance of instinctive behavior must be based upon the inheritance of some neural structure. The analogy at work was the thesis that inherited organic functions are ordinarily based upon or corelated with inherited organic structures.

Thought (or desires more properly) being hereditary it is difficult to imagine it anything but structure of brain hereditary, analogy points out to this. − Love of the deity effect of organization, oh you materialist! − Read Barclay on organization!! Avitism in mental structure a disposition & Avitism in corporeal structure are facts full of meaning. − Why is thought being a secretion of brain, more wonderful than gravity a property of matter? It is our arrogance, it is our admiration of ourselves. −[13]

This point about the neural basis of instinctive behavior was quickly generalized to stress its implications for human mental activity, and Darwin's self appraisal, "oh you materialist!" was clearly related to the assertion that the love of the deity could be explained in terms of the organization (and evolution) of the human brain. Although he reminded himself to read Barclay on this point, Barclay provided no arguments to dissuade him from his substantive conclusion: that to explain thought or mental activity as a "secretion" or function of the brain was no more "wonderful" and no less scientifically acceptable than to postulate gravity as a function of matter. Any apparent implausibility in the materialistic explanation of mental activity was rooted in human egocentricity.

This position was maintained in most of the entries in *Notebooks M* and *N*, but an extremely important strategy was formulated in July or August of 1838. Darwin decided to avoid stating his position concerning materialism by stressing only the *heritability* of such factors as emotions, instincts, and degrees of talent, and explaining such behavioral inheritance in terms of inherited neural structures.

To avoid stating how far, I believe, in Materialism, say only that emotions, instincts, degrees of talent, which are hereditary are so because brain of child resembles parent stock. − (& phrenologists state that brain alters).[14]

Since Darwin's materialism probably never consisted in much more than the claims that behavioral traits were inherited, and that the processes of heredity or generation were themselves physical in character, the strategy did not require much hedging. It did have certain consequences, I think, for the details of his published work. For example, he never published a claim as strong as the one which spoke of "thought being a secretion of brain," and he never publicly referred to his position as materialistic.

Notebook M also contains a note on a conversation Darwin had with his brother-in-law, Hensleigh Wedgwood, which describes Hensleigh as holding a position identical to that of the author of a text now included among the Darwin manuscripts in the University Library, Cambridge.

Hensleigh says to say Brain per se thinks is nonsense; yet who will venture to say germ within egg, cannot think — as well as animal born with instinctive knowledge, but if so, yet this knowledge acquired by senses, — then thinking consists of sensation of images before your eyes, or ears (language mere means of exciting association) or of memory of such sensation, & memory is repetition of whatever takes place in brain, when sensation is perceived. —[15]

This text was probably written between 22 July and 12 August 1838. Darwin's exchange with Hensleigh Wedgwood on the nature of the evidence relevant to the mind-body problem, as well as his careful annotation of Abercrombie's book, must both have been completed before September 1838, and probably during the summer months. In his annotations of the Wedgwood manuscript, Darwin sought to undermine the dualists' reliance on the distinction of objective knowledge and subjective or "internal consciousness." In making this point, he argued 1.) that the experiences or notions of sensation and of internal consciousness could not effectively be separated, and 2.) that while movement could be sensed, force and attractive force could not be.[16]

Darwin's continuing concern for the clarification of the concepts associated with consciousness was further expressed in a manuscript dated during the late spring or early summer of 1839. In this manuscript, he held that organic and inorganic laws were "different," that they made up "two great systems of laws in the world," and that organic laws "probably had some unknown relation" to the laws of electricity, chemical attraction, heat and gravity.[17] However, he thought "the vital laws act definitely (as chemical laws) as long as certain contingencies are present (contingencies as heat, light, etc.)." His position on the organic phenomenon of growth was broadly wholistic, i.e., he characterized it as the development or organization of tissue into a certain typical form. "Such tissue bears relation to whole, that is enough must be present to be able to exist as individual." In the next section he outlined the view that animal growth was identical to that in plants, but that the relation of animals to a "more extended space" required a comparable extension of its "powers of relation." These included a "sensorium" which would receive "communication from without" and gave the "individual power of willing." He did not distinguish the concepts of (conscious) will and of irritability, but held that it was easy to conceive such movements (as those of the arm of a polypus) as "obedience to certain stimulants without conscience in the lower animals, as in stomach, intestines, and heart of man (sic)." Next, he considered

Hensleigh Wedgwood's notes on the relation of thought and the brain, with annotations
by Charles Darwin
*Reproduced by courtesy of the Syndics of Cambridge University Library,
Cambridge, England*

The reason why thought &c. should imply the existence of something in addition to matter is because our knowledge of matter is quite insufficient to account for the phenomena of thought. The objects of thought have no reference to place.

[We see a particle move one to another, & the (or conceive it) & that is all we know of attraction, but we cannot see or else think: they are as incongruous as time & weight: all that can be said that though a regularity run in a parallel series: if though & weight always went together, & so a thing saw them it grew because yet it could not be said that the thought caused the weight, suppose that weight & thought, had less between them so depend on certain thought & organization; But if the thought were certain until the thought had a certain intensity (so the experiment was carried) then might it now be said, that thought caused weight, because both due to some common cause:— The argument reduces itself to what is cause & effect; & must uniformity of one to other: no end of this for if day was first, we should not think night an effect.]

coalescing the concept of conscious willing with that of regular response to
external contingencies, arguing that this would be a welcome simplification of
a problematic topic.

These willings have relation to external contingencies, as much as growth of tissue and
are subject to accident; the sexual willing comes on period of years as much as inflores-
cence. [in the margin:] Joining two difficulties into one common one always satisfactory,
though not adding to positive knowledge. Lessening amount of ignorance.

In a section he marked heavily with large '?', Darwin puzzled inconclusively
over the appropriate use of 'consciousness.'

How does consciousness commence Where other senses come into play; when relation is
kept up with distant object. When many such objects are present, & where will directs
other parts of body to do such. –
All this can take place & man not conscious as in sleep; or in sleep is man momentary
conscious, but is memory gone? –
    /where pain & pleasure is felt there
    /must be consciousness ???

Darwin made a graphic note to himself to explore the meaning of the words
'REASON,' 'WILL,' AND 'CONSCIOUSNESS.' Then he turned to the notion
of instinct, finding what he regarded as a solid argument showing that complex behavior (or a corresponding modification in the organization of the
brain) was in some sense heritable: "crows fear gun, – pointer's method of
standing – method of attacking peccari – retriever – produced as soon as
brain developed. . . ." From this he inferred that thought, "however unintelligible it may be" was as much a definite function of the brain as the production
of bile was a function of the liver. Nevertheless, he continued to find the
topic of materialism problematic. On the one hand, he labeled the question,
"What is matter?" a mystery. And on the other, he wrote, "This materialism
does not tend to atheism," since it provided an explanation of "so high a
mind" with a further, final end; i.e., the capacity for "looking back" and
"therefore consciousness, therefore reward in good life." He finally avoided
these quandries by means of the strategic decision outlined so briefly at p. 57
of *Notebook M*, "say only that emotions, instincts, degrees of talent, which
are hereditary are so because brain of child resembles parent stock."

3. EXPRESSION AND LANGUAGE

Darwin identified expression and language as key symptoms of the evolutionary continuity of mental and social phenomena from animals to men. The

philosophical significance of his position can best be represented by contrasting his views with those of the first English Hegelian, James Ferrier. Ferrier argued for a thesis which Darwin flatly denied.

It is impossible in principle to show that human consciousness has any analogue in brute animals, or even in children.

For Ferrier, consciousness was rooted in the active self-constitution of the ego. Since no person could teach another the true meaning of the word 'I,' this self-constitution was necessarily original and non-replicable in each case. Properly understood, 'consciousness' designated a completely free act, totally outside the "dominion of the law of causality." Consequently, consciousness could not be the subject of any scientific investigation, albeit the laws and facts of "passion, sensation, and reason" *were* appropriate subjects for the science of animal psychology. Ferrier concluded that only the absolute freedom of the self-creating ego was an appropriate subject of moral responsibility; all attributions of moral character to brutes or children were fallacious.

Darwin specifically denied that last proposition. In terms of his own genetic and social determinism, it was legitimate to assert that

A pointer ought to point

or that

These instincts (parental, conjugal and social) consist of a feeling of love (& sympathy) or benevolence to the object in question. Without regarding their origin, we see in other animals they consist in such active sympathy that the individual forgets itself, & aids & defends & acts for others at its own expense.[18]

These views were grounded on theses concerning the significance of *animal social behavior*. Darwin examined the role of expressive or communicative behavior and action more closely than he did any of the other so-called social instincts. His motive was quite clearly the denial of Ferrier's thesis:

The whole argument of expression more than any other point of structure takes its value from its connexion with mind, (to show *hiatus in mind not saltus between man & Brutes*) no one can doubt this connexion. – look at faces of people in different trades &c &c &c (emphasis added)[19]

Darwin's reflections concerning the transmission, reception, and interpretation of expressive signals were clearly intended to exhaust the gamut of human experience.[20]

How does social animal recognize & take pleasure in other animals. . . . It may be attempted to be said that young animal learns parent smell & look & so by association receives pleasure. . . . & hence idea of beauty.[21]

He saw it as part of his task to show that animal communication had strong analogies with human language.

The distinction [as often said] of language in man is very great from/all animals — but do not overrate — animals communicate to each other. . . . How far they communicate not easy to know, — but this capability of understanding language is considerable.[22]

Ferrier had characterized consciousness as ineffable, indescribable, and uncommunicable. Darwin came as close to directly denying this characterization as was possible, given an even stronger implicit tendency on his part to regard the concept of essentially private expression as *incoherent*.

Are the facts (about communication of ideas, etc.) of expression lawless, whilst they are the only steady & universal means recognized — no one can say expression was invented to conceal one's thought. —[23]

Expression was not only not "invented to conceal one's thought," but Darwin agreed with Burke and Dugald Stewart that *mimicry* of expressive behavior was conducive to the *experience* of the mental passion underlying that behavior.[24] In other words, the imitation of behavior led to the replication of feelings associated with the behavior. Darwin could have replied to Ferrier's central point about the ineffable and indescribable nature of the ego that the idealist was mistaken in looking for a *verbal* formula which could be mastered and communicated, as if the core of the ego could be shared by teaching another person the proper use of a word ('I') or a set of words. For Darwin, such communication had much deeper biological (and inarticulate) roots — a shared life, shared ancestry, shared social and expressive behavior. What could not be put into words could nevertheless the shared in non-verbal ways, e.g., by sympathetic experience of the same feelings.

Ferrier and Darwin stood at the antipodes concerning the metaphysics of consciousness, in spite of their considerable agreement concerning such subjects as reason in animals and the inadequacy of mechanistic theories of consciousness. For Darwin, expressive behavior, even if it were inarticulate, could nevertheless be the appropriate subject of scientific investigation. *Since there was no place in Darwin's universe of discourse for a feeling which could not be expressed, and since he thought that any expressible feeling could be sympathetically emulated, he took no notice of Ferrier's efforts to identify an isolated and indescribable core of consciousness.* Darwin sought to extend his own ideals and patterns of scientific inquiry to the analysis of expressive behavior, and he had seen no reason to agree with Ferrier's claims concerning free human acts, altogether outside the dominion of the law of causality. Finally, Darwin opposed Ferrier by attempting to formulate an ethical theory from the perspective of a naturalist, looking at man as he would any other social mammal. Darwin's account of moral behavior was as deterministic as his account of social behavior generally — but it should be remembered that Darwin never saw the "law of utility" as a simple calculus of pleasure and pain. The *utility* of human behavior had to be understood in the tripartite context of the *long and complex record of man's biological ancestors, of the diverse customs and tastes of distinct human populations, and of the possibility of a population's leaving descendants many generations into the future.*

His definition of expressive behavior, set forth during the month of August 1838 was almost identical to the "principle of serviceable associated habit" employed in his *The Expression of the Emotions in Animals and Man.*

Expression is an hereditary habitual movement consequent on some action, which the progenitor did when excited or disturbed by the same cause, which /now/ excites the expression.[25]

He had not so firmly marked the distinction between (acquired) habitual expression and that which was directly traceable to the "constitution of the Nervous System . . . independently to a certain extent of Habit" as he did later. He did note, however, that sighing, albeit expressive, had a direct physiological effect: "to relieve circulation after stillness."[26]

The list of expressive behaviors Darwin traced to particular biological functions was as lengthy in the *Notebooks* as in his much later published work on the subject. These included the grinning exposure of canine teeth;[27] the involuntary cry of pain;[28] the raised eyebrows of surprise;[29] the furious bellow of anger;[30] the side-long, narrowed look of suspicious inquiry;[31] the protruded lips of affection and desire;[32] the pallor of disease and languor;[33] the far-seeing, moist eyed look of hope;[34] and the short-sighted squint.[35] such behavior would be as subject to the laws of heredity as the organic structure and function upon which it was based.

Parents beget child like themselves. expression of countenances, organic diseases, mental disposition, stature, are slowly obtained & hereditary.[36]

Consequently, the capacity for interpreting facial expression ("physiognomical sensation") was as natural, and innate, in man as the capacity for vision itself, so children have no difficulty in expressing their "wants, pleasures or pains long before they can speak, or understand."[37] Darwin's older sister, Marianne, had four children of her own by 1838, and she had told him that "very young children express the greatest surprise at emotion in her countenance, — before they can have learnt by experience, that movements of face are more expressive than movements of fingers."[38]

In *Notebook N*, Darwin twice explored the thesis that music and particularly song was the form of pre-linguistic expression which had given rise to human language. He found "the taste for recurring sounds in harmony common to the whole kingdom of nature."[39] He noted the particular effectiveness of musical notes in communicating and exciting feelings of passion.[40] The identification of song as the prototypical form of language continued Darwin's stress upon the importance of the affective dimension of social organization, an emphasis which was also present in his linkage of the capacity for recognizing other conspecific individuals with responsiveness to beauty and ideas of beauty.[41] As he would later indicate, the capacity for musical expression would be directly favored in sexual selection. The net effect was to put the evolution of man's capacity for linguistic expression squarely in the context of the most powerful social instincts, and to subject that capacity to the immediate selective pressure which would follow from the evolution of assortative reproductive behavior. Darwin's discussions of the evolution of human language itself owed much to Lord Monboddo, to Horne Tooke, and to Benjamin Smart. They deserve separate and extensive consideration. All that can be indicated here is that these discussions, with their emphasis upon pantomime, poetry, and individual communication, laid great emphasis upon the *biological utility* of man's so-called *higher* capacities, his sense of beauty, wonder, and awe, and his awareness of his obligations to the society with which he is linked by heredity and by culture.[42]

4. SOCIAL INSTINCTS AND MORAL SENTIMENTS

Darwin's dedication to the task of providing an adequate scientific explanation of the origin of "intellectual man" led him to trace the so-called "higher" emotions, including that of love, to an evolutionary ancestry in the social instincts of animals. He freely used both moral language, e.g., 'love,' 'obligation,' and 'ought,' and mentalist language, e.g., 'recognition,' 'fear,' and 'pleasure,' in describing animal behavior and patterns of animal behavior or instincts.

There is textual evidence that he regarded sexual reproduction as *necessary* for significant evolutionary change.

If my theory be true, then the formation of sexes rigidly necessary. Without sexual crossing, there would be endless changes, & hence no feature would be deeply impressed on it, & hence there could not be improvements & hence not higher animals. It was absolutely necessary that physical changes should act not on individuals but on masses of individuals. − so that the changes should be slow and bear relation to the whole changes of country, & not to the local changes. This could only be effected by sexes.[43]

Only if populations of inter-breeding organisms were the units of evolutionary change could the variations which occurred in some fraction of the population be tested against the range ("country") of the whole population. The rate of change would be slow, but the population as a whole would be less vulnerable to extinction.

Darwin did not assume an ontology of unrelated individual organisms. For him, the unit of significant evolution was a group of organisms, a group structured by the capacity of its members to contribute to the next generation through the process of sexual crossing. Such populations need not be societies; since their members might be plants or the simplest proto-organisms, they might not exhibit social behavior.

It is essential to remember that this ontology of structured groups was in the background of everything that Darwin had to say about the social instincts and the moral sentiments. This is particularly important given the basic individualism of the British moral tradition which provided the vocabulary available for his comments concerning the moral or ethical implications of his theory. For example, there is *no* good reason to regard Darwin as assuming a typical Benthamite context for his understanding of the law of utility.

Law of utility. Nothing but that which has beneficial tendency through many ages could be acquired, & we are certain from our reason, that all which (as we must admit) has been acquired, does possess the beneficial tendency.[44]

Most basically, the notion Darwin labeled 'beneficial tendency' had to be interpreted in terms of survival and the prospects of leaving fertile progeny many generations hence. It could not be understood in terms of pleasure or happiness. Secondly, the ultimate subject of this "beneficial tendency" was, for Darwin, neither an individual organism nor a mere aggregate of such organisms, but a structured group.

In November of 1838, Darwin penned a strong statement claiming necessary links between sexual differentiation and the social instincts of animals, and between the social instincts and "all that is most beautiful in the moral sentiments of the animated beings."

I do not wish to say only cause, but one great final cause, nothing probably exists for one cause. My theory gives great final causes of sexes in separate animals: for otherwise there would be as many species as individuals, & though we may not trace out all the ill effects, − we see it is not the order in this perfect world, either at the present, or many anterior epochs. − but we can see if all species, there would not be social animals. hence not social instincts, which as I hope to show is probably the foundation of all that is most beautiful in the moral sentiments of the animated beings −.[45]

Darwin's first explicit statement of the link between the social instincts and man's moral sense seems to have resulted from his reading, in early August 1838, of Harriet Martineau's relativistic views in *How to Observe: Morals and Manners*. Martineau argued against an unchanging and universal moral sense, citing the historical variability of the moral approbation or disapprobation accorded such acts as taking the life of an enemy in battle, and claiming that "every man's feelings of right and wrong, instead of being born with him, grow up in him from the influences to which he is subjected." Nevertheless, he found her conceding Mackintosh's claim that there were *some* universal feelings of right and wrong, "which she seems to think are to make others happy & wrong to injure them without temptation."[46] He inferred "This probably is natural consequence of man, like deer, etc., being social animal, & this conscience or instinct may be most firmly fixed, but it will not prevent others being engrafted." He claimed that "friendship" among fellow animals in a social flock, herd, or tribe, since it was "necessary for long generation" (or the survival of a significantly large number of generations), was simply "good," and that a corresponding sense of pleasure eventually developed in association with such action.[47] Then toward the end of September, he sketched a more complete account of the implications of this insight for an account of man's moral and religious experience.

May not moral sense arise from our enlarged capacity/yet being obscurely guided/ (acting) on strong instinctive sexual, parental, & social instincts, giving rise "do unto others as yourself." "love they neighbour as thyself." Analyse this out, bearing in mind many new relations from language. The social instinct more than mere love. − fear for others acting in unison. − active assistance, etc., etc. ... ? May not idea of God arise from our confused idea of "ought," joined with necessary notion of "causation," in reference to this "ought," as well as the works of the whole world.[48]

Toward the close of *Notebook N*, Darwin began to connect the sense of beauty, particularly of musical beauty, with the need to *identify* and *communicate* with those to whom the social bond was particularly strong.

Does music bear any relation to the period when men communicated before language was invented. − were musical notes the language of passion & hence does music now excite our feelings.

How does Social animal recognize/ & take pleasure in? other animals, (especially as in some (instincts) insects which become in imago state social) by smell or looks, but it does not know its own smell or looks, & therefore there must be some instinctive feeling which is pleased by other animals smell & looks. − no doubt it may be attempted to be said that young animal learns parent smell & look & so by association receives pleasure. This/ will not do for insects. − if this view holds good, then man, a socialist does not know other men by smell, but by looks hence some obscure picture of other men, & hence idea of beauty.[49]

This theme was reiterated in the *Sketch of 1842*, and then developed in the

Essay of 1844 to the extent that the sexual struggle was seen to play a role equal to that of the struggle for life itself. This is, to be sure, more than adequate evidence that Darwin's concept of natural selection emphasized the variability of the chances of leaving progeny as much as it emphasized survival. Even more important, however, is its clear indication of his increasing confidence in a basically monistic view of the relation of mind and nature, and in the general adequacy of the metaphor of 'struggle' to express the wide range of selective forces covered by his theory.[50]

This sexual struggle might have been "less rigorous than the other" in that the less successful were usually not mortally wounded, but only suffered a reduction (even to zero) in the number of offspring they might produce. The usual consequence for evolutionary change was the alteration of "sexual characters," "no way related to their power of obtaining food, or of defending themselves from their natural enemies," but often concentrating upon "fighting one with another" among conspecific competitors for sexual opportunity. But Darwin's estimate of this selective agency grew enormously when he turned his attention specifically to the evolution of man.[51]

On 12 March 1839, Darwin wrote in *Transmutation Notebook E* that "it is difficult to believe in the dreadful but quiet war of organic beings, going on [in] the peaceful woods, & smiling fields."[52] Somewhat later in the spring of that same year, he wrote a ten-page manuscript commentary on a *Dissertation on the Progress of Ethical Philosophy, chiefly during the 17th and 18th centuries*, by Sir James Mackintosh. This manuscript stressed the foundation of man's sense of right and wrong in several social instincts which consisted of "a feeling of love (& sympathy) or benevolence" to the object in question. There was no indication, in this manuscript, that its author perceived any incompatibility or tension between the uses of 'war' in his theory of the transmutation of species and the centrality of 'love' in his ethics. If we are to have any idea of Darwin's perception of this problem, we need to begin with a commentary on this ethical manuscript. His general purposes, his method, and the vocabulary he employed in relating his position to the currents of ethical speculation recorded by Mackintosh must be examined.

One of Mackintosh's greatest concerns was to *distinguish* the question of the *psychological development* of the moral sense from that of the *criterion of morality*. This distinction was essential for his hopes to reconcile the universality and necessity of the dictates of conscience with the development of conscience through a process of mental association necessarily relative to individual or group circumstances. Darwin, on the contrary, always conflated these issues. On Darwin's terms, the genetic or historic *explanation* of the development of the moral sense also provided the best *justification* for the admission that man *ought* to act according to the instinctive inclinations which comprised it. Accordingly, his manuscript essay "On the Moral Sense" began with the announcement that he would study man from the same perspective that a natural historian would employ in analyzing the activity of any mammal.[53] His discussion involved a number of terms, 'instinct,' 'habit,' 'passion,' for which he provided no strict or technical definition, but which it is plausible to interpret as referring to behavioral patterns as more or *less* frequently repeated, and as more or less heritable. Thus 'passion' referred to episodic, short-lived behavior, 'habit' to a frequently repeated routine, and 'instinct' to a general pattern of behavior or behavioral repertoire, the capacity for which had become innate for a whole group of organisms. The essay admitted that man was the last in a series of animals in which the special instincts were increasingly less influential, but it nevertheless took man's possession of at least "parental, conjugal, and social instincts" as a basic premiss. With the same effortless Euclidean style which Paley used to define virtue as "the doing of good to mankind, in obedience to the will of God, and for the sake of everlasting happiness," Darwin asserted that "these instincts consist of a feeling of love (& sympathy) or benevolence to the object in question," and that they involved the animal "in such active sympathy that the individual forgets itself, & aids & defends & acts for others at its own expense." He also stipulated, without further analysis of the evolutionary significance of pleasure and pain, that action in "accordance to an instinct gives great pleasure, & such actions being prevented by (necessarily) some force give pain." Moral approbation or disapprobation of others was attributed to associated experiences of pleasure and pain contingent upon their conformity or non-confirmity to these same instinctive patterns.

Darwin was supremely confident that Mackintosh's account could be adapted to demonstrate that his own system was not selfish.[54] In his 1839 manuscript commentary on the moral sense and on Mackintosh's history, he insisted that feelings of love, benevolence, and sympathy were constituents of the basic social instincts. This is not to say that he provided much in the way of analytic clarification of the role 'love,' or its cognate terms, might play in the vocabulary of the naturalist. There was a paucity of occurrences of such terms, both in this manuscript and elsewhere in the Notebooks and manuscripts of the period 1837–1844.[55] This manuscript provided no more than an implicit definition of 'love' as an inner state associated with an instinctive social behavior which frequently came into conflict with the individual's own immediate needs for food or protection from danger.

His theory of the transmutation of species explained the characteristics of organisms or groups of organisms in terms of their contribution to survival, i.e., their relevance to past and present chances of leaving fertile progeny. The theory implied that the basic "laws of life" could be *adequately* expressed *only* in the context of a reasonable reconstruction of evolutionary history and an accurate statement of the laws of specific (evolutionary) change. The claim that some instinctive behavior consists in "such active sympathy that the individual forgets himself" must be seen in this same context.

Darwin's efforts to achieve this vision were sketchy and incomplete. In part, he was aware of the preliminary and fragmentary character of his position.

N.B. Until it can be shown, what things easiest become instinctive, this part of argument fails, or rather is weak.[56]

This admission was not unlike many others which expressed his inability accurately to identify, and his unwillingness to speculate about, those specific characteristics upon which the "checks" to the chances of leaving fertile progeny would fall most heavily. The difference is that as regards the evolution of social behavior Darwin already seemed to have taken sides, to have gone more than a few steps in the direction of the detailed claim that the "protection of others" had survival value, and more than that, that such "benevolence" would have some *advantage* in the struggle for existence. The grounds for this claim were sketchy. Yet they may have been adequate to account for the unusual forthrightness of the claim itself. Sexual crossing had been identified as a necessary condition of the kind of evolutionary change which Darwin saw himself as explaining. Related capacities for communication with and recognition of particular conspecific individuals could be advantageous in the most elementary animal societies. Music, language, and a sense of beauty could have evolved by such means. He found the notions of such "wholistic" characteristics as the organization of animal societies by instinctive social behavior very useful in sketching the evolutionary path from simple organisms to man.

There should be no blinking the fact that the results were uncritical and incomplete, both from the perspective of the biological theory and from that of the moral philosophy of his day. However, it could hardly have been otherwise in the initial stages of the elaboration of a new cosmological framework. His identification of moral approbation (or the judgment of conscience) with sensations of pleasure or pain associated with action (or failure to act) in accord with instinct rather than with passion or appetite, provided no more than a rhetorical basis for the assertion

By association one gains the rule, that the passions and appetite should (almost) always be sacrificed to the instincts.[57]

He obviously did not critically evaluate the difficulties involved in moving from a set of inter-locking descriptive theses concerning passion and instinct to a *rule* appearing to state what *should* be done. How significant was this lapse?

To answer this question fairly, and with appropriate attention to the scope of Darwin's thought, two points must be kept in mind. The first is that one of his basic premisses was that the evolution of social behavior was possible because some actions, i.e., those which had a "beneficial tendency, (not to any one individual, but to the whole past race)" became instinctive and innate. This first premiss might seem to imply a hopelessly biologized account of human behavior, were it not for the second, equally basic to Darwin's thought on this subject.

Now we know it is easy by association to give /almost/ any taste to a young person, or it is accidentally acquired from some trifling circumstance. – thus a child may be taught to think almost anything nasty ((accidentally)) . . . so a child may be taught, or will acquire from seeing conduct of others, the feeling that almost (rarely if opposed to natural instincts) any action is either right or wrong. –[58]

This second premiss could account for national or family customs, e.g., the "law of honor" or social etiquette. Such local norms, or patterns of expected performance, Darwin thought, might become instinctive. He toyed with the inference that the number of instincts which might give rise to distinctively moral obligations could not be limited to the original three ("parental, conjugal, social"), i.e., that different races of men might have different instincts. The social instinct might be associated with various attitudes toward leadership; the conjugal instinct might be monogamous or polygamous; the parental instinct might take various forms. His firmest conclusion from these disparate premisses was that *man had very few instincts*, and those he had were very general in their nature. But even a trace of instinctive action was "sufficient to give rise to the feeling of right & wrong. – on which/ almost/ any other might be grafted."[59] The parental and social instincts set a context within which moral authority could be invested in a pattern of education and custom (rules of etiquette, laws of honour) which might be "curiously modified by circumstances of country," but which nevertheless would be associated with the same moral feelings attached to the basic instincts. The breaking of a social custom would have effective consequences largely similar to a violation of the basic instincts (conscience) themselves.[60]

This account was designed to explain how man had evolved as an ethical animal, one who recognized that he ought to act in a certain way, or that he ought to accept a particular authoritative direction, even when his own appetites and passions struggled against such recognition of duty.[61] This framework was sufficiently loose to allow for any desired degree of historical and social relativism, and yet to insist upon the real moral authority of the diverse social norms. The theory led to a certain confidence, *a priori*, in a "Law of Utility" which implied that "Nothing but that which has beneficial tendency through many ages could be acquired." Since it was "probable that becomes instinctive which is repeated under many generations. . . . & only that which is beneficial to race will have reoccurred," the weight of success through many generations was on the side, not only of instinct, but also of parental teaching and even "general actions of community" which would strive for those same goals, enshrined in the experience of the race.[62]

Darwin's first drafts of the theory of the transmutation of species offered an evolutionary explanation of the presence of a moral sense, a sense of duty, or a feeling of right and wrong, in man. Some of his comments suggest that he hoped to do more, that he hoped to show that there was some connection between a group's prospects for leaving fertile progeny a number of generations into the future and its propensities for truth-telling rather than lying, or for love and sympathy rather than hostile selfishness. He was troubled by the fact that he was unable to infer anything about the details of those behavioral repertoires the capacities for which were most likely to become innate in all the members of a species. And there is the ambitious language of the opening paragraph of his fragment on Mackintosh, the language which claimed not only that man has "parental, conjugal, and social instincts, and perhaps others," but that "these instincts consist of a feeling of love (& sympathy) or benevolence to the object in question."

This language gives an interesting glimpse of Darwin's place in the ethical and political debates of the day, and tends to *refute* the view that he was the prototypical Social Darwinian, emphasizing individualistic selfishness and licensing any behavior which insured the pleasurable survival of one's individual enterprise.

Darwin's theory had the most radical implications, not only for the fate of religious orthodoxy, but also for the basic theses of the British ethical tradition, theses which had *not* been challenged by thinkers as diverse as Bentham, Paley, Mackintosh, and Whewell. On Darwin's terms, moral behavior had to be seen as a special case of adaptive behavior, which in turn was only one of the categories governed by the various laws of life. Consequently, neither pleasure, nor happiness, nor the stability of the established political order, nor the will of God, could function as the ultimate criterion of morality. That criterion could only be formulated in terms of "beneficial tendency" for the whole past race and the prospects of leaving fertile progeny indefinitely far into the future. *The issues were those of survival and survivorship.*

Darwin's *explanation* of the evolution of the moral sense, since it implicitly redefined 'right' and 'wrong,' 'duty,' and 'ought' in terms of the *survival* of a species, was easily conflated with a *justification* of the claim that the criterion of morality is survival. After all, the goal of the theory of transmutation of species, as Darwin was developing it, was an accurate formulation of the "laws of life" on the basis of a correct understanding of the adaptive interactions of members of organic populations and their environments. The curious blend of adaptation and inefficiency actually found in nature was not intelligible apart from an historical account of the development of the organism-popula-tion-environment triad. This implied, and it is of the first importance to note how really cogent this implication is, that *the natural historian could be justified* in claiming to give an answer to the question, "What is the moral sense?" On the assumption that behavior is as much subject to evolution as bone structure, all patterned behavior, even human moral and social behavior, was seen as subject to the implications of his theory. In offering an explana-tion of the origins of patterned behavior, he was also implicitly redefining the major features of those patterns. But the definition of 'moral behavior' is only a step away from the justification of a criterion of morality.

What are we to make of Darwin as a moralist? His particular reformulation of the 'law of utility,' a central term in the history of British moral thought, was "Nothing but that which has beneficial tendency through many ages could be acquired, & we are certain from our reason, that all which (as we must admit) had been acquired, does possess the beneficial tendency." The beneficial tendency in question accrued, not to any one individual, but to the whole *past* human species, not necessarily to the greater number living at any one time, but to some sub-population of adequate size to insure hereditary continuity (survival of descendants) over a significant number of generations (10^5). Nor was the expression 'beneficial tendency' understood or defined in such terms as 'pleasure,' let alone 'self-interest.' Darwin's use of 'beneficial tendency,' in 1839, was obviously and thoroughly dominated by the criterion of evolutionary success: the hereditary continuity (survival) of an inter-breed-ing population over a very large number of generations. Darwin may have become a Benthamite or a Spencerian by the time he wrote the *Descent of Man*, but the *evidence is not consistent* with the attribution of such views to him in 1839.[63]

PART III

CONCLUSIONS

CHAPTER NINE

THE CULTURAL CONTEXT OF THE FIRST DRAFTS
OF DARWIN'S THEORY

Darwin's published work developed some of the most fundamental concepts of his theory (struggle, selection, chance, design, and mechanism) in metaphorical and allegorical language. Close examination of this aspect of his linguistic practice indicates an almost poetic commitment to expression which was at once original, colorful, and controlled. Darwin's use of such figurative language did not flag with the passing years. Ten years after the publication of *The Origin*, he published the allegory of the architect choosing building stones from the shattered fragments at the base of a precipice to *explain* his notion of chance. In contrast, the allegory of the selecting being, infinitely more sagacious than man, but not an omniscient creator, received its fullest expression in the *Sketch of 1842*, and then was heavily modified by positivist disclaimers by the time the third edition of *The Origin* was submitted to the printer. The *Notebooks* and early manuscripts *did not develop or test* any of the figures of speech which were to become so famous. Nevertheless, these same early papers are essential for the interpretation of the figurative language which plays so large a part in the published expositions of the theory. Since the metaphors and allegories carried a heavy load of ambiguity, and since the critical responses of his readers made it quite plain that they were likely to be misinterpreted, or exploited to his disadvantage by his critics, his continued insistence that such expression was "almost necessary" for "convenience and brevity," has been examined closely.

Darwin compared his own usage, not to prestigious and safe precedents of the kind that might have been provided by Newton's generalization of the laws of terrestrial mechanics, but to some of the more controversial language in the science of his day: 'elective affinity' in chemistry and 'attraction' in place of 'gravitation' in physics. His metaphors and allegories did not function according to the "best" scientific practice. He did *not* take over the vocabulary and conceptual structure of a theory well established in a distinct but related field. He did not, e.g., follow the example of those who used the imagery and the mathematical apparatus associated with the familiar mechanics of wave motion to explore optical phenomena which were anomalous when approached in terms of the classic properties of particles. He did *not* develop his own views within the context of a field which had been mathematically codified, e.g., to the extent that this was true of the algebraic relationship of the concepts of pressure, volume, and rate of flow in hydrodynamics, nor did he use an established theory to model his own as hydrodynamics was used to model the major properties of electrical circuits.

To the contrary, the original referents of Darwin's metaphors and allegories were found in common experience, or at least in common, non-scientific belief, and ordinary agricultural practice. Where the categories and the vocabulary of other, well established scientific theories played a part, that part was *usually* negative and even antinomic: the eye was not an optimally designed photographic mechanism; the "rationality" of mountain burros *disproved* the hypothesis of "animated machines"; organisms were *much more complex than crystals* and were correspondingly intractable under the tools of mathematical analysis.

It is striking that Darwin's metaphors and allegories seem naive and even excessively "easy."[1] Their roots in colloquial language and common belief only partially explain this appearance. To the extent that his metaphors had algebraic, geometrical, or statistical connations, he left these undeveloped and largely unnoticed. The import of his metaphors and allegories was ontological rather than formal. Their "naivete" must be attributed to the requirements of the initial presentation of a theory such as Darwin's. He was tackling a subject which, in his view, not only lacked a dominant, generally accepted theory, but which did not yet exist as a legitimate, unified field of inquiry. No technique of empirical verification, taken alone, could have provided it with the required legitimacy. First, it was necessary to establish a *perspective* from which the significance of the available evidence could be recognized, and to which competent investigators, in the requisite numbers, could be attracted. Darwin's linguistic practice owed something to the rhetorician who wrote,

Language may more properly be said to help others to come at our thoughts, than to represent our thoughts: although it is likewise true, that we could not ourselves have come at them but by similar means (emphasis added).[2]

The concentration of figurative expression in his published work suggests a basically didactic (albeit occasionally autodidactic) intent. Since these metaphors and allegories also exacted a high cost in ambiguity and misunderstanding, their presumed pedagogical utility does not suffice to explain Darwin's dogged insistence upon their use.

One of the more remarkable features of Darwin's publication of his theory of the transmutation of species was its anticipation, fifteen to twenty years earlier, in relatively full-scale publication drafts. *The Sketch of 1842* and *The*

Essay of 1844, in their turn, were composed five years after the period of intense concentration which determined their basic conceptual structure. *The Essay of 1844* and *The Origin of Species* have not heretofore been subjected to comparative scrutiny. They exhibit a nearly identical sequence of topics, *no* basic differences in conceptual structure, and nearly identical metaphorical expression of the concepts of struggle, natural selection, and chance. The textual evidence alone is more than adequate to warrant the inference that *The Essay of 1844* furnished the structural and rhetorical model for Darwin's projected three volume work on natural selection, and for the hasty preparation and publication of *The Origin of Species*. There is a strong genetic resemblance between the expository rhetoric to be found in *The Sketch, The Essay*, and *The Origin*. The importance of the earliest drafts of the theory for the interpretation of Darwin's published work is like the importance of an organism's evolutionary history for an understanding of the details of its form and its functions.

Slight differences in the British cultural environment in 1839 and then in 1859 are of great importance for understanding Darwin's project. The names of J. S. Mill, Herbert Spencer, and Alexander Bain are *nowhere* to be found in the *Notebooks* and early manuscripts. In contrast, August Comte, Dugald Stewart, and William Wordsworth were not mentioned in work published after 1859. There are many other differences in the "environment" of "The Essay" and *The Origin*, including differences in Darwin's perceptions of his audience, his theory, and his own role as a creative scientist. Several aspects of the work which he published after 1859, and particularly the ontologically and morally significant metaphors and allegories to be found in that work, had a *more clearly identifiable function* in *The Sketch of 1842* and so are *more readily and accurately understood in the context of those earliest drafts of the theory*.

The dominant structural feature of Darwin's *Essay of 1844* was its clear division into two parts, the first showing "that the (natural) production, under existing conditions, of exquisitely adapted species, is at least possible," and the second taking this law-like network of possibilities and testing it against "direct evidence in favour or against" it. The explicit distinction of arguments for the "possibility" of the theory from arguments which weighed the theory against direct positive and negative evidence was not repeated in *The Origin*. In the *Notebooks* themselves, Darwin was aware of the methodological difficulty in compartmentalizing two kinds of evidence: one showing the cogency of the theory or the feasibility of investigating it further, and the second actually establishing its truth or falsity. Nevertheless, this division determined the sequence of topics in *The Essay*, and it identified statements concerning variability, the absence of certain kinds of natural limits to the range of organic variability, the inheritance of variations, and the struggle for existence, as constituting *the core* of the theory of transmutation of species. (*The Origin* adopted the same topic sequence as *The Essay*, and developed the core of the theory in nearly identical fashion, retaining much of the imagery and metaphorical expression to be found in the draft written fifteen years earlier.)

Darwin's diffident caution in the formulation of the conclusion of Part I of *The Essay* does much to explain the logical role played by the Part I metaphors, selection and struggle. The conclusion, as Darwin wrote it in both 1842 and then again in 1844, was a detailed and complex conditional proposition, a proposition which actually embedded a number of subsidiary hypotheses within the main thesis concerning the possibility of the transmutation of species. Schematically, it had the form

$$(V \,\&\, H \,\&\, M \,\&\, U) \to \Big\{ [\, (C_1 \,\&\, S) \,\&\, (C_2 \,\&\, R) \,\&\, (C_3 \,\&\, A) \\ \&\, (C_4 \,\&\, I) \,] \to 0 \Big\}$$

Or, in a succinct verbal variation:

Given the appropriately unlimited (U) variability (V) of an organic population, the inheritance (H) of that variability, and the probability that not all organisms will leave fertile progeny (M),

It follows that given the separate conditions for differential reproduction (S), the formation of adapted (A) races (R), and reproductive isolation (I),

New species will be formed (0).

For the reader in the last quarter of the twentieth century, the cogency and *heuristic power* of this hypothesis are so well known that it is often read as a categorical proposition. But in 1842–1844, Darwin had cause for concern. The plausibility of the hypothesis depended upon the exhibition of at least one instance in which its premises could truly be asserted in conjunction with its final consequent. He could not provide, obviously, a real-world illustration of the transmutation of species. Nor could he cast his premises in sufficiently precise mathematical form to justify an estimate of the prior probability of the truth of their conjunction and his conclusion. A believably plausible, if imaginary, *model* of the process which Darwin was hypothesizing as the explanation of the existence and of the variety of organic species was both a logical *and* a rhetorical necessity.

'Plausibility' in such contexts requires a pragmatic definition, i.e., it is relative to the beliefs of a particular group of people. Given the vagueness of the conditions for membership in this group, and the heterogeneity of the members' beliefs, it would be impossible to enumerate a set of logically necessary and sufficient conditions ensuring the group's affirmative judgment of the possibility or plausibility of *any* hypothesis. For example, Darwin could *not* have shown that his theory was as consistent as Euclidean geometry by developing a Euclidean model of his premises. He could and did elaborate a "likely story" to illustrate its cogency and significance. The principal ingredients of this story were the metaphors and allegories he deployed in the *Sketch of 1842* and *The Essay of 1844*.

The specific implications of the particular metaphors actually employed by Darwin were both scientific and in some sense extra-scientific (whether metaphysical or moral), but these diverse implications are intricately inter-connected and inter-dependent. The use of the *demiurge figure* ["a selecting being infinitely more sagacious than man (not an omniscient creator)"] in the *Sketch of 1842* was a significant instance of this interaction of scientific and metaphysical concerns. The classic roots of this allegory (in Plato's *Timaeus*) tapped a responsive vein among the religiously conservative and orthodox heirs of Cambridge Platonism. The battle was staged on home ground. To limit the ingenuity of the demiurge, or the variability of the material available to him, was to impugn the infinity of the omniscient creator, whose rhetorical symbol and surrogate the demiurge surely was. The allegory also tapped a source of methodological insight as old as Leibniz. To probe the consistency of a scientific hypothesis, it is useful to consider whether or not it maps a "possible world." One of the dimensions of such possibility is set by the laws of physics. Malthus had scornfully jibed at Godwin that no amount of careful selection for smaller skulls and shorter legs in sheep could reduce these unprofitable organs to evanescence. Darwin's survey assured him that no other kind of physical law limited the range of organic variability. The fact that the assumption of such a limit to variability had no secure scientific foundation was made particularly obvious in the context of the selecting demiurge, who had at his disposal indefinitely large numbers of organisms and indefinitely lengthy periods of time. The same absence of physical and biological laws limiting the variety of the parts of organisms (or embryological processes) was expressed in the demiurge's ability to "perceive differences in the outer and innermost organization quite imperceptible to man."[3] Allegorical expression allowed for the ambiguity of hyperbole and exaggeration. If "discrimination," "forethought," and "steadiness of object," as these were found in the demiurge, were "incomparably greater than those qualities in man," then it would follow that

With time enough, such a Being might rationally (without some unknown law opposed him) aim at almost any result.[4]

It was an explicit part of the allegorical account of the evolution of the mistletoe that *the demiurge was obliged to watch and wait and select* those seedlings which were even slightly more effectively co-adapted with the other organisms which comprised the major elements in the environment of that parasitic plant. Indirectly, this restriction on the demiurge's *patience* expressed a theme concerning which Darwin felt the deepest ambivalence: *chance*. Even though it was open to him to act on the reproductive system of an organism, to "keep its organization somewhat plastic," the activity attributed to the *demiurge* was *selection* and *emphatically not creation, design, or even manufacture*. Darwin's account implied that the *demiurge could not unite* the *causes of organic variability and the adaptive requirements of reproductive efficiency*. The sagacious selecting being was *unable to improve on the elementary strategy of trial-and-error*.

Darwin's allegorical account of the evolution of the mistletoe by the exercise of selective discrimination also provided a powerful rhetorical device for the didactic and autodidactic representation of the plausibility of the theory. Its power in this respect provides a partial explanation, but no more than a partial explanation, of his willingness to pay the considerable price of ambiguity which inevitably accompanied the use of figurative expressions with strong overtones of common speech. Since Darwin's theoretical and scientific vocabulary had few of the forbidding trappings of technical jargon, it was difficult, both for him and for his audience, to remember that he had the right to claim the privilege of stipulating the meaning of those parts of his vocabulary for which he might be prepared to assert a special technical status.

In one key sector of his logical vocabulary, his penchant for facile colloquial expression resulted in the blurring of a number of logical distinctions which both the scientific audience of 1839 and that of 1859 would have insisted upon maintaining in clear and rigorous fashion. The almost devastating *cost* of the ambiguity locked into the heuristically and persuasively powerful imagery of selection and struggle and economy was exacted in this sector. Darwin was unable to discriminate the explanatory modalities to be claimed for the various implications of his theory. He had completely failed to provide the logical equipment necessary to distinguish empirical propositions which were implied by his theory with *deductive necessity* from those to which it assigned varying degrees of statistical *probability*, or even from those which it merely *illuminated and reformulated* in terms which opened their subjects to empirical investigation.

It is impossible to make sense of this state of affairs without considering again the particular configuration and membership of Darwin's cultural circle, as well as the doctrines and idiosyncracies of its more prominent members.

1. THE LOGIC OF THE THEORY AND OF ITS RHETORICAL REPRE-SENTATION

Charles Lyell's and J. F. W. Herschel's views concerning the general nature of scientific method were the decisive influence upon Darwin's decision, probably in 1839, as to the most effective logical strategy to employ in the representation of his theory to a reading audience. But the highly significant, if implicit, role played by the careful and intricate *logical organization* of Paley's arguments must also be noted. At the time late in 1838 and into 1839 when this decision was being made, Darwin had no acquaintance with the work of J. S. Mill. He had read all three volumes of Whewell's *History of the Inductive Sciences*, but his annotations of his personal copy concentrated upon *teleological* and *taxonomic* topics *not* directly *relevant* to the *broadest logical articulation* of his argument. (Whewell's *Philosophy of the Inductive Sciences* was not published at this time; Darwin never purchased a copy, and seems to have decided he should read it only after noticing Herschel's comment on it in the *Edinburgh Review*.) For Herschel, the canonical form of laws of nature was clearly hypothetical:

If such a case arise, such a course shall be followed.

Rejecting Hume and the positivism of Brown, Herschel saw laws as structuring a realm of possible occurrences. Laws of nature, as distinguished from mere empirical generalizations, were in some way independent of particular trial and played a role like that of axioms in geometry, providing *a priori* for contingent events. Herschel was particularly critical of the view that causality could be analyzed solely in terms of regular temporal succession, and advocated the position, more compatible with deist imagery, that laws of nature expressed realities of power and agency, with conscious voluntary agency serving as the paradigmatic instance.

In another respect, the *Preliminary Discourse* set an almost impossibly rigorous precedent for Darwin's emulation. Herschel's criteria for laws of nature included the requirement that, when coupled with appropriate empirical detail, a law of nature implied mathematically precise observation statements as necessary logical consequences. The two part division of Darwin's argument — into a first part showing the possibility of his theory and a second part testing it against direct positive and negative evidence — surely reflected Herschel's estimate of the correct scientific strategy. At the same time, the vagueness, vacillation, and outright equivocity of Darwin's logical vocabulary — his confused and confusing uses of 'these facts all necessarily follow,' '*a priori* expectation,' 'manifestly possible if not probable,' 'throw light upon,' 'instead of being metaphorical becomes plain' — seem symptomatic of stress generated by an effort to satisfy criteria of mathematical precision and deductive necessity beyond the capabilities of his theory. He had every reason to think that Herschel would not accept the bare logical skeleton of his argument, and therefore every reason to clothe that skeleton with the plausible and relevant imagery of his metaphors and analogies. This was never a question of abandoning science for mere rhetorical fiction and fancy; Darwin's metaphors did a full job of scientific work. The point is simply that there was work to be done by figurative language in the context of his theory.

Darwin's figurative language tended to reflect the patterns of common speech rather than the technical idiom of other scientific theories, and it carried heavy mentalistic or anthropomorphic overtones. The philosophy of language to be found in the work of Dugald Stewart, and implicit in the etymological investigations of Darwin's brother-in-law, Hensleigh Wedgwood, is of prime importance here.[5] The Scottish common sense realists' assumptions of a language of nature, a natural language, and the progressive development of man's capacity for language, provided a congenial philosophical ambience within which to articulate a biological theory of the origins of man's "higher" — language related — capacities. The implications that all human language is a metaphorical or figurative elaboration of a system of human communication first elaborated in the context of the most primitive biological functions, and that the meaning of any given word in the language is best understood by juxtaposing it (or placing it in tension) with its earlier etymological uses, provided a strong antidote for the demands for an artificial technical language satisfying the requirements of mathematical precision and deductive logical connections. A theory of human evolution couched in the mathematical formalisms of Herschel's astronomy, in the fashion of Sewall Wright or R. A. Fisher, would have remained undiscovered or unnoticed much longer than was the fate of Gregor Mendel's far less threatening venture into mathematical biology.

The influential Scottish zoologist John Fleming and Darwin were in complete agreement on the thesis that "the intellectual powers of man differ, not in kind, but merely in degree, from those of brutes." Darwin's rhetoric reflected Stewart's sense of the primitive roots and progressive, figurative development of all human language, Fleming's nonchalant dismissal of the problem of materialism, and their common distrust of the intrusion of mechanistic metaphors into explanations of the natural history of life.

Comte and Whewell played a contrapuntal role in the development of Darwin's sense of scientific method. Darwin rejected Whewell's view that the category of final causality was beyond the range of scientific analysis, a condition for the possibility of biological investigation, rather than a topic for analysis and explanation. Comte provided the necessary antidote for the empirical vacuity of the assumption of one, general final cause operating throughout nature, and pointed the way toward a *scientifically reputable, limited functionalism*. There were strains of historicism and relativism in Comte which provided the critical tools Darwin required to distinguish his approach from that of the theological stage of zoology, but in 1838—1839, he failed to win Darwin's epistemological allegiance to the cause of positivism, and away from Herschel's more flexible, and more ambiguous, causal interpretation of the key phrase 'law of nature.'

Darwin's *Notebooks* and early manuscripts, together with the marginal annotations of the books in his personal library, provide essential evidence for the evaluation and the cogency of his resolution of the issues presented in powerful, dialectical fashion by his cultural circle. The *Notebooks*, early manuscripts, and marginalia contained *no* anticipatory testing of the allegories and analogies used in 1842 and in all the later drafts of the theory. It is possible that his reflections and investigations were guided by these metaphors, and that he simply failed to commit them to paper before 1842. His infrequent use of 'metaphor' reflected an interest in the evolution of man's capacity for aesthetic satisfaction and expression which was not extended, at least in 1837—1839, to an explicit appraisal of scientific language. He noticed and commented on the meaning of Stewart's critique of essentialist theories of predication, but made no effort to employ Stewart's logically flexible analysis of family resemblance to solve any of the contemporary disputes between nominalism and essentialism.

Darwin's *methodological self-image*, as it was reflected in the candid entries in his *Notebooks*, was in a state of *indecisive flux* during the all-important period from *August through October 1838*. On September 19th, an entry reflected the hypothetical-deductive structure advocated by Herschel and Whewell

The line of argument often pursued throughout my theory is to establish *a point as a probability by induction, & to apply it as hypotheses to other points, & see whether it will solve them* – (emphasis added).[6]

Later he admitted a considerable difficulty in keeping these two categories of evidence (for induction and for testing) separate.

I, from looking at all facts as inducing towards law of transmutation cannot see the deductions which are possible (emphasis added).[7]

The basic logical structure of the *Essay of 1844* was determined by the distinction of evidence for the possibility, cogency or plausibility of an hypothesis from evidence for its utility in explaining or solving facts about the real world. But this distinction was *not anticipated in the Notebooks*. Darwin gave *no preference* to either of the two conflicting attitudes just quoted. The major methodological text of the *Notebooks* dealt with the subject of natural history and the laws of life in a way which completely by-passed the distinction of induction and deduction as well as Herschel's distinction of laws of nature and empirical generalizations and Comte's claim that natural history was not properly part of biological science since it merely applied the laws of biology. Darwin's picture was more sensitive to the interplay of historical and systematic considerations in the articulation of the laws of life, and to the natural historian's difficulty in distinguishing laws of nature from empirical rules with merely local applications.

This program of investigation represented an important advance over the accounts of scientific methodology articulated by other members of the cultural circle. Its blend of evolutionary, ecological, and strictly physiological problems anticipated Darwin's long researches concerning barnacles. But it was not used to determine the sequence of topics, nor the logical structure, of the drafts of 1842, 1844, nor of the later published versions of the theory. *In drafting his theory for publication, he adopted a logical structure closer to the current consensus. Since this consensus had not been formulated for contingencies as complex as those of natural history, it provided no useable models for dealing with historical change in populations of highly diverse individual organisms, nor for basically statistical and generally non-predictive laws expressing the underlying regularities of such change.* The resultant slack in the argument was taken up by his artful invention and employment of allegories and metaphors for the *Sketch of 1842*.

One of the more significant and sharp variations in Darwin's vocabulary during 1837–1839 involved 'chance,' used frequently in the first two *Transmutation Notebooks* and then almost not at all after he read Comte and began to consider the difficulties which might be raised for his theory by any claims concerning human freedom. Such an attribute would have removed man from his field of investigation. As he worked out the implications of his commitment to psychological or behavioral determinism, he did not stop to rethink the importance of his earlier use of the "law of chances" as an anti-dote for progressivist hypotheses purporting to explain the migration and transmutation of organic populations. He did *not* negate the hypotheses that the sources of organic variation, and some of the causes of migration, were *random* in relation to the adaptive presures exerted by specific environmental "stations." But the *metaphors* of selection and struggle were employed to express (or mask) Aristotle's classic resolution of the dichotomy of chance and design or final causality.

Comte would have argued that *purely* hypothetical (theoretical) postulates were admissible, if they did not block the historical development of scientific inquiry. Some members of Darwin's circle would have licensed a more exten-sive use of allegory: a use based upon a theory of language and metaphor whose basic postulate was a thesis concerning the instinctive interpretation of natural signs and the figurative elaboration of these signs in an historically evolving community. In this context, metaphorical expression was essential to all human discourse, including the language of science itself. Only the cessation of inquiry and intellectual progress — whether because the tasks of research were complete, or because of a dogmatic imposition of a premature foreclosure — would insure that a definitive lexicon could be composed for an unchanging, completely literal technical language. This explains Darwin's willingness to use metaphorical and allegorical expression in the representa-tion of the central core of a scientific theory. But it falls short of an account of his use of the particular metaphors of 'selection,' 'struggle,' and 'economy.' These metaphors were not only non-mechanist and non-reductionist, they were thoroughly anthropomorphic and even moralistic.

2. "MATERIALISM" AND THE STATUS OF CONSCIOUSNESS AS A BIOLOGICAL CATEGORY

As we have seen, Darwin referred to himself with the terms, "O you ma-terialist!," and invented a strategy for the public avoidance of an admission of "how far I believe in materialism." The characteristic positions taken on this issue by his philosophical circle are particularly useful for the understand-ing of this aspect of his self-image. No member of the group whose positions have been reviewed in this study could be termed a materialist in the strict reductionist sense suggested by Maurice Mandelbaum. No one, certainly not the notorious pioneer of neurophysiology, Dr. William Lawrence, not August Comte, not even Lamarck himself, held that whatever properties living organisms exhibit are "ultimately explicable by means of general laws which apply equally to all of the manifestations of matter." Lawrence and Comte were particularly aware of the obstacles, for a biologist in the early years of the nineteenth century, in the path of an effort to unify biological explanation by a uniform application of the conceptual and mathematical apparatus of Newtonian physics. Moreover, Lawrence was also critical of the loose speculative analogies employed in Lamarck's account of "nervous" and "caloric fluids" whose agitations coordinated the movements of animals and plants, and in some sense "constituted" the emotions and sensations of animals. Even Lamarck was sufficiently insistent upon the radical significance of four distinctions in kind (between inorganic and living bodies, between plants and animals; between imperfect animals, devoid of feeling, and animals which experienced feeling but lacked intelligence; and finally that distinguishing intelligent animals from all the rest), to escape the reductionist implications of Mandelbaum's strict sense of materialism. Lamarck explicitly denied that sensation could be attributed to matter as such, following Hartley's lead and stating that "feeling is the result of an action and reaction, which becomes general throughout the nervous system." C. C. Gillispie's characterization of Lamarck as an Heraclitean, stressing the basic ontological status of *activity*, and particularly its priority and causal control over material structure, is accurate. The Rev. William Kirby's Bridgewater denunciations of Lamarck's materialism tell us somewhat more about Kirby and his desire to walk a tightrope between deism and orthodoxy than about Lamarck. Nevertheless, Lamarck's uncritical exploitation of chemical, electrical, and thermal analogies in physiology gave that strategy a bad odor among British physiologists and zoologists.

It is true that neither Lawrence nor Fleming would have satisfied the insistence by methodological dualists of the sort represented by Dugald Stewart that the difference in the sources of evidence concerning matter and mind (sensation and conscious reflection, respectively) were sufficient to ground a complete separation of the inductive science of mind from the other natural sciences. *Comte admitted no scientific status to psychology.* Lawrence most offended the moral sentiments which fed the frequently leveled charge of materialism when he spoke of insanity as a disease of the brain. Fleming clearly regarded the analysis of animal behavior as well within his province as a zoologist, regarding human behavior as basically similar in kind, differing only in degree from that of animals. Comte provided all the critical tools necessary to disqualify the ontological distinction of the human mind and the human body. In crucial respects, *the positions of Lawrence and Fleming had the flavor of a positivist denial of dualism rather than of a straightforward insistence upon the ontological priority (or exclusivity) of matter.*

Herschel and Whewell had little or nothing to say about the investigation of animal behavior, mental and social phenomena, and so the relatively obscure rhetorician, Benjamin Smart, whose book appeared precisely at the time Darwin was working out his views on expression and human evolution had considerable influence. Smart's position was plain and moderate, but thoroughly aligned with mainstream British skepticism concerning metaphysics. On the mind-body problem in particular, Smart's thesis was more in tune with the plain man's common sense than was Dugald Stewart's. *Darwin wrote in the Metaphysical Notebooks that Smart gave his views on the origin of language: both sentential forms and the various parts of speech were dictated by the "necessities and conveniences" of the social expression necessary for life, and not by an original effort of thought or mind considered independently of language.* In this view, *reason and language evolve concurrently*; each the instrument, and each the effect of the other.

Smart provided simple, blunt, and powerful dissolutions of the presumed "inductive science of mind," and incidentally of deistic natural theology. He took the Scottish criticism of the role of "ideas" in Locke's psychology to a rigorous conclusion, denying that the science of mind could establish the existence of its presumed subject matter, the regular relations among ideas. He turned the weapons of rhetoric *against both deism and atheism*, equating their cold and unembodied abstractions, and comparing both unfavorably to the folk imagery of "Guide, Friend, and Father."

In 1839, the time was not ripe for the reception of Hegel's philosophy of consciousness by British readers. It is not likely that many in Darwin's circle understood the seriousness of Ferrier's concession of the faculty of *reason* to brutes and children and his denial of the attribute of *consciousness* to either. There were no analogies between Darwin's concept of chance and Ferrier's account of the freedom and spontaneity of the self-creating ego.

Darwin's concern over the 'materialistic' implications of his theory was natural given the heated polemic associated with the epithet 'materialist' since the time of William Lawrence. But the possible applicability of the label "materialist" to Darwin is much less interesting than the details of his handling of "mental" phenomena. He rejected Stewart's distinction, repeated by Hensleigh Wedgwood, of introspection and sensation as means of access to mental and physical phenomena, respectively. He thought the distinction of "inner" and "outer" awareness without significance for the resolution of the question, "Does the brain think?" *His thoroughly biological perspective softened (or confused) the contrast between mental and physical phenomena.* He did not think of organisms as pieces of clockwork, and he can be labeled a mechanist only by retrospectively expanding the meaning of 'mechanistic.' *The Cartesian dichotomy of mind and matter meant little or nothing in a context where the processes or reproduction and embryological development were physical data as fundamental as those associated with inertial motion and simple machinery.* He also saw no need to concede the ground of this discussion to positivism or to empiricism. The basic concepts of physics, e.g., that of force, were not given as elementary sense data; nor could the principle of causality be given adequate explication in terms of the relative invariability of a sequence of phenomena. Darwin's insistence that every aspect of human capacity had developed within the process of evolution by natural selection *eluded the narrowly focussed Cartesian critique by shifting the meaning of 'matter'* in the direction charted by Hartley, Priestley, and Erasmus Darwin in the eighteenth century (interpreting it as a center of force or activity), and by insisting that *all thought was expressible and that expressive behavior had evolved in connection with the basic social instincts.* In this context, Charles Darwin would say, "The brain thinks," or "the brain secretes thought."

The *Notebooks* and early manuscripts contained *no* account of the *origins* of populations, societies of organisms, social instincts, nor of consciousness. The terms 'population,' 'society,' 'social instinct,' and 'consciousness,' functioned as primitive terms in the theory. They were not explicated by reference to other processes regarded as still more fundamental, but only through the propositions which linked them to each other and to the evolutionary process. In 1838, Darwin's account of instinct as inherited habit seemed thoroughly Lamarckian. His use of the proposition that "habits precede (and give) structure," however, has to be understood in Hartley's physicalist context where 'habit' does not connote 'consciousness' nor 'will,' but only regularity of behavioral response to definite environmental contingencies. 'Habit' was neither more nor less fundamental than 'conjugal, social, or parental instinct,' but expressed a greater degree of individual variability. This has been interpreted as a radical concession to the "Lamarckian" principle that the sources of organic variation and the adaptive needs of organisms are "coupled" through a process as teleological as human learning. It need not be. Darwin's insistence that "If my theory be true, then the formation of sexes rigidly necessary," *shifted the conceptual terrain so that the concept of sexual reproduction became fundamental and central*, and with it the concepts of population, society and "conjugal and parental instinct."

3. THE MORAL SENTIMENTS AND DEISM

Whewell's ethics had not been published in 1839, and the principal authors of moral treatises among the members of Darwin's philosophical circle were, at that time, Paley, Malthus, and the then famous but now hardly known barrister and historian, Sir James Mackintosh. Mackintosh's influence upon Darwin's thought during this period was of tremendous significance, and a more general understanding of it may transform our picture of the ethical significance of the theory of the transmutation of species. Mackintosh exerted a much greater influence upon the first expression of the theory of natural selection, as well as upon its author's crucial early reflections upon the theory's human significance, than that exerted by the two Mills and Jeremy Bentham together. Moreover, Mackintosh's departure from the major trends in British moral philosophy at the beginning of the nineteenth century was sufficiently great, and its influence upon the young Darwin sufficiently profound, to necessitate the most severe qualification of J. D. Bernal's thesis that his theory was a "reflection of the free competition of the full capitalist era."[9] Mackintosh was a strong advocate of *two anti-utilitarian theses* which Darwin wholeheartedly embraced. The propositions were:

> 1. The course of virtue consists in "following nature."

and

> 2. Self-interest is *not* the basic motive of all rational action.

Congenial as he found Mackintosh's views on these two points, and significant as that agreement was for his perception of the moral and aesthetic tone of his theory, Darwin found a third point in Mackintosh's *Dissertation* which evoked the unequivocal marginal epithet, "Trash!" The particular target of Darwin's philosophical disgust was Mackintosh's pretended final solution of a problem set by Whewell,

Why does the moral sense of man invariably approve that which increases the happiness of his species?

Mackintosh was correct, he thought, in identifying this coincidence as the necessary outcome of the "laws of human nature and the circumstances in which mankind are placed." But the famous barrister failed totally, in

Darwin's estimate, to pursue the basic task of *explaining* those laws of human nature in the context of man's capacity for adaptively modifying his behavior to meet the constantly shifting challenges of his environment. Darwin saw the assertion that the authority of conscience was to be attributed to its "mental contiguity" to the will as so much verbiage, signifying nothing but a complete absence of the requisite *empirical investigation of the social, historical, and environmental conditions of man's sense of duty, and of the conditioned and relative outcome of his particular judgments of right and wrong.* Mackintosh claimed a divine authority for the universality, necessity, and immutability of the judgments of conscience. But Darwin found it a "capital view!" that different nations of men might have a different moral sense just as different breeds of dog would have distinct patterns of instinctive behavior![10]

The major historiographic thesis of this monograph is that the accurate characterization of Darwin's scientific, as well as his philosophical and religious views, requires their precise location in the context of his "cultural circle." Because of the great cultural and social significance of the views of Paley and Malthus, it is essential to be particularly careful in comparing and distinguishing their views and Darwin's. Paley deserves and receives all the praise and ridicule appropriate for the author of theology textbooks once required for final examinations at one of the world's great universities. If he were the symbol of the established orthodoxy, his limitations would be perceived as limitations of that orthodoxy. To the extent that he confusedly defended religious orthodoxy by employing all the major theses and the argumentative modalities of deism, anyone who rejected Paley could easily be seen, by himself and by his contemporaries, as *rejecting deism* as well.

There was, in fact, much in Paley's deism which was not only in complete accord with the conceptual structure of Darwin's transmutation theory, but was seen to be so by Darwin himself. *Paley's logic, even more than Herschel's, was the logic of possibility.* Orthodoxy was shown to be possible (by showing that no absolutely decisive objection had been raised against it), and then direct evidence, for or against it, was considered. Paley's concept of purpose or contrivance, even while wrapped in its theistic context, was almost identical with Darwin's. "Variety obeying a rule, conducing to an effect, and commensurate with exigencies infinitely diversified." Paley and Darwin would have agreed that the rule in question was not simply one of the laws of physics; that, e.g., the woodpecker's tongue could not be understood as a natural consequence of the forces produced by the effort to feed on worms under bark, so long as one attended only to those forces catalogued in physical theories. Paley and Darwin could have agreed that nature's system was one of

'The Raising of Lazarus', Sebastiano del Piombo (1517–19)

"Many of the pictures in the National Gallery in London gave me much pleasure;
that of Sebastian del Piombo exciting in me a sense of sublimity." C. Darwin,
Autobiography, p. 61

beneficence rather than optimism. Neither man followed Leibniz in thinking that the key to rational biology was the allegory of the divine analyst seeking to achieve the greatest possible variety and perfection of design through the simplest possible means. *For each man, the dominant picture of nature was that of a collection of contrivances, exhibiting no one single and overriding purpose.*

Most surprising, and perhaps most important for the estimate of the true cultural significance of Darwin's theory, *Paley's theodicy* not only made room for a concept of chance identical to Darwin's, but its *ethical dimension absolutely required the metaphor of a lottery*: a fair lottery where the decisive circumstances of birth and social station were distributed without culpable divine bias. Paley provided as clear a picture of the individual struggle for eternal salvation as Malthus' political economy provided of the struggle for food by the individuals of one species.

It is important to note that those of Paley's theses with which Darwin was in greatest agreement were distinctive neither of religious orthodoxy nor of deism itself. Neither Comte nor Hume would have denied the claims that there is some order in the world and that some virtuous men are happy. What Comte and Hume denied was that such evidence is warrant for the typical theistic or deistic assertions concerning an infinite or transcendent creator of the universe. Darwin did not express himself on the basic issue which divided Hume and Comte on the one hand from Paley and the authors of the *Bridgewater Treatises* on the other. It is misleading to ignore his silence and place him in one camp or the other.

The centrality of the concepts of population and society in Darwin's theory marked a considerable *departure* from the *individualist ontologies* assumed by most members of his cultural circle. Darwin joined Dugald Stewart and William Wordsworth in thinking of nature itself as expressive, and this metaphor lay at the root of the more familiar allusions to selection and struggle. Both plants and animals modelled their "habits" (the botanical connotation of the term 'habit': the changing disposition of a plant in relation to changes in its environment or station, is very close to Darwin's usage) upon the regular contingencies of the diurnal, lunar, and solar cycles. Darwin spoke metaphorically of *plants having the notion of causality*. He linked the notion of beauty with the evolution of a capacity for recognizing or distinguishing various individuals of the same species, and speculated that the origins of language might be found in musical expressions of conjugal passion. He implied that language, thought, and emotion evolved together in connection with the conjugal, social, and parental instincts. 'Love' was understood as a feeling of (sympathy) or benevolence to the object in question. Without regarding their origin, we see in other animals they consist in such active sympathy that the individual forgets itself, & aids & defends & acts for others at its own expense.[11]

So understood, the moral imperatives of love were directly explained and justified by Darwin's unique reinterpretation of the "law of utility." For Darwin, this law had nothing to do with the greatest happiness of the greatest number, but provided a simple, stark, *retrospective* (or conservative) sanction for behavior which *had determined* the survival of some sub-population of appropriate size and structure to insure evolutionary continuity. In 1839, this proposition was ambiguous. Did it license a social morality or a political philosophy which would sacrifice the weaker and less productive members of the human economy? Did its author regard the accumulation of capital or military power as appropriate biological strategies for the survival of the species? There is no evidence that Darwin reflectively considered such questions during the interval 1837–1839, nor that he even hazarded an opinion on one side or the other of such controversy. He took at least one of the marks of human progress to be the development of a social structure and a culture which encouraged scientific activity. His examples of societies which had failed in this respect, and served as counter-examples to any thesis of "absolute tendency to progression," were the "dark ages" and "Spain now."[12] He made few or no correspondingly denigrating judgments of non-Western cultures. He did not describe the social processes which he thought would encourage scientific activity; he did not speculate about the possibility of a non-biological science of society itself.

He did see that his theory would cause the old "fabric to totter and fall!" and this was reflected in his own religious odyssey. Comte's role in this odyssey has not been noticed heretofore, and it was absolutely crucial. Darwin was greatly influenced by his account of the Law of Three Stages and its implication that biology should be taken beyond the "theological stage" which it occupied in contemporary England. *Hume and Comte exploded the scientific significance of the concept of divine design.* The issue was not creation; the issue was the empirical vacuity of the claim that *everything* was the product of *one design*. The concept of the divine will could not be given the character of a physical law: "we known nothing of the will of the Deity, how it acts & whether constant or inconstant like that of man." In the privacy of his personal manuscript reflections, Darwin dismissed this concept as "utterly useless."[13]

The label 'atheist' did not suit him, however. The central concepts of chance and struggle saved some meaning for the profound human experiences of love and hope. He had little sympathy for the cosmological premisses of natural theology, but he stopped short of thinking it meaningless to regard the universe as the causal consequence of anything. In *The Excursion*, the Wanderer and the Pastor found significance in the sweep, variety, and history of human experience, not in metaphysical formulas. Their sense of exhilaration in nature and natural powers and their chronicles of the meaning of suffering, struck and held the attention of the young Darwin.

4. DARWIN'S DIALECTICAL INDEPENDENCE OF HIS CULTURAL CIRCLE

Darwin's cultural circle had a remarkably diverse membership which presented him with a great variety of options in methodology, metaphysics, and ethics. The range of methodological positions represented was particularly significant, and captured almost all of the major contemporary themes concerning the logic of science. On the left there was Comte's complex web of historicism, instrumentalism, and positivism, implying that no thesis in theology or in metaphysics was above scientific criticism and that no extant theory or ideal of scientific inquiry had succeeded in achieving the generality and testability required of the final stage of positive science. On the right there was Whewell's version of orthodoxy, holding that some propositions were privileged or immune from scientific criticism, including those concerning the origins of things, and arguing strongly that certain conceptual structures (e.g., that associated with final causality) had to be accepted as untestable conditions for the possibility of inquiry. Lyell, J. F. W. Herschel and Dugald Stewart occupied intermediate positions, varying slightly with the issue being debated. Stewart's theory of natural language dissolved the sharp, fundamental distinction of metaphorical and literal expression essential for Comte's positivism. Herschel's critique of the concepts of law and causality loosened the grip of the phenomenalist strictures against anthropomorphic allusions to agencies and powers. Stewart and Herschel sought to preserve certain theses concerning the human mind or the divine agency from criticism of the kind Comte advanced, but their formulations were not secure against the reapplication of Hume's skeptical irony. In this context, the skeptical views of Benjamin Smart and John Fleming were highly influential.

The list of metaphysical positions represented on the circle was also reasonably complete. Dugald Stewart and Hensleigh Wedgwood argued for a dualism of mind and body, using the distinction of sensation and introspection and invoking the prerogatives of ordinary language against the neologisms of scientific languages and metalanguages when that served their purpose. Lyell insisted that human reason and the highest animal faculties were completely different in kind. August Comte, John Fleming, and Benjamin Smart refused, on positivist grounds, to accept questions concerning the distinction of mind and brain as meaningful. J.-B. de M. Lamarck and William Lawrence ranged more strongly in the direction of materialism, but they fell short of the mechanistic reductionism implied by Descartes' division of thought and extension.

The ethical debates among members of the circle were somewhat muted. Mackintosh and Whewell were critical of the opportunism and selfishness implicit in Paley's defense of the class bias and sexual chauvinism implicit in the "law of honor." But Mackintosh did not carry his advocacy of Bishop Butler's theory of benevolent altruism to the point of criticizing Thomas Malthus or Adam Smith. Malthus had no serious challenger among the members of the circle other than Darwin himself.

Darwin read and commented upon a number of works in natural theology during the years 1837–1839, including those by Whewell, Macculloch, Lord Brougham, Kirby, and Sir Charles Bell. There were few interesting differences among such authors. The more interesting debate might have been arranged between Philo of Hume's *Dialogues concerning Natural Religion*, and the Wanderer of Wordsworth's *The Excursion*. While it was likely that Darwin was aware of both, he made no comment concerning them. Philo's skepticism was philosophically complete and rhetorically devastating, at the same time it was urbane, sensitive, and tasteful. The religious faith of the Wanderer was non-dogmatic and, in comparison with that expressed in the *Bridgewater Treatises*, unpretentious. The Wanderer made no metaphysical claims, and it is difficult to discern the attributes of the god he found in nature. *The Excursion* cannot be said to include any character who defends philosophical theses in natural theology, no one like Paley, no one like Hume's deist, Cleanthes. Hume and Wordsworth might have agreed on the bankruptcy of the academic varieties of natural theology. Philo extolled the "smallest grain of natural honesty and benevolence" above orthodox piety, and the Wanderer would not have dissented. Nevertheless, the Wanderer's romantic prescription for the Solitary's despondency would have *amazed* Philo and even Hume: to rise at dawn, to chase the wild goat, to readopt the superstitions of folk religion in defiance of, and as a remedy for, the cold indifference of enlightenment.[14]

I hold a view of the scientific uses of metaphor which denies that Darwin's metaphorical expressions could have been replaced by completely literal statements setting forth the core of his theory. What is claimed is that attention to the contextuating features of Darwin's usage and to his estimate of his audience can assist in the more accurate interpretation of the first drafts of his theory. His metaphors had the flavor of idiomatic or colloquial speech and did not resemble the use of analogies and models in other fields of scientific inquiry. At least two key concepts, population and chance, were not readily expressible and manageable within the context of that scientific discourse which was the common and uncontested possession of Darwin and his contemporaries. Populations were not mere aggregates of organisms, they were structured groups, and the irreducibility of this usage of 'structure' could not have been more graphically portrayed than in his insistence that it would be preposterous to regard the mistletoe as the product of the direct, unmediated, interaction of the organism and its environment. The required mediation was to be found only in the simple process of biological reproduction, a process basic to the complex social structures of animal populations, the importance of which was expressed by the image of the demiurge constrained to await the outcome of the reproductive process in order to select those organisms which represented the slightest improvements in co-adaptation.

This irreducibility of distinct causal chains to a single source, whether in a previously identified natural force or in a *creative* design, was the core of the Darwinian concept of chance. This concept was basically analogous to Aristotle's account of chance in the sub-lunar world. Both Darwin and Aristotle linked the concepts of chance and design. Aristotle's account of chance identified it as the outcome of the intersection of two or more natural processes which, taken singly, exhibited all the regularity and order to be expected, but whose action in concert was unintelligible, haphazard, and in specific instances, infrequent. Aristotle's unmoved mover was not an omniscient creator.

Both the notions of populational intra-dependence and of chance were effectively captured in the metaphor of 'struggle,' particularly when that metaphor is seen in the etymological context provided by Wedgwood and by the *OED*'s references to Carlyle and Lyell. In Darwin's own stipulation, 'struggle' was an inherently equivocal term, with *no fewer than three meanings: interdependence, chance, and contest,* which graded into each other. The tension introduced by this stipulative combination of three meanings *transformed the meaning of each of them taken singly.*

One outcome of Darwin's considerable linguistic originality was the effectiveness with which he was able to articulate its basic theses so as to illustrate their power to connect the simplest organisms and the highest faculties to be found in man. The less carefully controlled rhetoric of later evolutionists can make nonsense of the human emotions of hope and love. To those whose understanding of the human experience is keyed upon the meaning and value of hope and love, Darwin's theory *has been made to seem an absurd expression of the alienation of science* from the slightest semblance of *care* or *concern* for the objects of its investigation.

In 1839, when the transmutation theory was put into its basic logical structure, self-sacrifice, benevolence, and love were the central imperatives of Darwin's ethic. The location of these imperatives within the massive context of a theory of the evolution of all life inevitably made them less likely guarantors of human *pleasure* or *happiness*. Their value was assured, however, so long as the *survival of the race and of the system of life upon which it depended were seen as values.* Darwin's was no theory of inevitable and constant progress. But his answer to the question,

Is man a child of hope?
On generations, without progress made

was basically identical to Wordsworth's own:

The vast Frame
Of social nature changes evermore
Her organs and her members, with decay
Restless, and restless generation, powers
And functions dying and produced at need, –
And by this law the mighty whole subsists:
With an ascent and progress in the main;
Yet, oh! how disproportioned to the hopes
And expectations of self-flattering minds.[15]

There is no question that the extreme diversity represented by the members of his philosophical circle occasionally overwhelmed Darwin's synthetic capacities. He resolved the difficult problem of responding to the influence of such a diverse group through the invention of strikingly colorful, colloquial, and detailed metaphors. The resultant ambiguities inevitably frustrate those who aim at their totally literal and rational reconstruction. The efforts of 1837–1839 were rewarded by a strikingly original and comprehensive synthesis of biological information, a synthesis which could have only been accomplished through the concurrent development of a new methodology, a new way of thought.

CHAPTER TEN

THE MEANING AND FUNCTION OF
DARWIN'S METAPHORS

Mary Hesse's account of the explanatory function of metaphor is particularly helpful in appraising the methodological significance of Darwin's metaphors. [1] Her discussion takes its illustrations from physics rather than biology. She adapts Max Black's *interaction view* of metaphors and models to the interpretation of the analogies built into, e.g., the kinetic theory of gases and the wave theories of sound and light. In this view, metaphoric usage functions in theoretical explanation by guiding the redescription of the domain of the explanandum. In contrast with the so-called *comparison view* of metaphor, the interaction view *denies* that the metaphor can be replaced without remainder by an explicit literal statement of the similarities between the field to which the metaphor is extended (the primary system of the explanandum, or phenomenon requiring explanation) and the proper field of the metaphor itself (the secondary system, for Hesse). For example, "Sound (primary system) is propagated by wave motion (taken from a secondary system)." [2] The comparison view, *rejected* by Hesse, implies that literal descriptions of both primary and secondary systems are independent of the metaphoric usage, and that the metaphor can be *eliminated* in favor of literal description. She asserts that the comparison view is presupposed by deductive models of scientific explanation which assume that the descriptions and descriptive laws of the primary system remain "empirically acceptable and invariant in meaning to all changes of explanatory theory." [3]

The interaction view holds that a "metaphor causes us to see the primary system differently and causes the meanings of terms originally literal in the primary system to shift toward the metaphor." [4] Hesse argues that it holds out the possibility of rational appraisal of that introduction of *new* observation predicates which is required by any theory of scientific confirmation involving *strong* prediction (the explanation of phenomena previously unknown and unrecognized). As Robert Young points out, Darwin's metaphors were certainly an invitation to "see" the evidence of natural history differently than it had been seen and described within the vocabulary of Cartesian mechanism. Taken in concert, the basic metaphors of 'selection,' 'struggle,' 'chance,' 'contrivance,' and 'economy,' created a perspective on this evidence which was altogether unique when compared with that of any of Darwin's scientific predecessors and peers. Bits and pieces of the ensemble have been traced to Malthus, Lamarck, Stewart, Lyell, Paley, and even William Wordsworth. Darwin's linguistic power and originality cannot really be appreciated by concentrating on any one of them to the exclusion of the others.[5]

The *orchestration* of all of these metaphors was required for that extension of the descriptive capacity of biology and natural history necessary for the recognition of the explanatory power and empirical warrant for Darwin's views. Hesse's account, however, offers *no* suggestions concerning the scoring of such a complex effort. She distinguishes a "good poetic metaphor" from a relatively tractable scientific model. Poetic metaphors are said to aim at imagery which is "initially striking and unexpected, if not shocking," and to "immediately give place to other metaphors referring to the same subject matter which are formally contradictory, and in which the contradictions are an essential part of the total metaphoric impact."[6] Her sharp distinction of such poetic expression from scientific metaphors meant to be "internally tightly knit by logical and causal interrelations" and exploited in "extreme quantitative detail," suggests an adverse criticism of Darwin's usage, both in 1844 and later in 1859.

On the other hand, Susan Gliserman has analyzed the effort by several early Victorian science writers, including Lyell and Whewell, to give "affective meaning to science, and especially to do this in order to persuade a general audience." She considered the "literary structure of the science writing as *no different* from that of Tennyson's poems" (emphasis added). My conclusions concerning Darwin's metaphors are in agreement with her that such language can be interpreted as a "self-dramatization" of "individual and shared tensions, ambivalences, and conflicts" concerning the meaning of a scientific theory.[7] Careful analysis of such metaphorical expression is essential for the reconstruction of the affective dimension of Darwin's work.

I want to argue, however, and here I follow Hesse, that the scientific significance, i.e., the descriptive, theoretical and methodological significance of these metaphors could not have been conveyed to Darwin's audience if the metaphors had been eliminated, from the very first, in favor of direct, literal expression. The metaphors had both an affective and a cognitive (scientific) dimension. The two dimensions were interdependent in a fashion which precludes the historical accuracy of any interpretation which isolates them from each other.

1. 'A BEING INFINITELY MORE SAGACIOUS THAN MAN'

In the *Sketch of 1842* and the *Essay of 1844* the metaphor of selection included the postulate of a selecting being infinitely more intelligent, percep-tive, and persistent than man (but not an omniscient creator).[8] This deliberate and explicit personification of the selecting being facilitated the articulation of several aspects of Darwin's argument — e.g., the allusion to "differences in the outer and innermost organization (of a living thing) quite imperceptible to man." Darwin's strong early interest in the 'laws of corelation' had been temporarily stymied by his relatively rudimentary and ancedotal knowledge of embryology. Such laws had not only not been established by 1844; but no clear statement of them had been proposed. Nevertheless, by the fall of 1838, Darwin had begun to reformulate the problem in a way which allowed him to bypass the obstacle represented by the missing embryological laws.

The by-pass depended upon the plausibility of a place-holding allusion to "organization" which did *not* depend upon accurate scientific knowledge of its nature. It was as if he were advancing the following argumentative ploy: "Patterns of biological organization, whatever they may be, are open to change. Instead of attacking the citadel of 'organization' directly, perhaps we can conquer it by discovering the means by which *changes* of organization occur." The metaphor of the intelligent selector provided a measured dose of hyperbole. Such a selector could perceive changes in "outer" and "innermost" organization imperceptible to man. Darwin quickly associated the notion of *forethought* with the notion of the selection of differences in organization. This implied that changes of organization occurring within individuals and in succeeding generations ("forethought extending over future centuries") could be fitted into an intelligible pattern or sequence of events. Nevertheless, the changes in outer and inner organization occurring in living things might have limits or antinomic properties which would frustrate the selector's exercise of intelligent forethought.

The lengthy illustration concerning mistletoe to be found in the *Essay of 1844* was put to succinct polemical use in *The Origin*, to distinguish Darwin's theory from those of Lamarck, Chambers, and others, who provided "no explanation" of the "coadaptations of organic beings to each other and to their physical conditions of life."[9] The *Essay of 1844* provided a detailed and elaborate illustration of the activities metaphorically or allegorically attributed to the intelligent selector in managing the evolution of the mistletoe. This selector, if his aim was "making a plant as wonderfully related to other organic beings as the mistletoe," had to proceed by the "continued selection of chance seedlings," and *not* by *directly producing*, however gradually, those variations which increased the coadaption of the mistletoe to its host, its pollinator, the birds which distributed its seeds, and so on.[12] The distinction of 'selection' and 'production' was underlined by allusions to the constraint upon the selector to "destroy all other seedlings with less of this power." In other words, the process of selection involved a distinctive additional step. Selection depended on the results of the *reproductive process* ("Supposing again, during these changes the plant failed to seed quite freely from non-impregnation . . .."). Darwin's metaphor of the intelligent selector was thereby distinguished from any hypothesis which implied God's direct causal production of biological variation.

The personification of nature implied a level of *possibility*. The consideration of what was possible for a being infinitely more sagacious than man bypassed the requirement that *only those physical laws known to be true* could be used in a scientific explanation. Asking whether or not a given process was possible for such a being was equivalent to describing the process with sufficient detail to enable one to understand a second question: "*Could there be laws of nature which would render this process either possible or impossible?*" The metaphor of the infinitely sagacious selector had both a critical and an investigative significance. It shifted the burden of proof by enabling Darwin to point out that a process of natural selection would not contravene any *known* law of nature; in that sense, it was *not impossible* (and that is an important part of the meaning of 'theoretically possible'). It also enabled him to *sketch* some of the laws which would support a process of natural selection, but which could neither be expressed in appropriate literal detail, nor advanced as if their truth had an adequate empirical warrant.

2. THE INSULAR ECONOMY

The significance of his visit to the Galapagos Islands for the development of the "species theory" is one of the most familiar features of Darwin's biography. Discussion of the role of "oceanic islands" and the evolution of their inhabitants remained an important part of all the published versions of the theory. In the earliest drafts, metaphorical allusions to the significance of an "insular economy" played an important transitional role.

On the one hand, the expression had relatively slight *affective* significance. It was more prosaic; its empirical significance was more directly and much less ambiguously apparent than that of 'selection' or 'struggle.' In both the earliest drafts and the published versions of the theory, references to oceanic islands and the concept of insular economy occurred in the *second part* of the Darwin's presentation. Such references were used to summarize what he regarded as "direct evidence" in favor of, or against, his theory. I have argued, however, that the second part of Darwin's presentation did not simply *test* an hypothesis whose *possibility* had been completely and independently established in the first part of that presentation. To the contrary, the second part added important information to the core of the theory and continued the effort to establish its general *possibility*.

For example, the model of an insular economy (together with specific references to oceanic islands, including the Galapagos) provided concrete illustration of several basic theses of the core of the theory:

1. The geological conditions of life are subject to persistent gradual change which is sustained through thousands of generations of living organisms.

2. The migration of organisms, together with geological changes, can insure the *reproductive isolation* of groups of organisms.

As it happened, in the earliest drafts of the theory, Darwin's most explicit allusions to sexual reproduction, as distinguished from asexual budding, as a crucial source of inter-generational variation in organisms, occurred together with his account of insular economies. However, the model also provided new information for the theoretical core of the theory:

3. Most continents originated as separate islands which gradually increased in size, but which continued to exhibit "oscillations of level" throughout geological time.

This implied a continuing source of new environmental stations, of new opportunities for, and of new barriers to organic migration. Biological theses concerning variation, heritability, and the checks to logarithmic population growth were corelated with the geological hypotheses of gradual continent formation for the first time in connection with the working model represented by the metaphor, 'insular economy.'

However, it should be noted that 'insular economy' also functioned rhetorically to enable Darwin to *imply*, rather than describe, the different sorts of "check" or selection pressure which would limit the size of organic populations. The connotations of 'economy' included the concepts of division of labor, and of social organization and stratification, and Darwin exploited these connotations to suggest the great range of new opportunities for evolution which would prevail on an oceanic island.

The expression 'insular economy' provided a working, natural model for the process of selection as important as the metaphor of the selector 'infinitely more sagacious than man.' Neither the cognitive nor the affective significance of these metaphors can be accurately determined if they are analyzed in isolation from each other. The same must be said of the expression whose metaphorical status was stated more unequivocally and persistently in the published versions of the theory, 'the struggle for existence.'

3. 'THE STRUGGLE FOR EXISTENCE'

It is not uncommon to read Darwin, and the views of Simpson and Rogers are cases in point, as if his use of 'struggle' had overtones not unlike those of 'war,' particularly as used in Hobbes' account of a primeval 'war of all against all.' 'Struggle' is understood to refer to a competitive process in which success for one organism implies failure for another.

A careful decision concerning the significance of Darwin's use of 'struggle' must reflect the context set in the chapter of *The Origin* which he entitled 'Struggle for Existence.' Extensive passages of that chapter are devoted to setting forth the web of relationships which bind together all the plants and animals which inhabit a particular region. For example, he noted that when the scotch fir on the heath at Maer were protected from grazing cattle by enclosure, the resulting stand of trees supported twelve species of plants and six of insectivorous birds not found on the open heath. The basic function of the chapter was to establish that living things are part of each other's environment; that 'environment,' in other words, does not denote a mere geographic site or station. Rather, 'environment' is used to refer to a matrix of possibilities for life — a matrix which is itself a function of the vital activities of still other organisms. Whether one speaks of these possibilities in terms suggesting a competitive struggle distinguishing "winners" and "losers," or as opportunities which call for co-adaptation, it is necessary to remember that Darwin set forth the 'struggle for existence' in the context of the basic thesis that the structure and function of "every organic being is related in the most essential, yet often hidden manner, to all other organic beings" in the same environment.[12]

Why did Darwin use 'struggle' for this purpose, and why did he characterize some of his uses of the term "far-fetched" and metaphorical? The *Oxford English Dictionary* distinguishes several senses of 'struggle' which may illuminate his intentions in using 'struggle for existence' in a "large and metaphorical sense."[13]

1. intr. To contend (with an adversary in a close grapple as in wrestling); also, in *wider use*, to make violent bodily movements in order to resist force or free oneself from constraint; to exert one's physical strength in persistent striving against an opposing force.[8]

The first element in this definition suggests a competitive relationship; but that is not true of 'a continued effort to resist force or free oneself from constraint,' nor of 'a strong effort under difficulties.' The only feature the three uses have in common is that of a strong effort against difficult circumstances, an effort which might be appraised as successful or unsuccessful. A secondary use of the term 'struggle' is distinguished by the *OED* and included within the first meaning cited above.

b. To make violent efforts to breathe (usually, 'to struggle for breath'); to be in the agony of death. Also (*nonce-use*) to pass out of (the world) with a struggle.

In this sense, 'to struggle' is like 'to gasp': it directly denotes the possibility that the effort may *not be successful*. But unlike 'race,' 'struggle' does not directly denote a competition. When an organism gasps for air, it may succeed or fail. But it is nonsense to ask "Who won?" if the gasper fails, or "Who lost?" if the gasper succeeds in resuming normal respiration. Not all terms which denote a set of processes which may be appraised or ranked in some order thereby denote competition. In the case of 'struggle' it is easy to assume that it *always* makes sense to ask, "Who (or what) won?" and "Who (which one or what) lost?" The question is, would Darwin have made such an assumption?

The *OED* quotes a paradigmatic passage from Charles Lyell in which 'struggle' is used in the particularly relevant phrase 'struggle for existence,' and where it is quite obviously also used as the name of a competitive process.

In the struggle for existence, the right of the strongest eventually prevails; and the strength and durability of a race depends mainly on its prolificness, in which hybrids are acknowledged to be deficient (1832: *Principles of Geology*, II, 56).

But Darwin was surely also aware of passages from Carlyle's *French Revolution*, where the verb 'to struggle' had the sense of 'to make progress with difficulty' or 'to maintain existence' or 'to continue one's course of action with difficulty.' "Either way, the world must contrive to struggle on" (1837; *French Revolution* III, vii, ii).

The aim of Hensleigh Wedgwood's *A Dictionary of English Etymology* was to trace the historic roots of English words. Wedgwood's etymology cannot settle the question of Darwin's understanding of 'struggle.' However, it may serve to tug at linguistic sensitivities dulled by the polemic and partisan reaction which greeted his use of 'the struggle for existence' from the start.[14]

Struggle. – Scruggle. Words of analogous formation and significance with straggle, scraggle, representing in the first instance a broken sound, then applied to broken confused movement. I *strogell*, I murmur with words secretly. He *stroggleth* at everything I do: il grommelle a tout ce que je fays. I *scruggle* with one to get from him. I *scruggel* with him: je me estrive a luy. I sprawle with my legs, *struggell*. – Palsgr. *Scriggle*, *scruggle*, to writhe or struggle. Forby. *Scriggins*, *scrogglings*, the straggling apples left on a tree when the crop has been gathered. Du. *struikelen*, Pl.D. *strukeln*, G. *straucheln*, to stumble.

To scraggle. Dorset to scramble. – Hal. In Northampton used in the tense of struggle, make efforts with different members of the body.

I'm often so poorly I can hardly *scraggle* along. Scraggling, irregular, scattered. Also applied to vegetation that grows wild and disorderly. – Mrs. Baker. Essentially the same word with *straggle* or *struggle*, and initial *scr* or *str* often interchanging. I scruggell with one to get from him, je m'estrive. – Palsgr. The word originally represents a broken sound, then a jerking irregular movement. N. *skrangle*, to jingle, rumble, rattle. Palsgrave gives murmur or grumble as the first sense of stroggell. He stroggleth at everything I do. Il grommell a tout tan que je fays.

Probably Fr. *excarquiller*, to straddle, is an equivalent of E. Scraggle, having first signified to throw about the legs, then to stretch them apart.

To straggle. To move irregularly, in varying directions, to separate from the regular line of march. From the figure of a broken rattling noise. Bret. *strake*, *strakla*, a clapper of a mill, rattle to frighten birds. A similar relation seems to hold good between Sw. *skramla*, to rattle, clash, and E. *scramble*, to get on by broken efforts, to move irregularly, confusedly. See Struggle.

A *broken or irregular sound* might be produced by an organism making some intense effort associated with irregular or otherwise uncoordinated movements of the whole body; for example, such extreme respiratory efforts as follow upon an obstruction of the trachea or lungs by some foreign matter or upon sustained exertion of some other part of the body. The picture which emerges from these etymologies has nothing to do with competition, and less with combat. It is strongly suggestive, however, of a more or less imperfectly organized but *vigorous* effort to maintain life and vital activities.

Both Wedgwood's etymologies and the *OED*'s distinction of various uses of 'struggle,' *disestablish* Gale's thesis that the three uses Darwin made of 'struggle' are contradictory. The three uses reflect a gradual growth in the meaning of the term, involving its application in contexts where it had not previously been applicable. The reconstruction of an etymological sequence exhibits a larger context of associated meanings within which it is pointless to distinguish the literal from the metaphorical, and the assertion that one of the uses *contradicts* the other is *false*. Rather, each of the meanings influences our understanding of the others.[15]

Wedgwood's etymology of 'struggle' implied an original or a paradigmatic use in which the term expressed a thrashing, sprawling or convulsive effort to get free of some obstacle or impediment to such normal vital activities as breathing, and unhindered, balanced, motion. The initial representations of broken sound and broken confused movement suggest the normal response of struggling to get one's breath while choking. This point is clearer in Wedgwood's etymology than it is in the *OED*'s account of 'struggle.' The sense captured by 'a broken sound' and 'broken confused movement' – which for Wedgwood were the first meanings of the earlier terms from which 'struggle' evolved – might be figuratively extended to capture the notion of contending with an adversary, but such an extension would be a special, limited usage. The *aesthetic* and *normative connotations* of 'a strong effort under difficulties' are not equivalent to those 'to contend with an adversary.' There is an imaginative and affective sense in which the allusion to *a broken sound* points to a resolution of the paradoxical juxtaposition of 'peaceful woods & smiling fields' and 'the dreadful but quiet war of organic beings.' It is as if the reality which Darwin sought to capture was neither that of war nor that of peaceful equilibrium, but that of *striving with difficulty*.

In Wordsworth's *The Excursion*, which replaced Milton's sterner vision as the focal point of Darwin's poetic interests after his return from his own excursion on the Beagle, the Wanderer learns the deeper human and religious significance of the stormy expanse of nature. Nature's revelation produced neither hopeless despair over the ravages of war, nor a giddy sense of meaninglessness. Instead, nature's broken sounds and confused movements pointed to the possibilities of life and love and understanding. Without *struggle*, without the impediment and obstacle of an almost imponderably complex web of natural and human intentions, love and understanding would remain trapped in a juvenile world without time and growth.

Robert Stauffer's edition of the "long version" of Darwin's account of natural selection throws more light upon the choice of the metaphor of 'the struggle for existence.' Stauffer points out that in the original draft of the relevant section, Darwin had used the title 'War of Nature' rather than 'Struggle of Nature,' and that he had chosen Hobbes' 'all nature is at war' as his topic sentence.[16] Darwin considered but set aside a phrase of Lyell's, 'equilibrium in the number of species.' It was, he wrote, "more correct," but it expressed "far too much quiescence." The choice of 'struggle,' therefore, was clearly a deliberate selection of a term intermediate between 'war' and 'equilibrium.' He used 'struggle' to refer to "several ideas primarily distinct but graduating into each other." These three ideas were

(1)   "The dependency of one organic being on another,"

(2)   "the agency whether organic or inorganic of what may be called chance, as in the dispersal of seeds and eggs,"

(3)   "what may be more strictly called a struggle whether voluntary as in animals or involuntary as in plants."

This use of 'struggle' can be connected with features of Wedgwood's etymology, particularly with 'broken confused movement,' 'the straggling apples left on a tree when the crop has been gathered,' 'jerking irregular movement,' 'broken rattling noise,' and 'to get on by broken efforts, to move irregularly, confusedly.' These uses of 'struggle' represent an important move away from the simple conceptions of a direct contest between competing organisms, and toward the more statistical concepts of varying chances of survival and of leaving fertile descendants.

Darwin's claim that the idea of dependence could be included among the meanings of 'struggle' was a more original linguistic invention. His earliest uses of 'struggle' occurred most frequently in his *Notebook* ruminations concerning the phenomena of "double personality," and of the effort to integrate conflicting behavioral tendencies.[17] These early uses of the term in contexts where it had roughly the sense of 'to struggle against impulse in order to realize one's true character' may have justified, at least for Darwin himself, his later stipulation that the idea of dependence was one of the three meanings of 'struggle.'

It hardly needs to be said that Darwin's emphasis upon his equivocal use of 'struggle' made little if any impression upon his readers. By far the most common misinterpretation has been to deal with 'the struggle for existence' as if it were simply equivalent to 'all nature is at war.' Darwin did not succeed in unifying the three meanings. The result was *ambiguity*; *not nonsense* but also *not technical precision*.

4. THE USES OF DARWIN'S METAPHORS

There is an interesting historical pattern of variation in the uses Darwin made of metaphorical expression in representing his theory. Nature was explicitly and uncritically personified in the description of the activities of an "all-seeing being," "infinitely more sagacious than man (not an omniscient creator)," who selected all the variations which tended to certain ends for thousands and thousands of years. No caveats or positivist disclaimers hedged this expression in 1842, but this same unqualified and unrestricted use of the metaphor of 'selection' occurred in *none* of the subsequent drafts of the theory.

The metaphor of 'war' dominated the presentation of "natural means of selection" in the *Essay of 1844*: "De Candolle, in an eloquent passage, has declared that all nature is at war, one organism with another, or with external nature," but this expression too was softened and qualified in later uses of the much more ambiguous term 'struggle' (116). In 1844, the bulk of the explanatory work was done by the more elaborate model of an "insular economy." The significance and empirical generalizability of this model enabled Darwin to bridge the rhetorical gap between the nearly mythical overtones of 'selection' and the entirely naturalistic (and empirical), if equivocal, use he made of 'struggle.'

This chronological development of Darwin's rhetoric is important for understanding his scientific uses of metaphorical expression. These uses fall into five broad categories: (1) critical-persuasive, (2) heuristic, (3) semantic, (4) explanatory and (5) affective.

First, it must be noted that Darwin's metaphors had persuasive and polemical uses. They distinguished his theory from contemporary positions to which it was opposed, and sought to attract support away from those positions to the side of the hypothesis of descent with specific transmutation. For example, the 'being infinitely more sagacious than man' was not the Creative Designer whose existence and attributes the authors of the *Bridgewater Treatises* sought to establish. Darwin insisted upon the *limited, relative infinity* of this being — whose designs, although they might exceed man's in penetration and foresight, were not to be regarded as absolutely perfect. This being could succeed, fail, or partially succeed. No category mistakes were involved in formulating secular analogies for his selective activities — no blasphemy could result from using the allegorical account of his concerns to bring into focus the possible role of "war" and "economic balance" in the transmutation of specific types. The characteristics of the selecting demiurge suggest that Darwin felt the force of Hume's skeptical arguments on natural religion more keenly than most of the English members of his intellectual circle.[17] This allegory may also reflect Wordsworth's vision of a god immanent in nature rather than the transcendent god of the physico-theologians. In any case, the demiurge of the selection allegory was *not* to be thought of as an omniscient creator, and thus not as infinite either in knowledge or in power.

The *limited* effectiveness of this being served to insinuate the importance of "undesigned" or chance factors in the process of transmutation and to distinguish Darwin's hypothesis from Lamarck's interpretation of evolution in terms larger than life, assigning an inner capacity for perfectibility to the simplest organisms. Darwin, in contrast, saw only a contextual (organism-environment) possibility for change in relative fitness. This same motif served to distinguish his program from that of E. Geoffroy St. Hillaire, whose account of the "unity of plan" imputed a more crystalline, mathematical regularity to organic nature than Darwin found there.

The allegory was persuasive as well as polemic because Darwin was able to formulate a complex set of models which carried suggestive echoes of those positions he sought to supplant. The allegory of selection implied the possibility of reconciliation with the view that organic nature is the product of intelligent design. In another vein, the conflation of the imagery of war with the mathematically impressive Malthusian ratios implied that the urge to mathematicize biology need not be foresaken entirely in the wake of the replacement of deterministic by statistical ideals of explanation.

Second, these metaphors had the broadly heuristic function of joining explanatory fictions with available information in order to organize and make plausible the search for additional "laws" and conditions which might explain the transmutation of species. The allegory of selection implied the reasonableness of a search for the "laws of corelation" (or "differences in outer and innermost organization"). The imagery of 'war' concealed the lack of empirical warrant for the supposition of *non-random* distribution of the chances of leaving fertile progeny and suggested the sort of evidence that might be sought. The representation of the insular economy took the preceding concepts from a merely ideal or theoretical level into the framework of a working, testable model — with a specific empirical interpretation — the Galapagos Archipelago. This enabled Darwin to build an enormous amount of background information into the statement of his hypothesis. In particular, he was able to allude to geological theories relevant to the continent building role of slowly rising "oceanic islands," to identify conditions left unspecified in the conclusions of Part I (e.g., isolation, and "powers of dispersal"), and to *tentatively* employ existing classificatory or taxonomic schemes and their reference to the several great classes of organisms.

The three images of the selecting demiurge, the war of nature, and the insular economy were increasingly specific and empirical, and their controlled use gradually set the stage for Darwin's claim that the transmutation theory had both *explanatory force* and *testable implications*. In part, the uses of the models to explain data and to test the theory were simple corollaries of their heuristic functions. To organize a particular program of research or investigation to the point where its pursuit seems more plausible and preferable to the available alternatives is to argue for both its testability and its explanatory power. After the model of insular economy had been employed, incorporating into this scientific project the immense amount of biogeographical and biogeographical data collected on the *Beagle* voyage, he was able to say,

This large class of facts being thus explained, far more than counter-balances any separate difficulties and apparent objections in convincing my mind of the truth of this theory of common descent.[18]

It should also be emphasized that the explanatory uses of these models were as fundamental as their heuristic employment. Apart from the allegory of the war of nature, Darwin had not established that the Malthusian ratios implied a *biased* distribution of the chances of leaving fertile progeny. The allegory of 'war' supplied a crucial step in an explanatory argument: it provided the *only* warrant for the move from "Not all organisms leave fertile progeny." to "Every organism maintains its place by an almost periodically recurrent struggle." Similarly, the allegory of the finite (demiurge) selector provided an interpretative background against which the unstated (and in the scientific atmosphere of the late 'thirties and early 'forties, perhaps unstateable) assumption concerning the random occurrence of heritable variation could be understood and by which it might even be said to be implied. The notion of randomness or chance necessary for an understanding of Darwin's premisses *is* necessary to establish that his antecedent premisses are causally independent of each other, i.e., that heritable variation occurs independently of the need for organic resources. The imagery of the demiurge waiting for and selecting from naturally occurring variation gave dramatic force and license to the assumption of this independence.

The same *co-ordination of* investigative, testing, and explanatory *functions* can be imputed to the model of insular economy. Much more concretely than any of the other expressions, it suggested how research might be done in order to discover the "checks" to population growth as they actually operate in nature and in nature's history. This model introduced new premisses into the argument (i.e., concerning "isolation," and the island hypothesis of continent formation), and had correspondingly independent functions.

All of the uses of metaphorical expression came to focus in its semantic function. They contributed to the formation of a new scientific vocabulary and, through it, to a new way of describing and perceiving nature. It is an intriguing fact that Darwin did not directly address the critical semantic problems surrounding the use of 'species' in either the *Sketch* or the *Essay*, even though the vocabulary of the established scientific community implied the *impossibility* of the thesis that species were formed by a process of transmutation from ancestors belonging to other species.

The combined models, but particularly the model of the selecting demiurge, mounted a rhetorically effective *tu quoque* argument against the assumption of the immutability of specific types. If the selecting being were truly immanent in nature, his power would be limited if naturally occurring variation could not be accumulated to the point of the reproductive isolation of distinct forms. All of the philosophical talk about secondary causality and the theological overtones of the prevalent understanding of 'law of nature' were channelled by Darwin into the claim that the god was *more* powerful, *if* there were no limit to the range of naturally occurring organic variation, and consequently no limit to the possibilities of the transmutation of species. He subtly inverted the prevalent relationship between the language of biology and that of physico-theology. Where many of his contemporaries saw nature as God's handiwork and found it necessary to bend their descriptions of it into patterns that seemed compatible with his omniscience, omnipotence, and benevolence, Darwin described nature as the relatively unsystematic outcome of an unpremediated struggle among random organic variants in slowly changing geological and environmental conditions, and shaped an old theological vocabulary to serve his new vision.

The three meanings of 'struggle' collected phenomena of considerable complexity and diversity under a common theoretical perspective, which was neither reductionist nor dualistic. The concepts of population and of social organization (including the notion of social behavior or social instincts) were embedded in all three senses of 'struggle,' and this was essential for the connection of the phenomena of natural selection and of sexual selection. The latter notion introduced considerations of conscious and tasteful purpose into the foundations of Darwin's theory, but such purpose was seen neither as an emergent nor as an epiphenomenon. It was *continuous* with the somewhat simpler organization of reproductive phenomena in plant populations.

The equivocity exhibited in Darwin's use of 'struggle' — the distinct references to competition, chance, and dependence — reflected the paradoxical tension of the other two key segments of Darwin's conceptual network: (a) the interconnection of the concepts of chance, design, and causal determinism, and (b) the problems associated with the uses of a vocabulary including both physicalist and mentalist terms to refer to the behavioral states of organisms. Recognition of this point should correct the current tendency to overemphasize the themes of reductive materialism and causal determinism in Darwin. For example, since the notion of chance was embedded in Darwin's usage of the central term 'struggle,' it is impossible to justify John Greene's failure to see "room for genuine chance in Darwin's view of nature."

Finally, I agree with Gliserman's (1975) identification of an *affective* use of scientific metaphor: the expression and occasional resolution of "individual and shared tensions, ambivalences, and conflicts" concerning the meaning of a scientific theory. In at least two of its aspects, centering on the concept of chance and the problem of materialism, Darwin's theory had implications which threatened the basic foundations of his understanding and emotional acceptance of the world of his experience. I have claimed that the metaphors of 'selection' and 'struggle' both expressed and masked the concept of chance. That is, the concept was expressed, indirectly, within a context which blocked the implication that the theory of transmutation of species was either basically unintelligible or alien to the human emotion of hope.

Darwin's uses of 'selection' and 'struggle' tended to personify nature and transformed the sense in which his account of human evolution might be called materialistic. With Dugald Stewart, he believed in natural signs and thought nature expressive. With John Fleming, he read human traits and the most profound human emotions in realms of nature which a Cartesian would have seen as merely mechanical. With Lamarck and other zoologists of the time, he rejected the Cartesian definition of matter as inert and conceptualized it instead in terms of activity or function.

Apparently Hume and Comte made it impossible for him to articulate his views within the context of a consistent and explicit deism, but Wordsworth pointed the way to a natural resolution of the themes of chance, suffering, hope and love which was, at least, not atheistic. Supported by the friendship of those, such as Lyell, whose delight in science as as ardent as his own, the young Darwin sought no theology beyond that of Wordsworth's poetic account of the excursive quest for the meaning of life within nature itself. His metaphors, read in cultural context, indicate that his emotional relation to the world of his theory was not one of alienation, but one of self-reflective acceptance.

CHAPTER ELEVEN

COMMUNITY AND INFLUENCE

1. VARIETIES OF SCIENTIFIC AND SCHOLARLY COMMUNITIES

An important limiting factor in current discussions of the explanatory uses of
metaphor in science is their omission of evidence of the *variety* of scientific
communities within which metaphor is an important means of communication. If *metaphor functions more or less radically to reform existing observation languages, the membership of groups of language users who share common metaphorical expressions must fluctuate widely.* It would be surprising if
these fluctuations exhibited a single pattern, identical in every instance; and
the same may be said for the sociological or disciplinary structure of the
groups of metaphor users. In *some* instances, these groups may be made up of
individuals who have been trained in the same academic discipline, attend the
same professional meetings, and submit to the judgment of a common group
of referees for a common group of journals. This is *not* true of the creation of
a new, interdisciplinary field. It is incredible as a description of the sociological phenomena underlying the influences which linked the young Darwin to
his audience and to those in whose audience he was to be found. Kuhn's
characterization of the relative unanimity among the members of sub-dis-
ciplinary "research fronts" has little relevance to those situations in which
one man (or a small group) espouses a comprehensive new theory, which will
create a number of new research fronts, if only a significant number of reputable converts can be made.[1] Darwin's distinctive task was to take both
evidence and conceptual machinery from a number of diverse fields, and
persuasively and coherently to represent his own novel integration of that
material.

Charles Kadushin's approach to the relationships of power and influence
which connect members of elite groups or "circles" has an appealing generality and may prove flexible enough to illuminate the common structure
of a greater variety of scientific and cultural communities. He offers the
following working definition of 'social circle':

(1) A circle may have a chain or network of indirect interaction such that most members
of a circle are linked to other members, at least through a third party. It is thus not a
pure face-to-face group. (2) The network exists because members of the circle share

common interests – political or cultural. (3) The circle is not formal – i.e., there are: (a) no clear leaders, although there may be central figures; (b) no clearly defined goals for the circle, though it almost always has some implicit functions; (c) no definite rules which determine modes of interaction, though there are often customary relationships; and (d) no distinct criteria of membership.[2]

Since this concept of social circle does not include the concepts of communication ("serious discussion about ongoing research"), of coauthorship, of apprenticeship, or of colleagueship ("two scientists work in the same laboratory"), it is sufficiently abstract and general to assist the structuring of a discussion of "historical influence" of the kind represented by the current book.[3] Neither the goals, the criteria and limits for membership, nor the norms for interaction among the members of such social circles need be clearly and formally defined. The perimeter and the structure of a social circle can be vaguely and flexibly determined by a fluctuating coincidence of shared interests. The vagueness and relativity of such social circles prevents their classification into *precise* categories, e.g., *cultural*, *utilitarian*, *political*, and *integrative*, (or sub-categories, e.g., the *valuational*, *expressive*, and *cognitive* sub-categories of the cultural category).

Diana Crane hopes to contribute to a sociology of culture by first analyzing the cognitive cultures of diverse scientific fields – examining the relations within the internal structure of various groups of collaborators and using these relations to interpret the cognitive products developed and accepted within such groups.[4] She concentrates upon groupings whose shared interests, goals, and norms of interaction are *relatively well defined and explicit*. Nevertheless, the analysis of 'social circle' upon which she relies suggests that such *well-defined and explicit* goals and norms of interaction are *characteristic only of special cases*. Crane relies upon citation analysis, survey questionaires, and interviews. Each of these sources of data finds the respondent in the position of a *spokesman* for a *group* which the *investigator* has implicitly *identified in advance*.

The result is the magnification of a cultural and historical artefact: the scientist as team-member, not unlike an employee in a well organized firm. Both proponents and critics of the role of the scientist in twentieth century (particularly post World War II) America have found this concept congenial, but its historical generality is not evident. What is needed is a more comprehensive and critical methodology for describing, analyzing, and appraising the *actual behavior* of members of elite groups at various periods in history. It is not a matter of ignoring what they say and watching what they do. It is a matter of carefully cataloguing and interpreting their *verbal*, *social*, *political*, and *economic behavior*. In *Invisible Colleges*, Crane concentrated upon a very narrow aspect of the *self-reporting verbal behavior* of sample populations of the scientific elite. She paid little or no attention to the linguistic content of the publications listed in the comprehensive bibliographies she employed.

According to Joseph Ben-David a comprehensive and systematic sociology of knowledge would depend on:

a) the existence of a systematic relationship between the conceptual structure of philoso-phies prevailing at the time, ... and the variables of the social situation, and b) a systematic relationship between those philosophies and science. [5]

He finds no relationship between class interests on the one hand and the concepts and methods of philosophy on the other, except in instances of what he calls "poor philosophy, *obiter dicta* which have little relationship to the theoretical part of the philosophies of otherwise good philosophers." These negative remarks are no more cogent than the content analyses upon which they are based. But here Ben-David's argument is damaged by a series of weak links. He uses Darwin's case to illustrate a conclusion that "the philosophical assumptions that had become part of the living tradition of science were selected by scientists from the array of competing philosophies for their usefulness in the solution of specific scientific problems and not for any socially determined perspective or motive."[6] He speaks as if the theory of natural selection had been "most unequivocally traced" to the ideas of competition and selection to be found in the individualistic model of society held by Malthus, and before him by Adam Smith and Hobbes. The present study has shown that Darwin's ontology was neither individualist nor atomist, and that instead it postulated the *structured population* as the basic unit of evolution.[7] In organisms possessing a capacity for the recognition of conspe-cific individuals, a *complex social organization had been favored by the processes of natural selection*, according to Darwin. Thus the premise of Ben-David's argument (that wholistic concepts were providing inspiration for new thinking in physics at a time when biology was more fruitfully inspired by atomism) is false.

Robert Merton put the issue in a more general context in his 1945 article, "A Paradigm for the Sociology of Knowledge."[8] What Merton found lacking in the sociology of knowledge thirty years ago was agreement upon the answers to the following questions:

(1)   Where is the existential basis of mental production located?
(2)   What mental productions are being sociologically analyzed?
(3)   How are mental productions related to the existential basis?

(4) Why are the mental productions related to the existential basis?
(5) Over what time span do the imputed relations of the existential base and knowledge obtain?

Comprehensive and adequate answers to these questions will be available only when philosophers, historians and sociologists of science begin *to cooperate* in the delineation and analysis of a significant variety of appropriate case studies. The present study, concentrating as it does upon a period of the life of a "great man," and upon the various beliefs which prevailed within a circle of influential authors whose works he *read*, does *not* claim to focus upon a *typical* event in the history of science, nor to have employed methods which will provide an adequate paradigm for the resolution of *all* the problems associated with the sociology of knowledge. It must be supplemented by a detailed account of Darwin's "face-to-face" contacts with those whose criticism of his "scientific" work would have been most influential. It also must be integrated with other studies of the "reception" given Darwin's theory. Such integration must avoid the trap of a dogmatic delineation of the boundary between "externalist" and "internalist" histories of science. It must take cautious notice of the historical and social relativity of uses of the term 'science' itself. This, in turn, will require that philosophers, historians, and sociologists take careful note of the complexity of the notions of "influence," "communication," and "cultural exchange." In the present study, the most careful attention has been given to the character of Malthus' *influence* upon Darwin. Certain features of that influence are important enough to merit reemphasis here.

2. THE MULTI-DIMENSIONAL STRUCTURE OF INFLUENCE

Darwin's debt to Malthus was substantial and its importance is often noted (Himmelfarb, Bernal, R. M. Young, Sandra Herbert, and P. Vorzimmer have written articles, chapters, or at least pages concerning it). Nevertheless, the conceptual dimensions of this debt have not yet received adequate analysis. The analysis offered in this book distinguishes 'struggle$_M$' employed by Malthus and 'struggle$_D$' used by Darwin.

> struggle$_M$ = zero sum competition for an inevitably scarce resource
> struggle$_D$ = vigorous effort to overcome a difficulty.

Darwin used 'struggle$_D$' to control three more detailed theses concerning struggle; theses not to be found in Malthus. These theses are:

1. The chances of overcoming the odds against survival and the leaving of fertile progeny in spite of the stress of disease, drought, extremes of temperature, predation, and the scarcity of various resources, are not distributed randomly in an organic population. Rather, these chances are biased by the distribution of heritable variation among the individuals in the population.

2. The environment of organic populations is subject to gradual but indefinite variation, in part as a function of relevant variation in the organic populations themselves: in their behavior, in migration, and in social organization.

3. Relationships of dependency, including parasitism and predation, but more strikingly those resulting from social organization, also work to bias the distribution of the chances of leaving fertile progeny in succeeding generations. There is no inherent limit in the variability of such relationships.

The importance of the distinction of 'struggle$_M$' and 'struggle$_D$' is partly indicated by the fact that Malthus saw the struggle for survival as a brake or retardant upon significant organic and social change. On his view, progressive change was not only not necessary, it was not possible outside definite limits. Darwin agreed that progressive changes in organic form were not a necessary consequence of his theory. On the other hand, it is of the first importance that his use of 'struggle' was intended to explain the gradual improvement of the adaptation of organisms to their environment and to each other.

It is crucial for those who think there is an important relation between Malthusian political economy and Darwinian natural selection, to note that *Darwin did not simply take over the Malthusian concept of struggle*. It is also true that Malthus' *Essay* provided a causally stimulating occasion for Darwin's inventive elaboration of the concept.

The fact that there were overwhelming differences in the views of Malthus and Darwin concerning the concept of struggle, does *not imply* that the *influence exerted by Malthus upon the structure of Darwin's concept should be seen*, from the perspective of a critical philosophy of science, *as a mere accident, a matter of chance to be attributed to historical vagaries of time and place*. The scientific community, or research front, to which Malthus and Darwin both belonged was structured by a loose but nontheless significant multi-dimensional consensus (in Kuhn's term, a 'shared matrix'). These dimensions included at least the following specific rows or sets of channels:

1.   Empirical evidence
    1.1.   Seed number is greater than required for replacement.
    1.2.   Populations of organisms surge widely in numbers.
    1.3.   In the long run, rate of population growth = 0.

2.   Mathematical analysis
    The comparison of corresponding members of arithmetic and geometric series.

3.   Metaphor (or evaluative and interpretative assumption)
    3.1.   Man is an animal, exhibiting no property not present in some degree in simpler forms of organic life.
    3.2.   Laws of nature must be interpreted realistically, as universal and necessary statements of objective fact.

It would be highly inappropriate, therefore, to suggest that Malthus and Darwin inhabited "different worlds" or that they employed scientific language in some fashion which renders their concepts, including the concept of struggle, "radically incommensurable." The links connecting Malthus and Darwin were *both causal and symbolic*. The methods I employ in this book call attention primarily to the latter by concentrating on the question, "What did Darwin make of what he read in Malthus?" My answer to that question cannot be forced into a simple *binary* model of *communication*. It is not the case, i.e., that Darwin either *affirmed* or *denied* what he read in Malthus. Instead, I claim, Darwin *critically reinterpreted* and *expanded* or *developed* what had been *a simple univocal term*, 'struggle', and constructed a complex (multivocal) metaphor of his own, in which three distinct senses of 'struggle$_D$' were placed in *interaction* with each other. *Communication* of this degree of subtlety and precision requires a *significant degree* of disciplinary or cross-disciplinary agreement, but it does *not* require *complete consensus*.

No causal analysis based upon an assumption that Darwin simply *agreed with* and then *generalized and applied* Malthus' concept of demographic struggle could be correct, and to that extent I *disagree* with J. D. Bernal.[9] I am in *greater disagreement*, however, with Joseph Ben-David's thesis that systematic causal analysis of the relationship between the logical structure and conceptual content of science, on the one hand, and the social conditions of scientific activity, on the other, is an *unpromising project*.

CHAPTER TWELVE

CONCLUSIONS CONCERNING THE YOUNG DARWIN

There are two basic reasons why study of the young Darwin and his cultural circle is important for Darwin studies generally, and for the history of biology as well. Both these reasons hinge on the length of the period intervening between his first formulations and representations of the theory and his eventual *publication* of it. The interval in question, twenty years, was lengthy enough to permit significant shifts in scientific opinion and in the general cultural ambience, in England and the rest of the world. If one knows that Darwin was influenced by Herschel, Whewell, and Malthus, but feels constrained to interpret that influence in a context where T. H. Huxley, Herbert Spencer, and J. S. Mill were equally important, the conclusions of such interpretation are already heavily predetermined. Huxley, Spencer, and Mill, however, had *no* influence upon the *discovery* and *first formulation* of the theory. Instead, when the theory was discovered and first articulated, the influence of Herschel, Whewell, and Malthus was contextuated by Darwin's reading of Dugald Stewart, John Fleming, David Brewster's review of Comte, Mackintosh's ethics, and the poetry of William Wordsworth. Such a difference in cultural context can, as should be clear by now, drastically transform the philosophical appraisal and interpretation of Darwin's theory. Second, the published versions of the theory were also influenced by Darwin's sensitivity to his social role as a scientist. His growing perception of this role led him to moderate and to some extent to suppress his personal estimate of the cultural significance of the theory. He would not indicate his views concerning materialism in print; he would certainly not publicly raise the possibility that his theory might cause the "whole fabric" of English culture and society to "totter and fall." Reliance on what he wrote on such subjects after the age of fifty and after the publication of *The Origin* may seriously distort the texture of his life as a scientist, and lead to equally serious misinterpretations of the meaning of the theory which he authored.

The first drafts of the theory, the early notebooks, the manuscripts and the marginalia associated with these materials, provide a perspective which is indispensable for the critical appraisal of the major theses of current Darwin scholarship.

For example, J. A. Rogers argues that Darwin used "unnecessary concepts" derived from the demographic theories of Malthus and Spencer. But Rogers assumes, without clarification or argument, a distinction of *biological meaning* and *social context*. He presumes it possible to isolate the properly *biological meaning* of Darwin's sentences and to express that meaning in some fashion less entangled with *extraneous* material from sources associated with it by historical *coincidence*. On his account, it should be possible to reformulate the core of Darwin's theory in technical language free of unwanted connotations of social context. To the contrary, the linguistic practice exemplified in Darwin's published scientific work was marked by a flexible and imaginative use of metaphorical expression which was heavy with social and cultural meaning. Darwin neither invented nor saw the need for the sort of unambiguous, unequivocal technical language required by Cartesian standards of theoretical adequacy. Darwin accepted Dugald Stewart's *critique* of the Cartesian cult of univocality, clarity, and distinctness. John Greene has argued that Darwin followed the tradition of Cartesian mechanism, but the *philosophic structure of the young Darwin's manuscript, notebook, and marginal annotation refutations of dualism do not support Greene's view*. Greene overlooked Darwin's share of the legacy of *Scottish Realism* and its basic axioms: there are *natural signs* and *nature itself is expressive*. The accurate appraisal of such influence is *indispensable* for the analysis of the *meaning* of Darwin's theory. The theory cannot be translated into a purely technical idiom without first determining the significance of the metaphorical language in which it was expressed.

When the theory is set in its original context, certain far-reaching questions are raised concerning the accuracy and cogency of generally received or prominent theses concerning the philosophical significance of Darwin's theory. For example, the young Darwin cannot usefully be located within the tradition of Cartesian mechanism. He was, instead, decisively influenced by Scottish realism and by romanticism. His penchant for metaphorical expression overrode the quest for mathematical clarity and distinctness in the expression of the core of his theory. Second, *he did not fail to develop a concept of chance*. He did express his views on chance in a vacillating and ambiguous fashion, and finally gave them their clearest expression in the central metaphors of "selection" and "struggle." Third, his moral views were not rooted in the individualism of Malthus nor of the English social philosophy articulated by Spencer or by Mill in the eighteen-fifties and 'sixties. Rudimentary as they were, his ethical views centered on the "social instincts" of love and benevolence. Darwin's ethics, at the time the theory of natural selection was first formulated, derived from the eighteenth-century views of Bishop Butler by way of James Mackintosh's account, and from the concepts of population, reproductive behavior, and social instinct as these were developed within the theoretical core of his views concerning biological species.

Fourth, the early drafts of the theory do not conform to the "hypothetico-deductive model" of scientific explanation, although they indicate Darwin's intent to represent his view *as if* they did conform to that model. Darwin himself flatly states in the *Notebooks* that he found it impossible to distinguish the inductive and deductive phases of his investigation. The first drafts of the theory do *not* articulate an hypothesis which could be subjected to the risk of falsification. The scientific significance and persuasive force of his views did not derive from a single definite prediction or retrodiction derived from the core of his theory. Nor did Darwin ever pretend that the consequences, e.g., of chance migration to a virgin oceanic island could be *deduced* from some law or general premise established by his theory.

Fifth, it can be a misleading oversimplification to refer to the young Darwin as a materialist, although he certainly did hold that thought was a function of the material brain — guessing that it might be permissible to say that the "brain secretes thought as liver secretes bile." The label 'materialist' can be misleading because Darwin did *not* hold that *any* biological laws (including those concerning expression or other aspects of animal or human behavior) could be reduced to or derived from the laws of physics and chemistry. Moreover, he considered it philosophically sound to read human traits into the description of animal behavior, to speculate concerning the animal origins of human language, and to insist upon the analogy of emotional expression in man and animals. Darwin did criticize and reject one form of metaphysical dualism. His position *cannot* be described as idealistic. He was more a philosophical realist than a positivist. It is difficult to imagine a single label which could capture all these features but it seems best to say that his position was naturalistic, not reductionist, and not adverse to the use of anthropomorphisms in the description of animal behavior.

Finally, the young Darwin's differences with the prevailing theologies (whether of Paley or of Whewell) were so great that it is misleading to refer to him as an orthodox member of the Church, as a deist, and perhaps even the label 'theist' should be withheld pending better evidence. The reason for this caution is *not* that the young Darwin held any view which implied the denial of the God of the Christians or of the deists. It is rather that he either held or was greatly influenced by so many beliefs and arguments which implied the denial of the prevailing *premisses* for deism and theism. The young

Darwin did not pause for explicit reflection upon the cosmological argument for the existence of God, and the *Bridgewater Treatises* and his other theological sources presented him with no other. But from the start his views concerning the evolution of man, his denial of free will as a distinctive human trait, and his insistence upon the significance of chance in the production of order, placed him at odds with the prevailing versions of that argument. If one were to accept theism, Darwin insisted that speculations concerning God had no implications for the form or content of any law of nature, except for the purely formal claim that laws of nature could be seen as the means or instruments by which God's will was worked on earth.

Under the influence of Comte and Hume, Darwin dismissed the concept of divine will as "utterly useless," arguing that it was empirically and scientifically vacuous since "we know nothing of the will of the Deity, how it acts and whether constant or inconstant like that of man." Thus his autobiographical claim to have been a theist during this period is on shaky ground. The labels 'atheist' and 'agnostic' are also inappropriate. Wordsworth's *The Excursion*, which he boasted he had read twice through during this period (and the nine books of the poem comprise a thick volume) portrayed a sense of significance and exhilaration to be found in nature, particularly in vigorous struggle with the suffering of life throughout the sweep, variety, and history of human experience. The young Darwin's positive theological views were similar to the central theses of the natural religion expressed by Wordsworth's character, the Wanderer.

Darwin's theory has seemed to most of its sternest critics and, surprisingly, to some of its most fervent advocates, as an expression of the indifference of science to the objects of its investigation, an echo of contemporary insouciance for those "who in the great lottery of life, have drawn a blank." But although it was "disproportioned to the hopes and expectations of self-flattering minds," Darwin found grandeur in his view of life. *Not* the glacial grandeur of deistic metaphysics, but the exhilaration of a scientific perspective which could guide the experimental search for the laws of life and provide an imaginative and affectively powerful representation of the great human themes of chance, suffering, hope, and love.

NOTES

CHAPTER ONE

1. See Allegard (1958), Hull (1973), Ruse (1974), de Beer (1963), Eiseley (1958), Glass, *et. al.* (1959), Greene (1959), Himmelfarb (1962), Ghiselin (1969), and Vorzimmer (1970).

Himmelfarb made extensive use of material from the *Transmutation Notebooks*. Herbert (1968) and (1971), concentrates upon the influence of Lyell and Malthus upon the young Darwin. Gruber and Barrett (1974), have edited and commented upon the early *Metaphysical Notebooks* and manuscripts. Freeman and Gautrey (1969) and S. Smith (1960), (1965), have given meticuluous accounts of important developments in Darwin's species work in the interval between 1837 and 1865. R. Stauffer (1975), has recently edited the materials which Darwin was working over in 1856–1858, before news of Wallace's "double" reached him. Nevertheless, no one has yet undertaken the reconstruction of the methodological and philosophical ambience within which Darwin formulated the first drafts of the theory.

2. David Hull (1967), writes, "Only since the so-called new systematics have biologists begun to realise that such a thing as a metaphysics of evolution *as a biological phenomenon* is not only desirable but also necessary. In fact, the development of evolutionary theory since Darwin might well be described as a scientific theory in search of a metaphysics" (p. 337). Hull gives Darwin a mixed review as a philosopher. He credits Darwin's "long, involved inductive argument," as setting forth a logic whose value we "only now are beginning to appreciate" (p. 335). But he finds Darwin's views on teleology insufficiently subtle, and states that Darwin "did not appreciate the consequences. . . evolutionary theory had for the logic of definition."

Hull (1973), examines the reaction to *The Origin of Species*, 1859, by "competent scientists," and by such philosophers of science as J. F. W. Herschel, Whewell, and J. S. Mill (pp. vii–viii). He finds that evolutionary theory did not meet the "standards of proof" established by Herschel, Whewell, and Mill "for the simple reason that no theory could possibly fullfill them, including the physical theories which these authors had chosen as a paradigm" (p. 16). Hull finds our current situation no better, "evolutionary theory and philosophy of science are still at odds" (p. 35). Philosophers of science have failed to provide an appropriate reconstruction or model for a *hypothetico-inductive* (HI) warrant for evolution theory. Biologists have not yet formulated a molecular version of evolutionary theory which could overcome the "indeterministic" character of its present form and bring it into conformity with the criteria of the so-called hypothetico-deductive (HD) model.

Hull addresses this difficulty by shifting the issue from logic to pragmatic considerations: "Scientific theories are accepted long before anything like direct proof is provided. For example, when Copernicus enunciated his heliocentric system, scientists immediately selected the observation of stellar parallax as the most significant test of the theory.

None was observed until the 1830's — long after all reasonable men had accepted the heliocentric system. Similarly, not until recently has anything like the observation of the evolution of new species of multicellular organisms been observed.... Yet, few reasonable men withheld consent to the theory that species have evolved and that natural selection is the chief (if not the only) mechanism involved" (pp. 50-51). Confirmation by "reasonably direct means" may come only "long after the theory has been established beyond all reasonable doubt." But Hull does not state explicitly what it is that overcomes such reasonable doubt, nor does he explicitly indicate whether (and why or why not) it was *reasonable* for *Darwin* to claim to have overcome such doubt. He does identify a metamethodological or metaphysical source for doubts *about* Darwin's theory: "here was Darwin's sin: he had not exercised enough caution. Science must be safe. The inductive method was calculated to make it safe.... As soon as a natural explanation was acknowledged for the origin and evolution of some species, nothing but time stood in the way of extending it to all species.... Unlike Wallace, Darwin insisted on telling a totally consistent naturalistic story or none at all" (p. 54). Perhaps Hull thinks that Darwin's theory was warranted as a "totally consistent naturalistic story," but he neither explicitly states nor argues for that position.

C. C. Gillispie (1959), sees Lamarck's theory as belonging to the "contracting and self-defeating history of subjective science," Darwin's to the "expanding and conquering history of objective science" (p. 286). Holding that "the significance of Newtonian physics for human affairs is that it has none" (p. 279), Gillispie writes that "Hypotheses non fingo" could have been said by Darwin as well as by Newton, and that the famous maxim meant that "theories (speculations are another matter) must just embrace the evidence" (p. 283). Gillispie partially agrees with those skeptical of Darwin's greatness. "His might be taken as the classic illustration of what Duhem meant when he described the English mind in science as weak and comprehensive. Nothing in the history of science is more familiar than his theory, or than the steps which led him to it by way of the Galapagos Islands and Malthusian political economy." He chides those among Darwin's "serious" opponents who wanted "from biology (what) science cannot give without ceasing to be science and becoming moral or social philosophy" (pp. 282–283).

On the other hand, John C. Greene (1959), writes of Darwin that "his *Descent of Man* showed clearly that he was a moral as well as a natural philosopher, a social as well as a natural scientist" (p. 327). Like Gillispie, Greene sees Darwin as Newton's heir, as "drawing out the ultimate implications of the Newtonian cosmology" (p. 307). Unlike Gillispie, Greene finds this legacy loaded with metaphysical implications, including "the death blow to traditional natural theology." Greene finds that Darwin, to the end of his days, "remained a prisoner in the rigidly deterministic system he had discerned in all the operations of nature, organic as well as inorganic." In *Death of Adam*, Greene made no use of Darwin's so-called *Metaphysical Notebooks*, and gave no consideration to the possibility that Darwin's moral and natural philosophy might itself have evolved in the years between 1837 and 1859 and beyond. In consequence, he sometimes deals with Darwin's views as if they were embedded in a hybrid Huxley—Darwin, Darwin—Huxley position. He quotes *Huxley* to the effect that a LaPlacean intelligence might have predicted the "state of the fauna of Britain in 1869," if that intelligence had known the laws of nature and the properties of the molecules in a primal cosmic vapour (pp. 304–05 and Note #36), but asserts there was no room for chance in *Darwin's* theory. Greene sees Darwin as following in the Cartesian tradition, or as agreeing with Robert Boyle that "the origin of forms and qualities in the physical world might be explained in terms of the local motions of ultimate particles of matter in a law-bound system of nature" (pp. 284, 303–307, 314). Greene sees "no room for genuine chance in Darwin's view of nature" (p. 304), and cedes to C. S. Peirce, William James, Henri Bergson, and A. N. Whitehead the laurels for finding "in the idea of organic evolution the key to a new philosophy of nature in which spontaneity, novelty, creativity, and purpose had a place – a place denied them earlier in the mechanical cosmology inherited from the seventeenth century" (p. 306). Greene might not affirm Gillispie's blunt dictum, "It was through no metaphor or analogy that Darwin prevailed" (Gillispie, 1959, p. 267), but he gave no consideration to the highly anomalous use of anthropomorphic metaphors ('select', 'economy', etc.) in a scientific theory presumably aspiring to the Cartesian explanatory ideal of a law-bound system of matter in motion. R. M. Young (1971), more correctly notes that Darwin *rejected* the Cartesian ideal.

None of these authors noted the importance for Darwin of the aesthetic and epistemological works of Dugald Stewart, a proponent of Scottish Realism. Darwin read an essay of Stewart's which set forth a theory of definition which anticipated that articulated more than a century later by Ludwig Wittgenstein. Stewart provided Darwin all the philosophical ammunition he needed to reject the Cartesian linguistic ideals of univocity, clarity, and distinctness, and to formulate *metaphorical* representations of the concepts of spontaneity, novelty, creativity, and purpose.

3. Darwin's *Notebooks M* and *N*, together with related manuscripts from the same period, have been edited and annotated by Paul Barrett and published together with a psychological study of Darwin's creativity by Howard E. Gruber (1974). The *Transmutation Notebooks*, *B*, *C*, *D*, and *E*, have been available in relatively complete form since 1967 (Gavin de Beer, *et. al.*, 1960–1967).

4. Darwin, *Notebook M*, p. 57. "To avoid stating how far I believe in Materialism, say only that emotions, instincts degrees of talent, which are hereditary are so because brain of child resembles parent stock – (and phrenologists state that brain alters)."

5. Young (1971), p. 480.

6. *Ibid.*, p. 447.

7. G. G. Simpson (1967), page 4, note #2, and page 226, note #6.

8. Charles Darwin, *The Origin of Species, in the Variorum Text*, edited by M. Peckham, (1959), IV. 14, 1–9c, p. 165. All references to published editions of *The Origin of Species* will be to the Peckham text, hereafter cited simply as *The Origin*. The details of these references are interpreted as follows:

'IV. 14, 1–9c, p. 165' =   'Chapter IV, sentence 14, sentences one through nine as inserted in the third edition, appearing on Peckham's page 165.'

9. *The Origin*. IV. 29–32e., pp. 167–168.

10. *Ibid.*, IV. 40., p. 168. Also see *The Origin*, VI. 256., p. 377. "In many cases we are far too ignorant to be enabled to assert that a part or organ is so unimportant for the welfare of a species, that modifications in its structure could not have been slowly accumulated by means of natural selection."

11. Page references for the *Sketch of 1842* and the *Essay of 1844* are to the edition by Francis Darwin (1909), republished by Gavin de Beer (1958). In this printed edition the

Sketch of 1842 occupies 48 pages; that of 1844, 160 pages. For the reference to the "being infinitely more sagacious than man," see the de Beer edition of the *Sketch of 1842*, at page 45.

12. Darwin's *Notebook E*, p. 150.

13. Darwin (1868), vol. 1, pp. 8–9.

14. Ghiselin (1969), p. 4.

15. de Beer edition (1958), pp. 57–58, 133–134.

16. The evidence which Darwin used to illustrate the Malthusian ratios (sudden increases in population size or "swarms," egg clutch size well above replacement level), did not include any information about specific forms of selection pressure. "We ought to feel no legitimate surprise at not seeing where the check falls in animals and plants." de Beer edition (1958), p. 118.

17. *Ibid.*, p. 54.

18. *Ibid.*, pp. 55–56.

19. *Ibid.*, p. 195.

20. *Ibid.*, pp. 196–198.

21. In 1842 and 1844, Darwin used a remarkable variety of terms to characterize the inferential relation holding between his theory and direct evidence favoring or opposing it:

> Now according to our theory during the infinite number of changes, we *might expect* that an organ used for a purpose might be used for a different one by his descendant, as *must have been the case* by our theory with the bat, porpoise, horse, etc., which are descended from one parent. And if it is chanced that traces of the former use and structure of the part should be retained, which is *manifestly possible if not probable*, then we should have the organs, on which morphology is founded and which *instead of being metaphorical becomes plain* and instead of being utterly unintelligible becomes simple matter of fact. (Emphasis added) de Beer edition, p. 77.

The concurrent use of these italicized expressions suggests that Darwin had not developed a definite pattern for the assignment of particular modalities to corresponding types of inferential or evidential relationships.

22. Stauffer (1975, p. 175ff).

23. *Ibid.*, p. 188.

24. *The Origin*. III. 25–32, pp. 146–147.

25. B. G. Gale (1972), gives a helpful discussion of scientific, political, and religious uses of 'struggle' in the first half of the nineteenth century. However, Gale conflates the meaning of 'struggle,' with those of 'battle,' 'war,' and 'conflict.' His failure to take adequate account of the diverse meanings of 'struggle' and of the complex inter-relationship of these meanings leads him to state without argument that the literal and metaphorical uses of 'struggle' describe "just about opposite" situations (p. 323).

26. Simpson (1967), pp. 221–222.

27. J. A. Rogers (1972).

28. Barlow, ed. (1958), p. 84.

29. Barlow, ed. (1958), pp. 67–68. For the autobiographical allusions to his reading of Paley, see p. 59.

30. *Ibid.*, p. 85.

31. Wedgwood, (1848), pp. 49—63. The handwriting of the second party to the manuscript dialogue is a close match to the handwriting found in manuscripts known to have been written by Hensleigh Wedgwood and available at the Cambridge University Library. It is a closer match to Hensleigh Wedgwood's hand than it is, for instance, to that of William Whewell or to that of Darwin's wife, Emma, or to that of Darwin's anamneusis, Covington. The identification is perhaps cinched by an entry in *Notebook M*, p. 61 where Charles Darwin wrote, "Hensleigh says to say 'brain thinks' is nonsense," and that is exactly the position defended by the second party to the dialogue. The manuscript in question was filed by Charles Darwin with his "Old and Useless Notes about the moral sense & some metaphysical points . . . ," and has been published by Barrett and Gruber (1974), pp. 396—398, and note #74, p. 411. The work of tracking down the mysterious second party was expertly assisted by Dr. Sydney Smith and by Paul Barrett, and they concur in my identification of Hensleigh Wedgwood.

CHAPTER TWO

1. Barlow, ed. (1958), p. 100.
2. Darwin's comments on Lyell's opinions on such topics may be found in the *Metaphysical Notebooks, M*, p. 128; and *N*, p. 19e and p. 115e.
3. Barlow, ed. (1958), pp. 77, 101.
4. See Leonard G. Wilson (1972), pp. 433—460, for the relationship between Darwin and Lyell during the years 1836—1841. Notebook references to Lyell occur in all six of Darwin's transmutation and *Metaphysical Notebooks*: *B*, pp. 10, 59, 96, 115—116, 155, 170, 201, 249e, and 272; *C*, pp. 39, 53, 74, 84, 135, 153, 167—169, 176, 266, and 270; *D*, pp. 60 and 133; *E*, pp. 37—38, 59e, 63—65e, 86e, 100—101e, 105, 134—135, 167e; *M*, p. 128; *N*, pp. 19e and 115e.
5. Barlow, ed. (1958), p. 101.
6. P. Roget (1840), vol. I, pp. 44—45, as cited in Gliserman (1975), pp. 87—88.
7. P. Roget (1840), vol. I, p. 474, as cited in Gliserman (1975), p. 88.
8. W. Whewell (1833).
9. S. Gliserman (1975), pp. 292—293.
10. (David Brewster, *anon*.), (1834), p. 457.
11. *Ibid.*, p. 429.
12. S. Gliserman (1975), p. 295.
13. W. Whewell (1833), pp. 223—284.
14. Barlow, ed. (1958), p. 82.
15. C. Lyell (1832), vol. 2, p. 160.
16. C. Lyell (1830), vol. 1, p. 155.
17. *Ibid.*, p. 30.
18. *Ibid.*, p. 48.
19. *Ibid.*, pp. 65—72.
20. *Ibid.*, p. 160.
21. C. Lyell (1833), vol. 3, pp. 384—385.
22. C. Lyell (1832), vol. 2, p. 13.
23. C. Lyell (1830), vol. 1, pp. 145—155.
24. C. Lyell (1832), vol. 2, p. 169.

25. *Ibid.*, pp. 135–136.
26. Stauffer, ed. (1975), p. 187, note   1, citing Lyell's heading of page 134 of volume 2 of the *Principles* (1832).
27. C. Lyell (1832), vol. 2, pp. 123, 145.
28. *Ibid.*, pp. 26–32, 37.
29. C. Lyell (1830), vol. 1, p. 112. See Martin Rudwick (1972), pp. 186–187.
30. C. Lyell (1830), vol. 1, p. 82.
31. C. Lyell (1832), vol. 2, p. 23.
32. *Ibid.*, pp. 64–65.

CHAPTER THREE

1. Dugald Stewart (1810), pp. 516–517 (from the *Essay* "On Taste"). For the influence of Hume upon the Scotch school see S. A. Grave (1960).
2. Dugald Stewart (1810), "On the Beautiful," pp. 262–263. Darwin's manuscript allusions to Stewart concentrated upon the *Essays* on aesthetic subjects and upon the development of sympathy and the system of the emotions. The text cited here is mentioned by Grave (1960), as anticipating a comparable passage in Wittgenstein, *Philosophical Investigations*, #65–67; see Grave, p. 231, note.
3. Dugald Stewart (1792), "Of Language," edited by Sir William Hamilton (1854), vol. 4, p. 22. Stewart argued that the primitive cognate of 'beauty' first expressed delight in the visual experience of color, and later acquired transitive associations with comparable experiences of form, motion, and finally even of moral character. He emphasized the contrast of the wild and savage beauties of Nature with the chaste, finished, classical beauties of Art. He claimed that forms and colors which operated chiefly by stimulating the wide ranging powers of imagination and memory had "important and obvious advantages over those which are more decidedly beautiful; inasmuch as these last, by the immediate pleasure which they communicate to the organ, have a tendency to arrest the progress of our thoughts, and to engage the whole of our attention to themselves." "Essay on the Beautiful," pp. 316, 321).
4. Stewart (1792) "Of Language," *Works*, vol. 4, p. 6.
5. *Ibid.*, p. 145.
6. Dugald Stewart (1810), "On the Beautiful," pp. 266, 269.
7. *Ibid.*, pp. 344–345.

Although ... our first notions of Beauty are derived from *colours*, it neither follows that in those complex ideas of the Beautiful which we are afterwards led to form in the progress of our experience, this quality must necessarily enter as a component part; nor, where it does so enter, that its effect must necessarily predominate over that of all the others. On the contrary, it may be easily conceived in what manner its effect comes to be gradually supplanted by those pleasures of a higher cast, with which it is combined; while, at the same time, we continue to apply to the joint result the language which this now subordinate, and seemingly unessential ingredient, originally suggested. It is by a process somewhat similar, that the mental attractions of a beautiful woman supplant those of her person in the heart of her lover. ...

In the progress of Taste, the word Beautiful comes to be more peculiarly appro-
priated (at least by critics and philosophers) to Beauty in its most complicated
and impressive form. . . . To Colour, and to the other simple elements which enter
into its composition . . we more commonly . . . apply the epithet pleasing, or
some equivalent expression.

8. Beckner (1968), pp. 22–25, analyzes the polytypic concepts to be found in biology.
Stewart's discussion of 'matter,' 'mind,' and their cognates gave an instrumentalist turn
to his theory of metaphor. See Hamilton edition, volume 4, pp. 57–58.

Strongly impressed with the errors to which we are liable, in the Philosophy of
the Human Mind, by the imperfections of our present phraseology, a philosophical
grammarian of the first eminence long ago recommended the total proscription of
figurative terms from all abstract discussions.[1] To this proposal D'Alembert
objects, that it would require the creation of a new language, unintelligible to all
the world; for which reason he advises philosophers to adhere to the common
modes of speaking, guarding themselves as much as possible against the false
judgments which they may have a tendency to occasion.[2] To me it appears, that
the execution of the design would be found, by any person who should attempt
it, to be wholly impracticable, at least in the present state of metaphysical science.
If the new nomenclature were coined out of merely arbitrary sounds, it would be
altogether ludicrous; if analogous, in its formation, to that lately introduced into
chemistry, it would, in all probability, systematize a set of hypotheses, as unfounded as those which we are anxious to discard.

Neither of these writers has hit on the only effectual remedy against this incon-
venience; to *vary*, from time to time, the metaphors we employ, so as to prevent
any one of them from acquiring an undue ascendant over the others, either in our
own minds, or in those of our readers. It is by the exclusive use of some favourite
figure, that careless thinkers are gradually led to mistake a simile or distant analogy
for a legitimate theory.

Such, indeed, is the poverty of language, that we cannot speak on the subject
without employing expressions which suggest one theory or another; but it is of
importance for us always to recollect, that these expressions are entirely figurative, and afford no explanation of the phenomena to which they refer. It is partly
with a view to remind my readers of this consideration, that, finding it impossible
to lay aside completely metaphorical or analogical words, I have studied to avoid
such a uniformity in the employment of them, as might indicate a preference to
one theory rather than another; and by doing so, have perhaps sometimes been
led to vary the metaphor oftener and more suddenly, than would be proper in a
composition which aspired to the praise of elegance." ([1]Du Marsais. Article
"Abstraction" in the *Encyclopedie.* [2]*Melanges*, tom. v. p. 30). (Eclair, #2.)
Emphasis added. Also see Stewart (1810), pp. 223–224.

Whence this disposition to attenuate and subtilize, to the very verge of existence,
the atoms or elements supposed to produce the phenomena of thought and
volition, but from the repugnance of the scheme of Materialism to our natural
apprehensions; and from a secret anxiety to guard against a literal interpretation

of our metaphorical phraseology? . . . Philosophical materialists themselves have
only refined farther on the popular conceptions, by entrenching themselves
against the objections of their adversaries in the modern discoveries concerning
light and *electricity*. . . . In some instances they have had recourse to the supposition of the possible . . . existence of Matter, under forms incomparably more
subtile than it probably assumes in these, or in any other class of physical phenomena. . . . It is evident that, in using this language, they have only attempted to
elude the objections of their adversaries, . . . divesting Matter completely of all
those properties by which it is known to our senses; and substituting, instead of
what is commonly meant by that word, – infinitestimal or evanescent entities, in
the pursuit of which imagination herself is quickly lost."

9. Charles Darwin, "Old and Useless Notes on Metaphysics," Barrett ed. (1974), pp.
386–388.
10. Stewart (1810), "On the Beautiful," p. 343.
11. David Brewster (1838), wrote the then anonymous review (see the *Wellesley Index
for Victorian Periodicals* 1966). Charles Darwin's allusions to Comte all occur in the
Metaphysical Notebooks and manuscripts, at *M*, pp. 72, 81, 135; *N*, p. 12; and "Old and
Useless Notes on Metaphysics," Barrett edition, p. 388, note a.
12. *Metaphysical Notebook M*, p. 69.
13. *Metaphysical Notebook M*, p. 137. This concurrence with the positivist critique of
theology and the theological stage of science was *not* consistent with Darwin's auto-
biological suggestion that, "although I did not think much about the existence of a
personal God until a considerably later period of my life," his views were those of a
theist or deist until *after* the publication of *The Origin*, when they gradually "weakened"
until he termed himself, with some appearance of reluctance, an agnostic, *Autobiography*,
pp. 87–94.
14. David Brewster (1838), pp. 275, 297–301.
15. August Comte, Martineau, trans. 1853, vol. 1, p. 395.
16. Brewster (1838), p. 280. Comte (1853), pp. 2–3, 225.
17. Brewster (1838), pp. 291, 302. Comte (1853), pp. 141, 393. Larry Laudan (1971a),
pp. 35–53, discusses the role of prediction and explanation in Comte's account of the
aims and nature of science.
18. Charles Darwin, *Cambridge Manuscript Collection*. 71. item 55-05. Published in
Barrett edition, pp. 417–418.
19. *Transmutation Notebook, D*, p. 67. "Law of monstrosity not prospective, but
retrospective in showing what organs are little fixed . . . . Although no new fact be
elicited by these speculations even if partly true they are of the greatest service towards
the end of science, namely prediction, till facts are grouped & called there can be no
prediction. – The only advantage of discovering laws is to foretell what will happen &
see bearing of scattered facts." Darwin distinguished "prospective" and "retrospective"
reference for laws in this passage, and linked them both with prediction as the end of
science. The passage, written by Darwin in the summer of 1838, clearly antedates the
Comtean text cited by Laudan (1971a), in support of his observation that, "In sharp
contrast to his predecessors and contemporaries, who generally insisted that the predictions were inevitably about future events, Comte argued that predictions were not
essentially temporal inferences but were chiefly distinguished from explanations by an

epistemic difference. Putting the matter another way, he believed that what was unique to a prediction (that is, what immediately distinguished it from an explanation) was not the 'leap' from past or present to future but rather the leap from known to unknown. Comte criticized the usual definition of prediction because it neglected the fact that we often predict the occurrence of events which have already happened, such as an eclipse in antiquity. I believe that this was one of the first occasions when a methodologist paid any serious attention to the question of 'retrodictions'." Laudan cites Comte, *Discours sur l'Esprit Positif*, Paris, 1844, p. 21, in support of this claim. Darwin's attention to this topic, which was serious if not sustained, followed his reading of Brewster's review of Comte, but preceded the publication of the *Discours* in 1844.

20. Brewster (1838), p. 288. Comte (1853), vol. 1, pp. 28–31.
21. Brewster (1838), pp. 303–306. Comte (1853), vol. 1, p. 182.
22. Comte (1853), vol. 1, p. 225, "The employment of this instrument must always be subjected to one condition, the neglect of which would impede the development of real knowledge. This condition is to imagine such hypotheses only as admit, by their nature, of a positive and inevitable verification at some future time, – the precision of this verification being proportioned to what we can learn of the corresponding phenomena. In other words, philosophical hypotheses must always have the character of simple anticipations of what we might know *at once*, by experiment and reasoning, if the circumstances of the problem had been more favourable than they are" (emphasis added).
23. Comte (1853), vol. 1, p. 226.
24. *Ibid.*, pp. 226–228.
25. *Ibid.*, p. 267.
26. *Ibid.*, p. 229. Comte's recognition of the need for a complex historiography, one which combined critical positivist themes with an appropriately flexible relativism, is well expressed in the following passage from vol. 1, pp. 265–266, of Martineau's translation, "The emancipation of natural philosophy from theological and metaphysical influence has thus far gone on by means of a succession of partial efforts, each isolated in intention, though all converging to a final end, amidst the entire unconsciousness of those who were bringing that result to pass. Such an incoherence is a valuable evidence of the force of that instinct which universally characterizes modern intelligence; but it is an evil, in as far as it has retarded and embarrassed and even introduced hesitation into the course of our liberation.... These observations are particularly applicable to the philosophical history of Optics – the department of Physics in which an imperfect positivism maintains the strongest consistence – chiefly through the mathematical labours which are connected with it. The founders of this science are those who have done most towards laying the foundations of the *Positive Philosophy* – Descartes, Huyghens, and Newton; yet each one of them was led away by the old spirit of the absolute to create a chimerical hypothesis on the nature of light."
27. Brewster (1838), p. 306. Also see *Positive Philosophy*, vol. 1, pp. 389–390:

"There seems no sufficient reason why the use of scientific fictions, so common in the hands of geometers, should not be introduced into biology, if systematically employed, and adopted with sufficient sobriety.... The process would be to intercalate, among different known organisms, certain purely fictitious organisms, so imagined as to facilitate their comparison, by rendering the biological series

more homogeneous and continuous. . . . It may be possible, in the present state of
our knowledge of living bodies, to conceive of a new organism capable of fulfilling
certain given conditions of existence. However that may be, the collocation of
real cases with well-imagined ones, after the manner of geometers, will doubtless
be practised hereafter, to complete the general laws of comparative anatomy and
physiology. . . ."

28. Comte (1853), vol. 1, p. 413; pp. 413–421. In this section, I have distinguished the
critical and the *relativistic* aspects of Comte's positivist account of hypotheses and the
principle of verifiability. Laudan (1971a), pp. 46–52, distinguishes what he terms 'CI'
("conservative, correlational interpretation") and 'LI' ("liberal interpretation") analyses
of the meaning of the text (1853, vol. 1, p. 225) quoted in note 22. CI would require of
all hypotheses that all of their non-logical predicates are drawn exclusively from observation. LI would accept hypotheses which are not "purely phenomenal ones, including the
atomic theory," from which it is possible for reason to deduce experimental consequences. I agree with Laudan that "what is clear is that Comte does not unequivocally
restrict positive science exclusively to those hypotheses which CI would allow" (p. 50).
29. Charles Darwin, *Autobiography*, pp. 67–68.
30. Charles Darwin, "Old and Useless Notes on Metaphysics," Barrett edition, p. 398.
The marks '/. . ./' set off Darwin's interlineal insertions. The double parentheses, '((. . .))',
contain a pencilled edition to a manuscript written in ink.
31. In an unpublished manuscript, Michael Ruse argues that "the Herschel–Whewell
notion of a consilience (of inductions) had a crucial influence on Darwin," p. 55, and
even more strongly, "the reason why Darwin set up his core arguments in the way that
he did was probably due essentially to the very influence of Herschel and Whewell,"
p. 22.
32. J. F. W. Herschel (1831), p. 35. "No one regards the night as the cause of the day,
or the day of night. They are alternate effects of a common cause, which their regular
succession alone gives us no sufficient clue for determining." Gunther Buttman's biography (1970), provides a striking portrait of Herschel's amazing breadth and depth
of interests. Buttman notes that although the section on method in the *Preliminary
Discourse* is "much more exhaustive than might be expected in a mere introduction,"
the underlying aim of the book was to "point out the spiritual and moral foundations of
scientific research," pp. 58–59. Buttman discusses Herschel's considerable interest in
poetry, his sympathy for Locke's deism ("John Herschel's own early religious ideas were
also along partly pantheistic and partly deistic lines.") and his later devout Christianity
(pp. 172–173). Buttman's account of Herschel's practice concerning the social role of
the scientist makes him seem like the very embodiment of the ideal of "disinterestedness," and shows that Herschel's impact upon the self-image of the British scientific
community was by no means limited to his methodology. Herschel refused offers of
research support from the Admiralty and the Royal Society (p. 111), never patented
his discovery of the use of sodium thiosulphate as a photographic "fixer" (p. 136), and
lobbied in scientific circles for a state supported system of education and greater participation by scientists in public education (p. 114). On "disinterestedness" as a norm of the
scientific community, see Norman Storer (1966), p. 79ff.
33. Herschel (1831), p. 36.
34. *Ibid.*, p. 95.

35. *Ibid.*, pp. 135–136.
36. *Ibid.*, p. 25. The emphasis of the phrase "precision in time, place, weight, and measure," has been added. Comte's understanding that biological phenomena were both too complex and too variable to be "accessible to the calculus," and the theme of historical relativism that was so important to his positivism provided an important counterbalance for the mathematical austerity of Herschel's position. Preoccupation with "crucial" and "essential" influences diverts attention away from issues more important for the understanding of science as an activity undertaken by *groups* of individuals. These issues include the determination of the nature and extent of consensus – in any given community of scientists – around the relevant substantive, methodological, and normative aspects of the activities of group members in formulating and presenting their scientific views. Elements of dissensus and active, adverse advocacy may be necessary for a truly "active society" (see A. Etzioni, 1968). In any case, Darwin's response to Herschel's ideal of mathematical deduction and precision was neither passive nor submissive. He developed his own mode of presentation, which – initially – was heavily allegorical. While he conceded nothing to the obvious point that his uses of 'law' and of 'necessary deduction' were, by some of Herschel's standards, erroneous, Darwin never challenged Herschel directly.
37. Herschel (1831), p. 36.
38. *Ibid.*, pp. 149, 152, 196, 203.
39. *Ibid.*, pp. 197, 144–148.
40. *Ibid.*, p. 167.
41. *Ibid.*, pp. 167, 170. Herschel provided no analysis of the relatively high confirmation he claimed for the subsumption of putative counter-examples under the theory or law being tested (a special case of the "consilience of inductions" to which Ruse refers).

While Darwin concurred in Herschel's estimate of the confirmatory value of such evidence, I think it is impossible to claim that Herschel provided him with a reasoned defense of their shared view.
42. Barlow edition (1958), pp. 66, 104, 113. Gerd Buchdahl (1971) and Larry Laudan (1971b) have recently examined different aspects of Whewell's contribution to mid-nineteenth-century controversy in the philosophy of science.
43. William Whewell, (1838, 1839).
44. Charles Darwin, *Cambridge Manuscript Collection*, 119, p. 29. Whewell was mentioned ten times in the *Notebooks* and early manuscripts, in the *Transmutation Notebooks*, *C*, pp. 55, 72, 91, 269; *D*, pp. 26, 49; and *E*, pp. 69, 128; in *Metaphysical Notebook N*, p. 14; and in the commentary on Mackintosh's ethics, Barrett edition, p. 403. Herschel's review of both the *History* and the *Philosophy of the Inductive Sciences* appeared in the *Quarterly Review*, (1841).
45. *Transmutation Notebook D*, p. 49.
46. Charles Darwin, "Commentary on Mackintosh and the Moral Sense," Barrett edition, p. 403. Darwin's one *manuscript* reference to the *History of the Inductive Sciences* commented on a point which was no more than an aside for Whewell. "All science is reason acting systematizing on principles, which even animals practically know. Art is experience + observation in balancing a body and an ass knows one side of triangle shorter than two. V. Whewell, *Induct. Science*, vol. I, p. 334," *Metaphysical Notebook N*, p. 14. *Darwin could not have been more mistaken if he thought he was accurately paraphrasing Whewell. The latter had been arguing that the architectural accomplishments*

of the middle ages no more implied a scientific grasp of the corresponding principles of mechanics than animal behavior implied knowledge of geometric axioms. The 1857 editions of the *History of the Inductive Sciences*, 3 vols., and the *Philosophy of the Inductive Sciences*, 2 vols., have been collected and edited by G. Buchdahl and L. L. Laudan (1967). I have transcribed the marginalia from Charles Darwin's personal copy of the 1837 edition of the *History of the Inductive Sciences*. Indications are that Darwin did *not* purchase the *Philosophy of the Inductive Sciences* when that work appeared in 1840. Darwin's personal copy of the *History* is in the Cambridge University Library.

47. *Transmutation Notebook C*, p. 55.
48. William Whewell, 1837, vol. 3, p. 456 (Darwin's copy).
49. William Whewell, *History* (1838), vol 3, p. 462 (Darwin's copy).
50. *Ibid.*, p. 476.
51. *Ibid.*, pp. 467–468.
52. *Ibid.*, pp. 469–470.

This asumption of an end makes his very definition of an organized being. 'An organized product of nature is that in which all the parts are mutually ends and means.' (*Urtheilskraft*. p. 296) And this, he says, is a universal and necessary maxim. He adds, 'It is well known that the anatomizers of plants and animals, in order to investigate their structure, and to obtain an insight into the grounds why and to what end such parts, why such a situation and connexion of the parts, and exactly such an internal form, come before them, assume, as indispensably necessary, this maxim, that in such a creature nothing is *in vain*, and proceed upon it in the same way in which in general natural philosophy we proceed upon the principle that *nothing happens by chance*. In fact, they can as little free themselves from this *teleological* principle as from the general physical one; for as, on omitting the latter, no experience would be possible, so on omitting the former principle, no clue could exist for the observation of a kind of natural objects which can be considered teleologically under the conception of natural ends.'

53. *Ibid.*, p. 473.
54. *Ibid.*, pp. 578–579.

CHAPTER FOUR

1. Some time between February and June of 1838, Darwin wrote the following in his *Transmutation Notebook C*, pp. 76–78.

Once grant that species and genus may pass into each other, – grant that one instinct to be acquired (if the medullary point in ovum has such organization as to force in one man the development of a brain capable of producing more glowing imagining or more profound reasoning than other, if this be granted!!) & whole fabric totters & falls. – Look abroad, study gradation, study unity of type, study geographical distribution, study relation of fossil with recent. The fabric falls! But man – wonderful man "divine ore versum coelum attentior" is an exception. – He is mammalian, his origin has not been indefinite. – he is not a deity, his end (under present form) will come, (or how dreadfully we are deceived) then he is no exception. – He possesses some of the same general instincts all & feelings as animals. They on the other hand can reason – but man has reasoning powers in excess, instead of definite instincts – this is a replacement in mental machinery, so analogous to what we see in bodily, that it does not stagger me. –

The enthusiastic tone of the preceding passage may have turned to irony a few weeks later (*Transmutation Notebook C*:, p. 166): "Thought (or desires more properly) being hereditary it is difficult to imagine it anything but structure of brain hereditary, analogy points out to this. – Love of the deity effect of organization, oh you materialist! – Read Barclay on organization!!" In spite of the exclamation points, the pages of Darwin's copy of Barclay (1822) remained uncut.

The subject of materialism was not one which Darwin took lightly. In his *Metaphysical Notebook M*, he proposed a strategy to himself for dealing with the touchy subject (p. 57): "To avoid stating how far, I believe, in Materialism, say only that emotions, instincts degrees of talent, which are hereditary are so because brain of child resembles parent stock. – (& phrenologists state that brain alters)," the text trailed off. June Goodfield (1969), points out that the early nineteenth century was a time of "great debate over physiological method and physiological explanation," and that this debate was "closely tied in" with current disputes in philosophy, theology, and politics.

2. Maurice Mandelbaum (1971), discusses metaphysical idealism, positivism, and materialism as major philosophic currents in the nineteenth century (pp. 6–28, p. 22).

3. *Transmutation Notebook C*, p. 267, and *Metaphysical Notebook M*, p. 155. James Ferrier, (1838a), (1838b), (1839). See Robert Brown's (1970) brief discussion of Ferrier, pp. 447–449.

4. James Ferrier (1838a) pp. 437–439, note, and 450.

5. Ferrier (1838a), p. 198. Ferrier quoted T. Brown in his note on p. 194: "That which perceives is a part of nature as truly as the objects of perception which act on it, and as a part of nature is itself an object of investigation purely physical. It is known to us only in the successive changes which constitute the variety of our feelings; but the regular sequences of these changes admit of being traced, like the regularity which we are capable of discovering in the successive organic changes of our bodily frame."

6. Ferrier (1838a), pp. 784–786; (1838b), pp. 239–243.

7. Barclay (1833), p. 31. For Barclay's views on the distinction of the "living internal principle" and "organic structure," see pp. 103–413 of his *Inquiry*.

8. *Ibid.*, pp. 487–489, citing Cudworth's *Intellectual System*, 139–172.

9. John Abercrombie (1838), p. 218. Darwin's copy, extensively annotated, is in the Cambridge University Library. Abercrombie's basic views on causality and materialism are set forth in the first thirty four pages. Darwin also wrote extensively in the margins of Abercrombie's discussion of determinism, pp. 197–205.

10. John Fleming (1922), vol. 1. pp. 214–215. "Of the essence of mind we absolutely know nothing; and hence the various phrases, Unity, Indivisibility, Immateriality, and others, which have been employed to express the nature of this essence, are, in fact, expressions of our own ignorance and presumption. When we witness the mind capable of exciting action in matter, and of being excited to action by matter, – exhibiting its identity by its local residence – variable in its relations to matter, – variable relatively to its own conditions, capable of exercising different functions at the same time, and, last of all multiplying with an increases of population, we feel overwhelmed with the

incomprehensible phenomena which it presents, and admit the suitableness of an expression of our Divine Master, when applied to the present case, "Ye know not what manner of spirit ye are of."

Darwin's annotated copy of Fleming's book is in the Cambridge University Library.

11.   Fleming (1822), pp. 242–272.

12.   Fleming, *op. cit.*, pp. 4–20. For the distinction of "descriptive and "explanatory" vitalism and mechanism, see June Goodfield (1960).

13.   Charles Darwin, "Old and Useless Notes on Metaphysics," Barrett ed., pp. 382–383. "In Athenaeum. Smart Beginning of a New School Metaphysics, – give my doctrines about origin of language – & effect of reason. Reason could not have existed without it – quotes Ld Monboddo language commenced in whole sentences. – signs –? were signs originally musical !!!?? – At least it appear all speculations of the origin of language. – must presume it originates slowly – if they have, then language was progressive. – We cannot doubt that language is an altering element, we see words invented – we see their origin in names of People. – sounds of words – argument of original formation – declension etc. often show traces of origin –"

14.   Smart (1839), 2nd Essay, p. 184.

15.   Smart (1839), 3rd Essay, pp. 456 and 504. Smart's claim that all existence claims were to be assessed by a single method, that of physics, amounted to no more than a reaffirmation of the classic distinction of physics, logic, and ethics. It was not based on an analysis of nineteenth century science, and had no reductionist implications. On the other hand, it was clearly antimetaphysical in intent; see page 499. Smart's discussion of theological language continued to p. 515.

16.   Thomas Rennell (1819). Lawrence lost the copyright to his lecture as a result of an action brought under a Star Chamber Act of 1637, and reaffirmed by Lord Eldon in the 1820's, that "where there was blasphemy, sedition, or immorality, there was no property." Goodfield, (1969), p. 307.

17.   David Thompson (1950).

18.   William Lawrence (1816, 1819) pp. 15–16.

19.   *Ibid.*, pp. 95–96.

20.   *Ibid.*, p. 105. "Shall I be told that thought is inconsistent with matter; that we cannot conceive how medullary substance can perceive, remember, judge, reason? I acknowledge that we are entirely ignorant how the parts of the brain accomplish these purposes – as we are how the liver secretes bile, how the muscles contract, or how any other living purpose is effected – as we are how heavy bodies are attracted to the earth, how iron is drawn to the magnet, or how two salts decompose each other. Experience is in all these cases our sole, if not sufficient instructress; and the constant conjunction of phenomena, as exhibited in her lessons, is the sole ground for affirming a necessary connexion between them. If we go beyond this, and come to inquire the manner how, the mechanism by which these things are effected, we shall find everything around us equally mysterious, equally incomprehensible: – from the stone which falls to the earth, to the comet traversing the heavens. . . ."

21.   *Ibid.* (1816), pp. 160–161. "The science of organized bodies should therefore be treated in a manner entirely different from those, which have inorganic matter for their object. We should employ a different language, since words transposed from the physical sciences to the animal and vegetable economy, constantly recall to us ideas of an order altogether different from those which are . . . treated in chemistry, mechanics, and other

physical sciences: the reference therefore to gravity, to attraction, to chemical affinity, to electricity or galvanism, can only serve to perpetuate false notions in physiology, and to draw us away from the proper point of view, in which the nature of living phenomena and the properties of living beings ought to be contemplated. We might just as rationally introduce the language of physiology into physical science; explain the facts of chemistry by irritability, or employ sensibility and sympathy to account for the phenomena of electricity and magnetism, or for the motions of the planetary system." The second of the two lectures in Lawrence's *Introduction of 1816* was "On Life."

22. Charles Darwin, "Old & Useless Notes on Metaphysics," #36. Barrett edition, p. 394n.

23. Rev. William Kirby (1835), Introduction, vol. I, xxxi.

24. All of Darwin's explicit manuscript references to Lamarck are to the latter's *Philosophie Zoologique*, 2 vols. (1830). He possessed and annotated only the first of the two volumes, but the Notebooks allude to the second as well (*C*, p. 269).

Quotations are from the translation by Hugh Elliot, *Zoological Philosophy*, by J. B. Lamarck, Hafner, 1963 (1st published by Macmillan, 1914).

Lamarck quoted Naigeon, "every idea must in the last analysis be resolved into an image perceived...all that issues from it (i.e., the understanding) and can find no perceptible object to fasten upon is absolutely chimerical," with approval.

"To set up a reasonable opposition to the views stated above, it would be necessary to show that the harmony existing throughout the nervous system is not capable of producing sensations and the individual's inner feeling; that intellectual acts, such as thoughts, judgments, etc., are not physical acts, and do not result immediately from relations between a subtle agitated fluid and the special organ containing it; lastly that the results of these relations are not transmitted to the individual's inner feeling. Now the physical causes named above are the only ones that can possibly give rise to the phenomena of intelligence. If therefore the existence of these causes is denied, and if consequently it is denied that the resulting phenomena are natural, it will then be necessary to seek another source of these phenomena outside nature. It will be necessary to substitute for the physical causes rejected, fantastic ideas of our own imagination, ideas that are always baseless since it is quite obvious that we can have no other positive knowledge than that derived from the actual objects which nature presents to our senses," (Elliot trans., p. 365).

25. *Ibid.*, pp. 191–194, 260. In dealing with the label, 'radical, positivist, materialist,' which has been applied to Lamarck by John Greene (1959, pp. 158, 351), it is important to remember that Lamarck did not characterize his own position as 'materialistic,' and that it was neither monistic nor reductionist in form. Greene's label suggests that Lamarck was a reductionist and that he was required to generate the progressive series of organic forms with no more than a "law bound system of matter in motion" at his disposal. Thus Greene sees Lamarck's allusions to the "law" that nature proceeds from the most imperfect to the most perfect forms of vital organization as an inconsistent escape into "semi-purposive" psychologism. On the other hand Gillispie (1959) sees Lamarck as sacrificing all the reality and objectivity of the taxonomic hierarchy in an attempt to capture the dynamic aspect of life's history.

26. *Ibid.*, p. 217. For the identification of caloric and the animating force, p. 195, 217, 205–206; for the distinction of plants and insensate animals, pp. 97–104; for the vague upper boundary of sensate animals (as distinct from those which might be called

intelligent), p. 93.
27. *Ibid.*, p. 227.
28. *Ibid.*, pp. 335, 347.

CHAPTER FIVE

1. Leslie Stephen (1876, 1927 reprint), vol. 1, pp. 404—420.
2. William Paley (1794).
3. Charles Darwin. *Autobiography* (N. Barlow, ed., 1958), p. 59. Although Darwin's autobiographical reflection upon his religious odyssey attributes "the old argument of design in nature" to Paley (p. 87), I know of no evidence that he reread Paley after his undergraduate days. The Cambridge University Manuscript Collection contains (CD mss. folio 91, number 114) brief handwritten notes on Paley that appear to have been written during Darwin's student days. Darwin did, of course, read other books on natural theology – e.g., by Whewell, Kirby, Lord Brougham, and J. Macculloch, M.D. – during the years between 1837 and 1839.
4. William Paley (1794), vol. I, pp. 4—11.
5. Charles Darwin. Cambridge University Manuscript Collection. #91, 114.
6. William. Paley (1802), p. 90.
7. Paley (1802), pp. 82, 180, 252. Leslie Stephen, *op. cit.*, p. 409, note 1, identified possible sources for the illustration of the watch as Paley used it.
8. Paley, (1802), pp. 169, 172. Paley was also impressed by the "prospective contrivances" exhibited in embryological development, where such organs as teeth, eyes, and lungs developed at a tempo corresponding to their functional utility. The *foramen ovale* and the *ductus arteriosus*, advantageous for the embryo, *atrophied* at birth. Paley thought the match between male and female sexual organs was so completely inexplicable without the concept of design that "were every other proof of contrivance in nature dubious or obscure, this alone would be sufficient," p. 185.
9. Paley (1802), p. 145. Stephen (1876), vol. 1., p. 411.
10. Paley (1794), vol. II, p. 343; and (1802), p. 3: "It is not necessary that a machine be perfect, in order to show with what design it was made: still less necessary, where the only question is, whether it were made with any design at all."
11. Paley (1802), pp. 236—237.
12. *Ibid.*, p. 27.
13. *Ibid.*, p. 304.
14. *Transmutation Notebook C*, pp. 76—78. See Chapter 4, note #1.
15. Thomas Malthus (1798), p. 201.
16. *Ibid.*, p. 205.
17. Paley (1802), p. 326.
18. *Ibid.*, p. 352.
19. Malthus (1798), p. 143.
20. Paley (1802), pp. 344—345.
21. Malthus (1798), pp. 207, 210.
22. Paley (1802), pp. 353, 361.
23. Sandra Herbert (1971, 1968); Peter J. Vorzimmer (1969); Robert M. Young (1969, 1971); Gertrude Himmelfarb (1959, 1968); J. D. Bernal (1965), vol. 2, p. 662, and vol.

4, p. 1233; Joseph Ben-David (1971), p. 11.

24. "Charles Darwin to A. R. Wallace, Down, April 6th, 1859," in Francis Darwin, ed. (1903), vol. I, p. 118.

25. Nora Barlow, ed. (1958), p. 120.

26. de Beer, et. al., eds. (1967), pp. 162–163 (pages 134–135 of D). The text quoted is that which Vorzimmer (1969) attributes to the corrections of the published transcript by Dr. Sidney Smith of St. Catharine's College, Cambridge.

27. S. Herbert (1971), pp. 212–213.

28. C. Lyell (1835), 4th edition, vol. II, p. 391.

29. Herbert (1971), p. 216.

30. T. Malthus (1826), vol. 1, pencilled annotations on blank pages at rear of volume. The complete set of listed pages was as follows: 3, 23, 29, 41, 81, 343, 499, 517, 519. Darwin's personal copy of volume 2 was left uncut. His autograph in volume 1 is dated, "April, 1841."

31. T. Doubleday (1842), p. 7, cited in W. Petersen (1969), p. 157.

32. Malthus (1826), vol. 1, p. 343.

33. Transmutation Notebook D, pp. 134–135, and "Essay on Theology and Natural Selection," P. Barrett, ed. (1974), p. 419.

34. J. R. Poynter (1969), pp. 109, 325–326.

35. Vorzimmer (1969), p. 538.

36. Herbert (1971), p. 217.

37. Himmelfarb (1959), p. 160.

38. Bernal (1965), vol. 2, p. 662, vol. 4, p. 1233.

39. For general discussion of the interaction of science and the social and political conditions of scientific activity see D. Crane (1972), J. Ben-David (1971), S. Toulmin (1972), pp. 200–319, and N. Mullins (1973).

40. T. Kuhn (1970), p. 177; Toulmin (1972), pp. 484–503.

41. Malthus (1798), pp. 97–101.

42. See A. Macintyre (1966), pp. 157–177, for a review of eighteenth century British arguments on the basis of ethics. Also see the discussion of J. Mackintosh (1837), to follow below.

43. Malthus (1830), Flew, ed., pp. 223–224.

44. Malthus (1798), Flew, ed., pp. 206–207.

45. "Essay of 1844," de Beer, ed. (1958), pp. 116–121.

46. Metaphysical Notebook, N, p. 47.

47. Transmutation Notebook, E, p. 97: "Considering the Kingdom of nature as it now is, it would not be possible to simplify the organization of the different beings (all fishes to the state of the Ammocoetus, Crustacea to – ? &c) without reducing the number of living beings – but there is the strongest possible [erasure, leaving a blank, E.M.] to increase them, hence the degree of development is either stationary or more probably increases. –"

48. "Old and Useless Notes on Metaphysics," Barrett, ed. (1974), p. 398.

49. Charles Darwin's Natural Selection, R. C. Stauffer, ed. (1975), pp. 172–173, 186–188.

50. For Darwin's anthropomorphism, see especially Metaphysical Notebook N, p. 49: "Arguing from man to animals is philosophical, viz. (man is not a cause like a deity as N. Cousin says), because if so orangoutang, – oyster & zoophyte; it is (I presume, see

p. 188 of Herschel's Treatise) a "travelling instance" a "frontier instance" – for it can be shown that the life and will of a conferva is not an antagonist quality to life and mind of man. – & we do not suppose an hydatid to be a cause of itself – (by my theory no animal as now existing can be cause of itself.) & hence there is great probability against free action. – on my view of free will, no one could discover he had not it. –"
51. *Metaphysical Notebook M*, p. 151.

CHAPTER SIX

1. Charles Darwin, *Sketch of 1842*, de Beer edition (1958), p. 86. Basil Willey's (1940, pp. 136–154), account of Hartley is an extremely useful analysis of the eighteenth century uses of this idea.
2. Charles Darwin, "Commentary on Macculloch," Barrett edition, pp. 417–418.
3. *Notebook M*, pp. 103–104. W. B. Huntley (1972), did not succeed in clarifying the meaning of this passage, see his attempt at p. 468. At p. 155 of *Notebook M*, Darwin mentions "Hume's essay on the Human Understanding well worth reading" in a fashion which raises the possibility that he had not yet read it when he wrote the passage cited at pp. 103–104.
4. *Metaphysical Notebook N*, p. 101.
5. Side 52 of the "Old and Useless Notes. . . . ," see Barrett edition (1974), p. 403.
6. Huntley (1972), p. 470.
7. Charles Darwin, *Essay of 1844*, de Beer edition, p. 250. Quoted by Huntley, *op. cit.*, p. 464.
8. David Hume, (1779).
9. Norah Barlow, ed. (1958), pp. 138–139; pp. 84–85.
10. *Ibid.*, pp. 85–96; particularly 92–93: "Another source of conviction in the existence of God, connected with the reason and not with the feelings, impresses me as having much more weight. This follows from the extreme difficulty or rather impossibility of conceiving this immense and wonderful universe, including man with his capacity of looking far backwards and far into futurity, as the result of blind chance or necessity. When thus reflecting I feel compelled to look to a First Cause having an intelligent mind in some degree analogous to that of man; and I deserve to be called a Theist."
11. *Ibid.*, p. 85; "About this time (1837–1839) I took much delight in Wordsworth's and Coleridge's poetry, and can boast that I read the *Excursion* twice through. Formerly Milton's *Paradise Lost* had been my chief favourite, and in my excursions during the voyage of the Beagle, when I could take only a small volume, I always chose Milton'" For Wordsworth's impact on the nineteenth century, see L. Stephen (1876), vol. 2, p. 452; also A. O. J. Cockshut, pp. 9–15.
12. William Wordsworth (1814), *The Excursion*, Book VIII, lines 15–20.
13. *Ibid.*, Book VI, line 979.
14. *Ibid.*, Book VIII, line 184.
15. *Ibid.*, Book VI, line 1186.
16. *Ibid.*, Book V, line 905.
17. *Ibid.*, Book V, line 1013.
18. *Ibid.*, Book V, line 465.
19. *Ibid.*, Book IX, line 470.

20. *Ibid.*, Book V, lines 560–570.
21. *Ibid.*, Book VIII, lines 200–205.
22. *Ibid.*, Book IV, lines 1250–1270.
23. *Ibid.*, Book IV, line 330 (citing *The Book of Daniel*).
24. *Ibid.*, Book I, lines 185–195.
25. *Ibid.*, Books III and IV (titles).
26. *Ibid.*, Book VII, lines 1000–1005.
27. *Ibid.*, Book IV, line 1205.
28. Cockshut (1964), pp. 9–15.
29. For the view that science makes contact with the life-world only through technological extensions of theory, see Jurgen Habermas (1971), pp. 50–53.
30. Charles Darwin, *Metaphysical Notebook M*, pp. 39–41.
31. Basil Willey (1940), p. 137. "As we have seen, there existed in the eighteenth century a widespread desire to equate the moral with the physical world: to see in it an order comparable with the order of Nature. Newton's principle of gravitation had bound together all physical bodies into a harmonious unity; could not some principle be found which should unite moral phenomena into an analogous synthesis? Sometimes it seemed that the principle of self-love was the true moral counterpart of gravitation; sometimes, that it was the principle of universal benevolence. . . . The most important of these varieties of moral gravitation was the principle of the Association of Ideas." Darwin's brother-in-law, Hensleigh Wedgwood had married Mackintosh's daughter, Fanny; Charles Darwin's first meeting with Sir James Mackintosh had been at the Wedgwood estate, Maer, in 1827 (*Autobiography*, p. 55). Darwin composed his reflections on Mackintosh while staying at Maer in May of 1839, annotating a personal copy which is now with other books from his library at the University Library, Cambridge University. Sir James Mackintosh (1837).
32. William Whewell, "Preface," to Mackintosh, (1837), pp. 40–41. See Darwin's *Autobiography*, p. 66.
33. Mackintosh (1837), pp. 193, 196.
34. *Ibid.*, pp. 249–250.
35. *Ibid.*, pp. 368–369; 390–331.
36. *Ibid.*, p. 354.
37. *Ibid.*, p. 366. Alasdair McIntyre (1966), pp. 166–167, provides a critique of Butler's individualism.
38. Mackintosh, (1837), p. 202.
39. *Ibid.*, p. 377.
40. *Ibid.*, p. 383.
41. Charles Darwin, marginal comment on Mackintosh's *Dissertation*, p. 41.
42. Mackintosh (1837), p. 202. Also see A. McIntyre(1966), p. 166.
43. Charles Darwin, marginal comment on Mackintosh's *Dissertation*, p. 194.
44. Mackintosh (1837), p. 198.
45. *Ibid.*, pp. 200, 201, 202.
46. *Ibid.*, pp. 393–395. "It is the nature of an emotion to withdraw the mind from the contemplation of every idea but that of the object which excites it. . . . The emotions and desires which compose conscience, while they occupy the mind, must exclude all contemplation of the cause in which the object of these feelings may have originated. To their eye the voluntary dispositions and actions, their sole object, must appear to be the first link of a chain."

PART II INTRODUCTION

1. Berger, P. and Luckmann, T. (1967), pp. 92–128; Habermas (1971), pp. 50–61, and (1972); Burrows (1970), pp. ix–23; and Young (1969, 1970, 1971a, 1971b).

CHAPTER SEVEN

1. R. B. Freeman and P. J. Gautrey (1969). The reference to selection was on the inside cover of *Notebook D*.
2. *Transmutation Notebook E*, p. 128.
3. *Sketch of 1842*, de Beer ed. (1958), p. 86; also see *Transmutation Notebook C*, p. 138; *Transmutation Notebook C*, pp. 139–141; *Transmutation Notebook B*, pp. 22–26, 36–37; *Transmutation Notebook C*, p. 154; and *Transmutation Notebook D*, pp. 58–59.
4. "Old and Useless Notes...," #19, #20, Barrett (1974), pp. 387–388.
5. See Chapter 3, note #2.
6. *Transmutation Notebook E*, pp. 53–55.
7. Comte (1853), Martineau trans., vol. I, p. 22.
8. *Essay of 1844*, de Beer ed. (1958), p. 252.
9. Herschel (1831), pp. 178–179.
10. *Transmutation Notebook E*, p. 51.
11. *Variation in Animals and Plants*, Vol. I, pp. 8–9.
12. *Transmutation Notebook B*, p. 14.
13. *Ibid.*, p. 101; pp. 227–228.
14. *Origin*, V. 5.
15. *Variation*, II, 431.
16. *Variation*, II, p. 253.
17. Charles Darwin, *The Descent of Man*. 2nd ed., revised and augmented, (London 1879), p. 613. Hereafter cited as *Descent*.
18. *Origin*. VI: 234–236. 1. f.
19. *Origin*. XIV. 124, p. 738; Charles Darwin. *The Various Contrivances by which Orchids are Fertilised by Insects*. 2nd ed., revised. New York, 1892. p. 277, pp. 284 286. Hereafter cited as *Orchids* also see *Descent*, 141.
20. *Descent*, 177–178; *Origin*, f XI. 21–24e, p. 523; *ibid.*, I. 9: 4–5e & 9–12e, pp. 78–79; *ibid.*, IV 9. c., p. 164.
21. *Descent*, 24, and note. Also see the "Essay of 1844," in *Evolution by Natural Selection*, de Beer, ed. Cambridge, 1958, pp. 208–209. "The homological construction of the whole frame in the members of the same class is intelligible if we admit their descent from a common progenitor, together with their subsequent adaptation to diversified conditions. On any other view, the similarity of pattern between the hand of man or monkey, the foot of a horse, the flipper of a seal, the wing of a bat, &c., is utterly inexplicable. It is no scientific explanation to assert that they have all been formed on the same ideal plan."
22. *Transmutation Notebook B*, pp. 40–43.
23. *Ibid.*, p. 148.
24. *Transmutation Notebook C*, p. 100.

25. *Transmutation Notebook B*, 55e.

26. *Ibid.*, p. 221.

27. *Notebook B*, p. 73, "Whether species may not be made by a little more vigour being given to the chance offspring who have any slight peculiarity of structure. Hence seals take victorious seals. Hence deer victorious deer, hence male armed & pugnacious. All orders cocks all warlike." *Notebook C*, p. 61, "Study the wars of organic being. The fact of guavas having overrun tahiti, thistle pampas show how nicely things adapted then aberrant varieties will be formed in any kingdom of nature, where scheme not filled up. Most false to say no passages Nature is full of them. Wading birds partially webbed &c., &c., & in round of chances every family will have some aberrant groups. But as for number five in each group absurd."

28. *Transmutation Notebook E*, p. 26.

29. J. F. W. Herschel (1850).

30. Comte (1853), H. Martineau trans., vol. II, p. 121. Jacques Monod (1971), pp. 110–117, claims that molecular biology has finally (since 1953) succeeded in providing a conclusive scientific argument assuring the place of Darwin's concept of chance in any warranted theory of organic evolution.

31. Herschel (1831), p. 37.

32. D. Brewster (1838), p. 280.

33. *The Origin*. IV: 14.8c. "So again it is difficult to avoid personifying the word Nature; but I mean by Nature, only the aggregate action and product of many natural laws, and by laws the sequence of events as ascertained by us." Darwin made extensive use of the "if . . . then . . ." schema in summarizing part one of both the *Sketch of 1842* and the *Essay of 1844*, de Beer, ed. (1958), pp. 57, 133–134.

34. *Notebook D*, p. 67.

35. Darwin manuscripts, #91:39–41. I am particularly indebted to Paul Barrett and to Sydney Smith for consultation in the identification of this manuscript.

36. Herschel (1831), p. 35. See Darwin's reference, dated Jan. 21, 1839, at *Notebook N*, p. 60.

37. Comte had condemned the career of the "fanciful mathematical theory of chances," from its inception, which he attributed to James Bernoulli, to its use by both Condorcet and Laplace, as equivalent to "offering our own ignorance as the natural measure of the degree of probability of our various opinions." Martineau trans. (1853), vol. 2, pp. 120–121.

38. Charles Darwin, "Old and Useless Notes on Metaphysics," Item 41, side 6 (Barrett ed., p. 398).

39. Charles Darwin, "Old and Useless Notes on Metaphysics," Item 33 (Barrett ed., p. 391). "Westminster Review. March 1840. p. 267 – says the great division among metaphysicians – the school of Locke, Bentham & Hartley, & the school of Kant & Coleridge is regarding the sources of knowledge – whether "anything can be the object of our knowledge except our experience" – is this not almost a question whether we have any instincts, or rather the amount of our instincts – surely in animals according to usual definition, there is much knowledge without experience. So there *may* be in men – which the reviewer seems to doubt." The *Wellesley Index of Victorian Periodicals* does not identify reviewers for the Westminster. Darwin referred to a review of seven of Coleridge's works in the *London and Westminster Review*, no. 65, for March, 1840, pp. 257–302. The author of this review may have been John Stuart Mill. If so, this was

Darwin's only citation of J. S. Mill before 1844. There is no indication the two men met during this interval.

CHAPTER EIGHT

1. "People often talk of the wonderful event of intellectual man appearing. the appearance of insects with other senses is more wonderful. it's (*sic*) mind more different probably & introduction of man nothing compared to the first thinking being. although hard to draw line. not so great as between perfect insects and forms hard to tell whether articulate or inarticulate, or even a mite. − A bee compared with cheese mite − with its wonderful instincts. The difference is that there is a wide gap between man and next animals in mind, more than in structure." *Transmutation Notebook B*, pp. 207−208.

2. C. Darwin, *Transmutation Notebook C*, pp. 76−78.

3. *Ibid.*, p. 154.

4. *Metaphysical Notebook M*, p. 151.

5. *Metaphysical Notebook N*, p. 49.

6. Charles Darwin, Manuscript Folio #91, sides 25−28. University Library, Cambridge University. See Barrett (1974), pp. 388−390.

"September 6th 1838.
    Every action whatever is the effect of a motive.[x]

p. 1

[Must be so, analyse[a] ones feelings when wagging ones finger − one feels it in passion, love −́ jealousy − as effect of bodily organism − one knows it, when one wishes to do some actions (as jump off a bridge to save another & yet dare not one could do it, but other motives prevent the action. See Abercrombie conclusive remarks p. 205 & 206.]

Motives are units in the Universe.

[Effect of hereditary constitution, − education under the influence of [others] varied capability of receiving impressions − accidental (so called like chance circumstances. As man hearing bible for first time, & great effect being produced. − the wax was soft, − the condition of mind which leads to motion being inclined that way] one sees this law in man in somnambulism or insanity. free will (as generally used) is not then present, but he acts from motives, nearly as usual//
difference is from imperfect condition of mind all motives do not come into p. 2
play. −

It may be urged how often one try to persuade person to change line of conduct, as being better & making him happier. − he agrees & yet does not. − because motive power not in proper state. − When the admonition succeeds who does not recognize an accidental spark falling on prepared materials.

From contingencies a man's character may change − because motive power changes with organization.

The general delusion about free will obvious. − because man has power of action, & he can seldom analyse his motives (originally mostly *instinctive*, & therefore now greater effort of reason to discover them: this is important explanation) he thinks they have none –

Effects. – One must view a wicked man like a sickly one[p] – We cannot help loathing a diseased offensive object, so we view wickedness. – It would however be more proper to pity than to hate & be//
disgusted with them. Yet it is right to punish criminals; but solely to *deter* others. – It is not more strange that there should be necessary wickedness than disease.

This view will not do harm, because no one can be really *fully* convinced of its truth, except man who has thought very much & he will know his happiness lays in doing good & being perfect, & therefore will not be tempted, from knowing everything he does is independent of himself to do harm. –

Believer in these views will pay great attention to Education –

p. 4

These views are directly opposed & inexplicable if we suppose that the sins of a man are, under his control, & that a future life is a reward or retribution. – it may be a consequence but nothing further. –

Footnotes: x, a, and p, were all written overleaf of page 1.

[x]A man may put himself in the way of contingencies. – but his desire to do arises from motives. – & his knowledge that it is good for him effect of education & mental capabilities. –

[a]One well feels how many actions are not determined by what is called free will, but by strong invariable passions – when these passions weak, opposed & complicated one calls them free will – the chance of mechanical phenomena. – (mem: M. Le Comte one of philosophy, & savage calling laws of nature chance)

[p]Animals do attack the weak & sickly as we do the wicked. – we ought to pity and assist & educate by putting contingencies in the way to aid motive power – if incorrigibly bad nothing will cure him.

7. Darwin's personal copy of John Abercrombie, M.D. (1838), is in the University Library, Cambridge University. Pages 202–203, deal with psychological determinism and are extensively annotated.

8. Charles Darwin, *Metaphysical Notebook M*, pp. 27, 31.

9. Discussions of chance occured in *Transmutation Notebook B*, pp. 40–44, 55, 146–148, 221, *Notebook C*, pp. 61, 268; *Notebook D*, p. 152.

10. Allusions to Comte occurred on pp. 70 and 72, *Metaphysical Notebook M*.

11. Abercrombie (1838), p. 10.

12. *Transmutation Notebook C*, p. 166; and *Metaphysical Notebook N*, p. 44. *Notebook N*, p. 44 had been excised by Darwin; Paul Barrett has recovered it and published it in place with his edition of *Notebook N*.

13. *Transmutation Notebook C*, p. 166.

14. *Metaphysical Notebook M*, p. 57.

15. *Metaphysical Notebook M*, p. 61 (excised; relocated and published by Paul Barrett (1974), pp. 276–277.

At almost this same time, Darwin read either Comte's *Cours de Philosophie Positive* (first two volumes) or the review of Comte which appeared in the *Edinburgh Review* for

July, 1838. The review acquainted Darwin with the positivist move for undercutting the argument between the dualists and the materialists. Abercrombie's mystifying references to the substratum or ultimate essence of the principles of vegetable life, animal life, and matter, might have sufficed to lead Darwin to question the significance of extra-scientific comments on the nature of life. Comte's account of the three stages provided some philosophical authority (the reviewer compared Comte's work quite favorably to Whewell's then recent *History of the Inductive Sciences*) for the conclusion that there simply was no knowledge to be gained beyond the determination of the "close relation of kind of thought and structure of brain." Hensleigh Wedgwood had completely failed to convince him that consciousness could plausibly be divided into a subjective, internal aspect and an objective aspect involving the senses. Instead, Darwin's own boundless interest in the discovery of scientific laws, now supported by his reading of both Herschel and Comte, was extended to the confident assumption that positive science could solve the mind-body problem by formulating the laws which corelate brain states and mental states. These laws, just as all the other "laws of life," could only adequately be formulated in a theoretical context which included the laws of specific change. "To study metaphysic as they have always been studied appears to me to be like puzzling at astronomy without mechanics. – Experience shows the problem of the mind cannot be solved by attacking the citadel itself. The mind is function of body – we must bring some stable foundation to argue from." *Metaphysical Notebook N*, p. 5.

"I suspect the endless (source) round of doubt and scepticism might be solved by considering the origin of reason as gradually developed. See Hume on Sceptical Philosophy." *Metaphysical Notebook N*, p. 101.

16. This manuscript had neither title, date, nor any indication of authorship. The manuscript was written out in ink by someone other than Darwin, but there were interlineal and marginal comments – mostly in pencil – written in by Darwin himself. The author of the manuscript on which Darwin commented was his brother-in-law, Hensleigh Wedgwood. Darwin manuscript folio #91; sides 39–41. University Library, Cambridge University. See Chapter One, note #31.

C. DARWIN

H. WEDGWOOD

Why may it not be said thought perceptions will, consciousness, memory, etc. have the same relation to a living body (especially the cerebral portion of it) that attraction has to ordinary matter.

The relation of attraction to ordinary matter is that which an action bears to the agent. Matter is by a metaphor said to attract; & hence if thought, etc. bore the same relation to the brain that attraction does to matter, it might with

[living]
Well the heart is said to feel

equal propriety be said that the [   ] brain perceived.

Now this would certainly be a startling expression, & so foreign to the use of ordinary language

NOTES — page 221

C. DARWIN / **H. WEDGWOOD**

that the onus probandi might fairly be laid with those who would support the propriety of the expression. They would do well to ask themselves the converse [ ] of the question above stated, & indeed until we know what answer they would give in support of their view it is impossible to show satisfactory its erroneousness.

[because there are living bodies without these faculties]

In the absence of such a guide we can only point out the mode of perceptive action by which we come to conceive of matter as attracting & show that the new groundwork is entirely wanting by which thought or memory might be in like manner attributed to the brain.

it is point of indifference.

There are two modes of perceptive action by which bodily action is made known to us, revealing respectively what are called its subjective & objective aspect.

The subjective aspect of bodily action is revealed to us by the effort it costs to exert force or by internal consciousness; the objective, by our external [ ] senses in the way in which we apprehend the force of inanimate bodies. How we identify the two aspects as different phases of the same object of thought is a question which ought to be clearly comprehended by anyone who wishes to fully understand this subject, but the answer to it would require a considerable degree of attention.

[what]
How do the senses affect us except by internal consciousness.

As recognized by our external senses
i.e. movement?

We must endeavour to do without it as well as we can. The objective-aspect of (sic) Bodily action // consists in the manifestation of force // capable of being traced to the body of the individual to whom the action is attributed: force (be it remembered) being a phenomenon apprehended by the same faculty with matter & being necessarily exhibited in & by matter.

[Underlining and lining out is by Darwin.]
By our external senses

The phenomena of gravity considered in themselves consist in a force manifested in every particle of matter directed towards every other particle; but *force* (objectively (sic) considered), // is a phenomenon the essence of whose existence consists in its communication to other matter in the course of its *direction*, & thus when

C. DARWIN

How can force be recognized by our external senses – only movement can.

as known by the exertion of our own power & consciousness of it

?

?

Attraction of sulphuric acid for metal.

??We do not know attraction objectively

H. WEDGWOOD

we apprehend force in inanimate matter we feel dissatisfied until we can point out the source from which it arises.

But coming round to the subjective aspect of action // we are conscious that we ourselves can originate in any point an opposition of forces balancing each other & moving in opposite direction. We are satisfied therefore if we can trace any force in inanimate matter up to the action of some animated agent. Now the phenomena of gravity are manifestly the same as if every particle of matter were an animated being pulling every other particle by invisible strings & as on this supposition the forces manifested would be fundamentally accounted for, we prefer this metaphorical mode of stating the fact to the mere statement of the ~~force exhibited - in - every-~~ (sic) phenomena actually apprehensible by sense.

There is nothing analogous to this in the relation of thought, perception, memory, etc. either to our bodily frame or the cerebral portion of it.

Thoughts, perceptions, etc., are modes of subjective action – they are known only by internal consciousness & have no objective aspect. If thought bore the same relation to the brain that force does to the bodily frame, they could be perceived by the faculty by which the brain is perceived but they are known by courses of action quite independent of each other. A person might be quite familiar with thought & yet be ignorant of the existence of the brain. We cannot perceive the thought of another person at all, we can only infer it from its behavior.

Thought is only known subjectively // the brain only objectively.

The reason why thought etc. should imply the existence of something in addition to matter is because our knowledge of matter is quite insufficient to account for the phenomena of thought. The objects of thought have no reference to place.

C. DARWIN

We see a particle move one to another, & (or conceive it) that is all we know of attraction. but we
cannot see an atom think: they are as incongrous
as blue & weight: all that can be said that thought
& organization run in a parallel series, if blueness &
weight always went together, & as things grew bluer
it /uniquely/ grew heavier yet it could not be said
that the blueness caused the weight, anymore than
weight the blueness, still less between things so
different as action thought organization: But if the
weight never came until the blueness had a certain
intensity (& the experiment was varied then might
it now be said, that blueness caused weight, because both due to some common cause: − the
argument reduced itself to what is cause & effect:
it merely is /invariable/ priority of one to other: no
not only thus, for if day was first, we should not
think night an effect. //Cause and effect has relation to forces & mentally because effort is felt//

Darwin's annotations of the Wedgwood manuscript should be compared with his marginal comments in Abercrombie's *Inquiries*, pp. 27–34.

DARWIN	ABERCROMBIE
p. 27	p. 27
functions of the nervous system, as gravitation of matter	*The former* (matter) *we know only by our senses, the latter* (mind) *only by our consciousness.* In regard to their essence or occult qualities, we know quite as little about matter as we do about mind . . . no ground for believing that they have anything in common.
	Does the materialist tell us that the principle which thinks is material or the result of organi- zation, we have only to ask him what light he expects to throw upon the subject by such an assertion. For the principle which thinks is known
& by their laws, such as of gravity, of crystalline arrangement arrange- ment of particles	to us only by thinking and the substances which are solid and extended are known to us only by their solidity and extension.
p. 29	p. 29
?? will my theory apply here? By materialism, I mean merely the intimate connection of kind of	Facts . . . accord equally with the supposition that the brain is the organ of communication between the mind and the external world. When

DARWIN   ABERCROMBIE

thought with form of brain – like   the materialist advances a single step beyond this,
kind of attraction with nature of   he plunges at once into conclusions which are
element   entirely gratuitous and unwarranted.

Generation!   (There is) a broad and obvious distinction be-
Here organ produces life!   tween phenomena of mind and functions of
& life & thought intimately re-   bodily organization.
lated.
Elective Affinity is a thing not
analogous to other qualities of
bodies, yet is supposed property
of matter, so would I say thought
was – from analogy of organ. –

p. 31
From the myriads of animals that
have existed we may assume
thought as function of matter, &
then say to what function of
matter, shall we compare the
phenomena of attraction? This
assumption is as justifiable as the
other
We only know thought as a
phenomenon attendant on structure, and we only know electric
attraction as function of matter.

But why should not matter have   To what function of matter shall he like that
function, as plain facts indicate,   principle by which he loves and fears and joys
as well as they have attraction   and sorrows. . . .

p. 32   p. 32
!? What a poor argument   Matter cannot explain memory.
Liver continues to secrete bile, &
testes same vivifying semen!

p. 33   p. 33
As the elective affinity of a salt   (If materialism is true, animals are immortal.)
changes when its elements unite
in composition, so my mind.

Good   There are in the lower animals many of the
                                          phenomena of mind. . . .

                                          There are other principles superadded to material

DARWIN   ABERCROMBIE

things, of the nature of which we are equally
ignorant: − such, for example, as the principle
of vegetable life, and that of animal life. To say
that these are properties of matter, is merely
arguing about a term. . . .

p. 34   p. 34

It is sufficient to point out close   Whether in their substratum or ultimate essence,
relation of kind of thought and   they are the same, or whether they are different,
structure of brain.   we know not, and never can know in our present
                                       state of being. Let us, then, be satisfied with the
                                       facts, when our utmost faculties can carry us no
                                       farther; let us cease to push our feeble specula-
                                       tions, when our duty is only to wonder and
                                       adore."

17. Charles Darwin, manuscript folio #91, sides 34−38; University Library, Cambridge University. See Barrett (1974), pp. 392−395.
18. C. Darwin, "On the Moral Sense," manuscript folio #91, side 42 (Barrett, p. 398).
19. *Metaphysical Notebook M*, p. 151.
20. *Transmutation Notebook C.*, p. 154.
21. *Metaphysical Notebook N*, pp. 107−109.
22. *Metaphysical Notebook M*, pp. 96−97.
23. *Metaphysical Notebook N*, p. 35.
24. *Metaphysical Notebook N*, p. 10.
25. *Metaphysical Notebook M*, p. 107.
26. *Notebook M*, p. 94.
27. *Notebook C*, p. 243.
28. *Notebook M*, pp. 92, 94.
29. *Ibid.*, p. 95.
30. *Ibid.*, p. 147.
31. *Notebook N*, pp. 7, 8.
32. *Notebook M*, p. 146; N, p. 9.
33. *Notebook N*, p. 13.
34. *Notebook N*, p. 9.
35. *Notebook N*, p. 104.
36. *Transmutation Notebook D*, p. 18.
37. *Metaphysical Notebook M*, p. 145, N, 11, 64, 65.
38. *Metaphysical Notebook N*, p. 37. See Paul Barrett, *op. cit.*, p. 354, note 161.
39. *Metaphysical Notebook N*, p. 18. Since expressive behavior exhibits individual variability and can, as in the decoying behavior of a bird feigning injury to lead a predator from its nest, have deceptive effects, claims that *human language* is an altogether different kind of behavior have to rest on traits other than man's obvious capacity for individually innovative or deceptive speech. One possibility is the syntactic organization of human speech. Darwin did *not* raise this or a comparable question. But his *Notebooks*

did anticipate a curiously syntactical theme from his later published work on expression: the principle of opposition.

> Why does dog put down ears when pleased. – it is opposite movement to drawing them close on head, when going to fight, in which case expression resembles a fox – I can conceive the opposite muscles would act, when in a passion. – dog tail curled when angry & very stiff. back arched. just contrary, when pleased tail loose & wagging – (*Metaphysical Notebook M*, pp. 146, 147; excised – published by Barrett (1974), p. 294.

Darwin's theory led him to consider the evolutionary and biological significance of all behavior, and of all behavioral forms. Naturally, he looked for parallelism in the opposition of emotional states, and in the organ systems (e.g., antagonistic muscles, or the antagonistic actions of the same muscles) used in expressing those states. He found that opposed intentions were expressed by the action of antagonistic muscles.

40. *Metaphysical Notebook N*, p. 107.

41. *Metaphysical Notebook N*, p. 109.

42. *Metaphysical Notebook N*, pp. 31, 65. Manuscript folio #91, sides 5, 13 ("Old & Useless Notes on Metaphysics").

43. *Transmutation Notebook E*, pp. 49–50. This theme appears for the first time at p. 167 of *D*, "One of the final causes of sexes to obliterate differences, final cause of this because the great changes of nature are slow. If animals became adapted to every minute change, they would not be fitted to the slow great changes really in progress. –"

44. Charles Darwin, "On the Moral Sense," manuscript filed with "Old and useless notes about the moral sense & some metaphysical points written about the year 1837 and earlier." *Charles Darwin manuscripts*, no. 91, Cambridge University Library. See Barrett edition, p. 402, note 2.

45. Charles Darwin, *Transmutation Notebook E*, pp. 48–49.

46. Harriet Martineau, *How to Observe. Morals and Manners*, Knight, London, 1838, p. 22. See Barrett edition, p. 300, note 50. Darwin's *Metaphysical Notebook M*, p. 76 (Barrett, p. 279).

47. *Metaphysical Notebook M*, p. 132e. (This page was excised by Darwin, but found and replaced by Paul Barrett, see his edition, p. 291.)

"Sept. 8th. I am tempted to say that those action which have been found necessary for long generation, (as friendship to fellow animals in social animals) are those which are good & consequently give pleasure, & not as Paleys rule is then that on long run *will* do good. – alter *will* in all such case to *have*, & origin as well as rule *will* be given. –"

I do not agree with Barrett (p. 303, note 100) that 'Paleys rule' here refers to Paley's "law of honour." Instead, the reference is to Paley's utilitarian interpretation of all moral rules. Where Paley sought to use theology to buttress an otherwise unsupported claim that virtuous action was that which would do good "in the long run," Darwin sought to develop a naturalistic focus upon *evolutionary origins* of the moral sense.

48. *Metaphysical Notebook M*, pp. 150–151.

49. *Metaphysical Notebook N*, pp. 107, 109.

50. *Essay of 1844*, de Beer ed., p. 120. "Besides this natural means of selection . . . there is a second agency at work in most bisexual animals tending to produce the same effect, namely the struggle of the males for the females. These struggles are generally decided by the law of battle; but in the case of birds, apparently, by the charms of their

song, by their beauty or their power of courtship, as in the dancing rock-thrush of Guiana."

51. Charles Darwin, *Descent of Man*, 2nd ed., Murray, London: 1879, pp. 616–617. "He who admits the principle of sexual selection will be led to the remarkable conclusion that the nervous system not only regulates most of the existing functions of the body, but has indirectly influenced the progressive development of various bodily structures and of certain mental qualities. Courage, pugnacity, perseverance, strength and size of body, weapons of all kinds, musical organs, both vocal and instrumental, bright colours and ornamental appendages, have all been indirectly gained by the one sex or the other, through the exertion of choice, the influence of love and jealousy, and the appreciation of the beautiful in sound, colour or form; and these powers of the mind manifestly depend on the development of the brain."

52. *Transmutation Notebook E*, p. 114.

53. "On the Moral Sense," side 42, Barrett (1974), p. 398.

54. *Ibid.*, side 51, Barrett, pp. 402–403.

55. See Table VI.

56. "On the Moral Sense," side 50, Barrett, pp. 401–402.

57. *Ibid.*, side 45, Barrett, p. 399.

58. *Ibid.*, side 47, Barrett, p. 400.

59. *Ibid.*, side 49, Barrett, p. 401.

60. *Ibid.*, side 48, Barrett, pp. 400–401.

61. C. H. Waddington (1961), caught the tenor of Darwin's approach most accurately.

62. Charles Darwin, "On the Moral Sense," side 50, Barrett, pp. 401–402.

63. The following note, filed by Charles Darwin with his "Old and useless notes on the moral sense. . . ." demonstrates the basically antithetical relationship of Darwin's views and those of Bentham. Darwin sought to show that his view would unite, or show to be almost identical, the doctrines of utilitarianism and the moral sense school. But since Darwin's view was that the moral sense was truly hereditary, or innate, he could not have been more solidly opposed to Bentham's position.

[OUN$_{30}$] October 2^{d}. 1838

Two classes of moralists: one says our rule of life is what *will* produce the greatest happiness. – The other says we have a moral sense. – But my view unites** both /& shows them to be almost identical /& what *has* produced the greatest good/ or rather what was necessary for good at all/ (& this alone explains why our moral sense <points> [prevents?] <is> to revenge). In judging of the rule of happiness we must look *far forward* /& to the general action/ – certainly because it is the result of what has *generally* been best for our good *far back* – (much further than we can look forward: hence our rule may sometimes be hard to tell)

The difference between civilized man & savage, is that the former is endeavoring to change that part of the moral sense which experience (education is the experience of others) shows does not tend to greatest good. – Therefore rule of happiness is to certain degree right. – The change of our moral sense is strictly analogous to change of instinct among animals. –

    **Society could not go on except for the moral sense, anymore than a hive of Bees without their instincts.

Michael Ghiselin, "Darwin and Evolutionary Psychology," *Science* (1973), 179, pp. 964–968, completely ignores Darwin's account of the moral sense and his critique of utilitarianism.

CHAPTER NINE

1. C. C. Gillispie (1959), makes this point.
2. Benjamin Smart (1838), p. 52.
3. *Essay of 1844*, de Beer ed., p. 114.
4. *Ibid.*, p. 115.
5. The theory of metaphor which was explicitly stated by Dugald Stewart and elaborated by Benjamin Smart has interesting similarities to the "interaction" interpretation of scientific metaphor advocated by Mary Hesse (1964).
6. *Transmutation Notebook D*, p. 117.
7. *Transmutation Notebook E*, p. 51.
8. Gillispie (1959), pp. 268–277.
9. Bernal (1954), vol. 4, p. 1233.
10. *Metaphysical Notebook N*, p. 3.
11. The quotation is from Darwin's manuscript commentary on Mackintosh's history of ethics. See side #42 from folio #91 ("old and useless notes. . .") from the Charles Darwin manuscripts, Cambridge University Library. Published on p. 398 of the Barrett edition (1974).
12. *Metaphysical Notebook N*, p. 47.
13. Quoted from the manuscript commentary on Macculloch (1838), published in the Barrett edition, pp. 417–418.
14. William Wordsworth, *The Excursion*, Book IV, lines 489 and following.
15. *Ibid.*, Book VII, lines 1000–1005.

CHAPTER TEN

1. Mary Hesse (1964), "The Explanatory Function of Metaphor," pp. 157–177. Professor Hesse's views on this subject have been more fully set forth in the context of the Duhem-Quine *network model* of scientific inference in her *The Structure of Scientific Inference* (1974), particularly pp. 197–222. In the latter work, Hesse writes "A normative critique of method may disclose the implicit aims of a methodology and judge the appropriateness of its means to its ends. A science whose aim is application and prediction may have different normative requirements from one which desires truth, beauty or morality. Sometimes comprehensive theories of maximum empirical content are appropriate, sometimes instrumentalist predictions, sometimes inductive inferences. It is a naive reading of the history of science to suppose that different methodologies are necessarily in conflict, given their different aims. The logic of science should provide a comparative study of such methodologies, rather than a partisan polemic on behalf of some against others" (p. 7).
2. Hesse, (1964), p. 158.
3. *Ibid.*, p. 164.

4. *Ibid.*, p. 167.
5. Both Robert Young (1971a) and B. G. Gale (1972) focus upon *one* of Darwin's metaphors to the exclusion of the others, Young dealing with 'selection,' and Gale with 'struggle.' Consequently, neither of them comes to grips with the *general* problem of the scientific uses of metaphor.
6. Hesse (1964), p. 169.
7. Gliserman (1975), p. 456.
8. de Beer, ed. (1958), pp. 45, 114–115.
9. *The Origin*, "Introduction," 25 (Peckham ed., p. 37).
10. de Beer, ed. (1958), pp. 115–116.
11. *The Origin*, III. 146, p. 160.
12. *Oxford English Dictionary* (1963), volume X, pp. 1166–1167.
13. Wedgwood (1872).
14. Gale (1972) says that the literal and metaphorical uses of 'struggle' describe "just about opposite" situations.
15. Stauffer, ed. (1975), pp. 175ff.
16. C. Darwin, *Notebook M*, pp. 15, 19, 80. "The possibility of the brain having whole train of thoughts, feeling & perception separate from the ordinary state of mind, is probably analogous to the double individuality implied by habit, when one acts unconsciously with respect to more energetic self, & likewise one forgets what one performs habitually. – Agrees with insanity, as in Dr. Ashe's case, when he struggles as it were with a second & unreasonable man." Dr. Ashe suffered from recurrent delusions of economic ruin, which he struggled against by "keeping the sum-total of his accounts in his pocket." Charles Darwin had discussed this case with his physician father.
17. de Beer, ed. (1958), p. 116.
18. Hume's *Dialogues concerning Natural Religion* suggest that the deistic argument from design (formulated by Cleanthes in the *Dialogues*) did not really establish the existence of a creator distinct from the world itself. The skeptical protagonist of the *Dialogues*, Philo, further insinuated that not only was there no reason to assume that the god of the deists could be distinguished from the soul of the world, but there was no evidence to support the claim the so-called natural and moral attributes of the divine being (power, intelligence and benevolence) were united in a *single* being.
19. de Beer, ed. (1958), p. 204.

CHAPTER ELEVEN

1. Kuhn (1970), p. 177. It is plausible that different research communities in different sciences at different stages in history are characterized by different degrees of consensus, ranging from near unanimity to strong conflict and polemical advocacy. At this point, no philosopher, historian, nor sociologist studying the processes of science has provided an effective measure of such variations in consensus. Toulmin (1972, pp. 200–319, 484–503), provides the most extensive philosophical discussion of this problem, but gives no attention to the implications of alternatives to consensus or "exchange" models of the social structure to be found in scientific communities. See Mitroff (1974), 229–250.
2. Kadushin (1968), p. 692.
3. See N. Mullins (1973), pp. 18–33, and (1975), for a discussion of the relations

connecting members of what he calls "small coherent, activist theory groups." Mullins distinguishes four stages in the historical development of a theory group. His model requires the production of an exemplary paradigm development in the *first* of these four stages and provides a sociological explanation of the "gestalt shift" or change in perception of the topic or topics under investigation which, as he seems to agree with Kuhn, is necessary for the production of significant cognitive novelty. The notions of metaphor, cultural influence, and cultural circle employed in my account of the paradigmatic accomplishment of the young Darwin suggests that no purely sociological explanation of such "shifts" will be adequate. A satisfactory explanatory model must include historical studies of social and cultural circles and philosophical studies of the uses of *language* which underlie the cognitive products of those circles.

4. Diana Crane (1972), pp. 1–21.

5. Ben-David (1971), p. 8.

6. *Ibid.*, p. 11.

7. The development of the concepts of population structure and social instincts in the young Darwin's private papers and notebooks has been discussed above in Chapter 8, Sections 3 and 4, on expression and language, and social instincts and moral sentiments.

8. Merton (1973), Storer, ed., pp. 7–40.

9. Bernal (1954), as in Pelican (1969) edition, vol. 3, pp. 558, 662, vol. 4, pp. 1233–1235.

BIBLIOGRAPHY

I. PRIMARY SOURCES

A. PAPERS

The Darwin Collection, Anderson Room, University Library, Cambridge University, Cambridge, England.

Darwin, C.: 1837a–1838a, *Transmutation Notebook B.*
Darwin, C.: 1838b, *Transmutation Notebook C.*
Darwin, C.: 1838c, *Transmutation Notebook D.*
Darwin' C.: 1838d–1839a, *Transmutation Notebook E.*
Darwin, C.: 1838e, *Metaphysical Notebook M.*
Darwin, C.: 1838f–1839b, *Metaphysical Notebook N.*
Darwin, C.: 1837b–1840a, "Old and Useless Notes about the moral sense & some metaphysical points written about the year 1837 & earlier."
Darwin, C.: 1838g, "On Macculloch, Attributes of the Deity."
Darwin, C.: 1842, *The Sketch of 1842.*
Darwin, C.: 1844, *The Essay of 1844.*

B. LIBRARY

Books from Darwin's personal library at the Anderson Room, University Library, Cambridge University, Cambridge, England.

Abercrombie, J.: 1838, *Inquiries Concerning the Intellectual Powers and the Investigation of Truth*, 8th ed., Edinburgh.
Barclay, J.: 1822, *Inquiry into the Opinions, Ancient and Modern, Concerning Life and Organization*, Edinburgh.
Fleming, J.: 1822, *Philosophy of Zoology*, 2 vols., Edinburgh.
Herschel, J.: 1831, *A Preliminary Discourse on the Study of Natural Philosophy*, Lardner's, London.
Lamarck, J.: 1830, *Philosophie Zoologique*, Paris.
Lawrence, W.: 1822, *Lectures on Physiology, Zoology and the Natural History of Man, Delivered at the Royal College of Surgeons*, London.
Lyell, C.: 1830, 1832, 1833, *Principles of Geology*, 3 vols., John Murray, London.
Mackintosh, J.: 1837, *Dissertation on the Progress of Ethical Philosophy*, Edinburgh.
Malthus, T.: 1826, *An Essay on the Principle of Population*, 6th ed., 2 vols., London.
Wedgwood, H.: 1848, *On the Development of the Understanding*, Taylor and Walton, London.
Wedgwood, H.: 1872, *A Dictionary of English Etymology*, 2nd ed., Trubner, London.
Whewell, W.: 1837, *History of the Inductive Sciences*, 3 vols., London.

232 BIBLIOGRAPHY

C. PUBLISHED PRIMARY SOURCES

Barlow, N. (ed.): 1958, *The Autobiography of Charles Darwin*, Cambridge University Press.

Barrett, P. and Gruber, H. (eds.): 1974, *Darwin on Man*, Dutton, New York. (*Notebooks M, N*, "Old and Useless notes on the moral sense. . . ," and the Commentary on Macculloch.)

Darwin, C. 1868, *The Variation of Animals and Plants under Domestication*, 2 vols., Murray, London.

Darwin, C.: 1879: *Descent of Man*, 2nd ed., Murray, London.

Darwin, F. (ed.): 1908, "Charles Darwin, The Sketch of 1842 and The Essay of 1844," in G. de Beer (ed.), *Evolution by Natural Selection*, Cambridge University Press, 1958.

Darwin, F.: 1887, *The Life and Letters of Charles Darwin*, 3 vols., John Murray, London.

Darwin, F. and Seward, A.: 1903, *More Letters of Charles Darwin*, 2 vols., John Murray, London.

De Beer, G., *et. al.* (eds.): 1960–1967, *Darwin's Notebooks on Transmutation of Species*, Parts I–VI, in *Bulletin of the British Museum* (Natural History, Historical Series), London, vol. 2, nos. 2–6, vol. 3, no. 5.

Peckham, M. (ed.): 1959, *Charles Darwin, The Origin of Species, in the Variorum Text*, University of Pennsylvania, Philadelphia.

Stauffer, R. (ed.): 1975, *Charles Darwin's Natural Selection, Being the Second Part of His Big Species Book Written from 1856 to 1858*, Cambridge University Press.

II. OTHER PRIMARY AND SECONDARY SOURCES

anon.: 1840, "Review of Coleridge," *London & Westminster Review* 65, 257–302.

Barbour, I.: 1976, *Myths, Models and Paradigms, A Comparative Study in Science and Religion*, Harper & Row, New York.

Basalla, G., *et. al.* (eds.): 1970, *Victorian Science, a Self-Portrait from the Presidential Addresses to the British Association for the Advancement of Science*, Doubleday, New York.

Beckner, M.: 1968, *The Biological Way of Thought*, University of California Press, Berkeley (1st published, 1959).

Ben-David, J.: 1971, *The Scientist's Role in Society*, Prentice-Hall, Englewood Clifts, New Jersey.

Berger, P. & Luckman, T.: 1967, *The Social Construction of Reality*, Doubleday Anchor, New York (1st published, 1966).

Bernal, J.: 1953, *Science and Industry in the Nineteenth Century*, Routledge & Kegan Paul, London.

Bernal, J.: 1954, *Science in History*, 4 vols., C. A. Watts & Co., Ltd. (3rd ed. published by C. A. Watts and Pelican Books, 1969).

Black, M.: 1962, *Models and Metaphors*, Cornell University Press, Ithaca, New York.

Brewster, D. (anon.): 1838, "Review of Comte's *Cours de Philosophie Positive*," *Edinburgh Review* 67, 271–308.

Brewster, D. (anon.): 1834, "Review of Astronomy and General Physics considered with reference to Natural Theology. by Rev. Wm. Whewell," *Edinburgh Review* 58, 422–457.

Brown, R. (ed.): 1970, *Between Hume and Mill*, Modern Library, New York.

Buchdahl, G.: 1971, "Inductivist vs. Deductivist Approaches in the Philosophy of Science as Illustrated by Some Controversies between Whewell and Mill," *Monist* 55, 343–367.

Burrow, J.: 1970, *Evolution and Society, A Study in Victorian Social Theory*, Cambridge University Press, Cambridge, (1st published, 1966).

Buttman, G.: 1970, *The Shadow of the Telescope: A Biography of John Herschel*, trans. B. Pagel, New York.

Cockshut, A.: 1964, *The Unbelievers: English Agnostic Thought*, 1840–1890, London.

Coleman, W.: 1971, *Biology in the Nineteenth Century: Problem of Form, Function, and Transformation*, John Wiley, New York.

Crane, D.: 1972, *Invisible Colleges*, University of Chicago Press, Chicago.

de Beer, G.: 1963, *Charles Darwin*, Nelson, London.

Doubleday, T.: 1842, *The True Law of Population Shown to be Connected with the Food of the People*, Simpkin, Marshal, London.

Douglas, M.: 1970, *Natural Symbols, Explorations in Cosmology*, Random House, Vintage Books, New York.

Eiseley, L.: 1958, *Darwin's Century: Evolution and the Men Who Discovered It*, Doubleday, New York.

Ellegard, A.: 1958, *Darwin and the General Reader: The Reception of Darwin's Theory of Evolution in the British Periodical Press*, Goteborgs Universitets Arsskrift, Gothenberg.

Elliot, H., trans.: 1914, *Lamarck's Zoological Philosophy*, Macmillan, London (republished, Hafner, 1963).

Etzioni, A.: 1968, *The Active Society*, Free Press, New York.

Ferrier, J.: 1838a, "An Introduction to the Philosophy of Consciousness," *Blackwood's Magazine* 43, 187–201, 437–452, 784–791.

Ferrier, J.: 1838b, "An Introduction to the Philosophy of Consciousness," *Blackwood's Magazine* 44, 234–244, 539–552.

Ferrier, J.: 1839, "An Introduction to the Philosophy of Consciousness," *Blackwood's Magazine* 45, 201–211, 419–430.

Freeman, R. and Gautrey, P.: 1969, "Darwin's *Questions about the Breeding of Animals*, with a Note on *Queries about Expression*," *Journal of the Society for Bibliography in Natural History* 5, 220–225.

Gale, B. G.: 1972, "Darwin and the Concept of a Struggle for Existence: A Study in the Extra-scientific Origins of Scientific Ideas," *Isis* 63, 321–344.

Ghiselin, M.: 1969, *The Triumph of the Darwinian Method*, University of California Press, Berkeley.

Ghiselin, M.: 1973, "Darwin and Evolutionary Psychology," *Science* 179, 964–968.

Gillispie, C.: 1959a, *Genesis and Geology, the Impact of Scientific Discoveries upon Religious Beliefs in the Decades before Darwin*, Harper, New York (1st published, 1951).

Gillispie, C.: 1959b, "Lamarck and Darwin in the History of Science," in B. Glass, et. al. (eds.), *Forerunners of Darwin*, The Johns Hopkins Press, Baltimore, 1959, pp. 265–291.

Giere, R.: 1973, "History and Philosophy of Science: Intimate Relationship or Marriage of Convenience," *British Journal for the Philosophy of Science* 24, 282–297.

Glass, B., *et al.*: 1959, *Forerunners of Darwin*: 1745–1859, The Johns Hopkins Press, Baltimore.

Gliserman, S.: 1975, "Early Victorian Science Writers and Tennyson's 'In Memoriam': A Study in Cultural Exchange," *Victorian Studies* 18, 277–308, 437–459.

Goodfield, J.: 1969, "Some Aspects of English Physiology: 1780–1840," *Journal of the History of Biology* 2, 283–320.

Grave, S.: 1960, *The Scottish Philosophy of Common Sense*, Oxford University Press.

Greene, J.: 1959, *The Death of Adam*, Iowa State University Press, Ames.

Grene, M.: 1966, *The Knower and the Known*, Basic Books, New York.

Grene, M. and Mendelsohn, E. (eds.): 1975, *Topics in the Philosophy of Biology*, Boston Studies in The Philosophy of Science, vol. 27 (Synthese Library) Reidel, Dordrecht, Holland.

Habermas, J.: 1971, *Toward a Rational Society*, J. Shapiro, trans., Beacon Press, Boston.

Habermas, J.: 1972, *Knowledge and Human Interests*, trans. J. Shapiro, Heinemann, London.

Handlist of Darwin Papers at the University Library, Cambridge: 1960, Cambridge University Press.

Hartley, D.: 1749, *Observations on Man, His Frame, His Duty, and His Expectations.* 2 vols., London (Facsimile published in 1971, Garland, New York).

Herbert, S.: 1968, *The Logic of Darwin's Discovery*, Unpublished dissertation, Brandeis University.

Herbert, S.: 1971, "Research Note: Darwin, Malthus and Selection," *Journal of the History of Biology* 4, 209–217.

Herschel, J.: 1841, "Review of Whewell's History of the Inductive Sciences and Whewell's Philosophy of the Inductive Sciences," *Quarterly Review* 68, 177–238.

Herschel, J.: 1850, "Review of Quetelet," *Edinburgh Review* 92, 1–57.

Hesse, M.: 1964, *Models and Analogies in Science*, University of Notre Dame Press, Notre Dame.

Hesse, M.: 1974, *The Structure of Scientific Inference*, University of California Press, Berkeley.

Himmelfarb, G.: 1962, *Darwin and the Darwinian Revolution*, Doubleday, New York.

Himmelfarb, G.: 1968, *Victorian Minds*, A. Knopf, New York.

Houghton, W. (ed.): 1966, *Wellesley Index for Victorian Periodicals: 1824–1900*, Toronto.

Hull, D.: 1967, "The Metaphysics of Evolution," *British Journal for the History of Science* 3, 309–337.

Hull, D.: 1973, *Darwin and His Critics: The Reception of Darwin's Theory of Evolution by the Scientific Community*, Harvard University Press, Cambridge.

Hume, D.: 1779, *Dialogues concerning Natural Religion*, in C. Hendel, Jr. (ed.), *Hume Selections*, Scribner's, New York, 1927 and 1955.

Huntley, W.: 1972, "David Hume and Charles Darwin," *Journal of the History of Ideas* 33, 457–470.

Huzel, J.: 1969, "Malthus, the Poor Law, & Population in Early Nineteenth Century England," *Economic History Review* 22, 430–452.

Kadushin, C.: 1968, "Power, Influence and Social Circles: A New Methodology for Studying Opinion Makers," *American Sociological Review* 33, 685–699.

Kirby, W.: 1835, *On the Power Wisdom and Goodness of God as Manifested in the*

Creation of Animals and in Their History, Habits and Instincts, 2 vols., London.

Kuhn, S.: 1970, *The Structure of Scientific Revolutions*, 2nd ed., University of Chicago Press.

Lakatos, I. and Musgrave, A.: 1970, *Criticism and the Growth of Knowledge*, Cambridge University Press.

Laudan, L.: 1971, "Towards a Reassessment of Comte's 'Methode Positive'," *Philosophy of Science* 38, 35–53.

Laudan, L.: 1971, "William Whewell on the Consilience of Inductions," *Monist* 55, 368–391.

Lyell, C.: 1835, *Principles of Geology*, 4th ed. 3 vols., John Murray, London.

MacCormac, E.: 1971, "Meaning Variance and Metaphor," *British Journal for the Philosophy of Science* 22, 145–159.

Macculloch, J.: 1838, *Proofs and Illustrations of the Attributes of God*, London.

MacIntyre, A.: 1966, *A Short History of Ethics*, Macmillan, London.

Malthus, T.: 1798, *An Essay on the Principle of Population*, J. Johnson, London, reprinted in A. Flew (ed.) *Malthus: An Essay on the Principle of Population*, Penguin, 1970.

Mandelbaum, M.: 1958, "Darwin's Religious Views," *Journal of the History of Ideas* 19, 363–378.

Mandelbaum, M.: 1971, *History, Man & Reason: A Study in Nineteenth Century Thought*, Johns Hopkins Press, Baltimore.

Mandelbaum, M. (trans.): 1853, *August Comte, the Positive Philosophy*, 2 vols., London.

Martineau, H.: 1838, *How to Observe, Morals and Manners*, Knight, London.

McMullin, E.: 1975a, *History and Philosophy of Science: A Marriage of Convenience?* Boston Studies in the Philosophy of Science, vol. 32, pp. 515–531, Reidel, Dordrecht, Holland.

McMullin, E.: 1975b, "Philosophy of Science and Its Rational Reconstructions," for the Kronberg Conference on Progress in Science and Methodology. Forthcoming.

Merton, R.: 1970, *Science, Technology and Society in Seventeenth-Century England*, Harper, New York (1st published, 1938).

Merton, R.: 1973, "A Paradigm for the Sociology of Knowledge," in N. Storer (ed.), *The Sociology of Science*, University of Chicago Press.

Mitroff, I.: 1974, *The Subjective Side of Science*, Elsevier, Amsterdam.

Monod, J.: 1971, *Chance and Necessity*, A. Wainhouse, trans., A. A. Knopf, New York.

Mullins, N.: 1973, *Theories & Theory Groups in Contemporary American Sociology*, Harper & Row, New York.

Mullins, N.: 1975, "A Sociological Theory of Scientific Revolution," in *Determinants and Controls of Scientific Development*, K. D. Knorr, et. al. (eds.), D. Reidel, Dordrecht, Holland.

Muret, M.: 1766, *Memoires, etc., par la Societé Economique de Berne*, Berne.

Murphy, A.: 1976, *Lyell's Principles of Geology*, unpublished dissertation, University of Notre Dame.

Paley, W.: 1794, *A View of the Evidences of Christianity*, 16th ed., 2 vols., London, 1817.

Paley, W.: 1802, *Natural Theology*, 18th ed., Alnwick, 1818.

Petersen, W.: 1969, *Population*, 2nd ed., Macmillan, London.

Poynter, J.: 1969, *Society and Pauperism: English Ideas on Poor Relief, 1795–1834*,

Routledge & Kegan Paul, London.

Ravetz, J.: 1971, *Scientific Knowledge and Its Social Problems*, Oxford University Press.

Rennell, T. (anon.): 1819, "Review," *Quarterly Review*, 1–34.

Rogers, J.: 1972, "Darwinism and Social Darwinism," *Journal of the History of Ideas* 33, 265–280.

Roget, P.: 1840, *Animal and Vegetable Physiology*, 3rd ed., Pickering, London.

Rose, H. and Rose, S.: 1970, *Science and Society*, Pelican, London.

Rudwick, M.: 1972, *The Meaning of Fossils: Episodes in the History of Palaeontology*, Elsevier, New York.

Ruse, M.: 1974, "The Darwin Industry – A Critical Evaluation," *History of Science* 12, 43–58.

Ruse, M.: (forthcoming), "Darwin's Debt to Philosophy."

Rutherford, H.: 1908, *Catalogue of the Library of Charles Darwin now in the Botany School, Cambridge*, Cambridge University Press (P. Gautrey's current annotation in the Anderson Room, University Library, Cambridge).

Scheffler, I.: 1963, *The Anatomy of Inquiry*, Knopf, New York.

Scheffler, I.: 1967, *Science and Subjectivity*, Bobbs-Merrill, New York.

Simon, W.: 1963, *European Positivism in the Nineteenth Century*, Cornell University Press, Ithaca, New York.

Simpson, G.: 1967, *The Meaning of Evolution*, revised ed., Yale University Press, New Haven.

Smart, B.: 1839, *Beginnings of a New School of Metaphysics*, London.

Smith, S.: 1965, "The Darwin Collection at Cambridge with One Example of Its Use: Charles Darwin and *Cirripedes*," *Actes du XIe Congres International D'Histoire des Sciences. Extrait*, 96–100.

Smith, S.: 1960, "The Origin of 'The Origin,'" *Advancement of Science* (British Association for the Advancement of Science) **64**, 391–402.

Stephen, L.: 1876, *History of English Thought in the Eighteenth Century* 1902, 3rd ed., 2 vols., London (Reprinted in New York, 1927).

Stephen, L. and Lee, S.: 1921–1922, *The Dictionary of National Biography*, Oxford University Press.

Stewart, D.: 1792, "Elements of the Philosophy of the Human Mind," in W. Hamilton (ed.), *The Collected Works of Dugald Stewart*, Edinburgh, 1854 (Reprinted in 1971, International Publishers, Westmead, Farn Borough, Hauts).

Stewart, D.: 1810, *Philosophical Essays*, 3rd ed., 1818, Edinburgh.

Storer, N.: 1966, *The Social System of Science*, Holt, Rinehart & Winston, New York.

Thompson, D.: 1950, *England in the Nineteenth Century*, Penguin, London.

Toulmin, S. and Goodfield, J.: 1965, *The Discovery of Time*, Harper & Row, New York.

Toulmin, S.: 1972, *Human Understanding*, Oxford University Press.

Vorzimmer, P.: 1969, "Darwin, Malthus, and the Theory of Natural Selection," *Journal of the History of Ideas* 30, 527–542.

Vorzimmer, P.: 1970, *Charles Darwin: The Years of Controversy*, Temple University Press, Philadelphia.

Waddington, C.: 1961, *The Ethical Animal*, Atheneum, New York.

Whewell, W.: 1838, 1839, "Presidential Addresses," *Proceedings of the Geological Society*, 2–642ff., 3–61ff.

Whewell, W.: 1857, *History of the Inductive Sciences*, 3 vols. and *Philosophy of the*

Inductive Sciences, 2 vols., in G. Buchdahl and L. Laudan (eds.), *The Historical and Philosophical Works of William Whewell*, Frank Cass & Co. London, 1967.

Whewell, W.: 1833, *Astronomy and General Physics considered with reference to Natural Theology*, Pickering, London.

Willey, B.: 1940, *The Eighteenth Century Background*, reprint, Boston, 1961.

Wilson, L. G.: 1970, *Sir Charles Lyell's Scientific Journals on the Species Question*, Yale University Press, New Haven.

Wilson, L. G.: 1972, *Charles Lyell, The Years to 1841: The Revolution in Geology*, Yale University Press, New Haven.

Wordsworth, W.: 1814, "*The Excursion*," in E. de Selincourt and H. Darbishire (eds.), *Wordsworth's Poetical Works*, Oxford, 1949.

Young, R.: 1969, "Malthus and the Evolutionists," *Past and Present* 43, 109–145.

Young, R.: 1970, *Mind, Brain and Adaption in the Nineteenth Century, Cerebral localization and its biological context from Gall to Ferrier*, Clarendon Press, Oxford.

Young, R.: 1971a, "Darwin's Metaphor: Does Nature Select?" *Monist* 55, 442–503.

Young, R.: 1971b, "Evolutionary Biology and Ideology: Then and Now," *Science Studies* 1, 177–206.

INDEX

Abercrombie, J. 20, 59–60, 127, 129, 218 n. 6, 223–25 n. 16
adaptation 54, 122
agnosticism 88
alienation 84, 93, 186, 196
analogy 7, 16, 49, 77, 106, 111
animal psychology 57
anthropomorphism 6, 42, 84–85, 213 n. 50, 217 n. 33
atheism 31, 66, 186
audience created by Darwin's metaphors 150–51, 153

Barclay, J. 20, 58–59
beauty, origin of idea of 140
Beckner, M. 39
Ben-David, J. 189
benevolence 142
Bernal, J. D. 79, 84, 192
biologism in political economy 84
Brewster, D. 28–29, 40, 123
Brown, T. 59–60
Butler, Bishop Joseph 97–98

capitalism 79, 163, 192
Carlyle, T. 178
cause 3, 47–48
chance 3, 117–23, 194; Aristotelian theory of, 118, 159, 170; Comte's critique of, 217 n. 37; Malthus' and Paley's views on, 74–75; metaphorical expression of, 118, 186; and 'war' in Darwin's usage, 121
circle, cultural 1, 14–18, 20, 151, 168–71, 187–90; social, Kadushin's definition of 187–88
classification of sciences 43
colleague 23
communication, scientific 79–85
communities, scientific 187

Comte, August 15, 20, 40–47; distinction of fundamental laws and historical laws, 113; fictions in science, 44, 205 n. 27; functionalism, 157, 168; historical relativism, 205 n. 26; influence on Darwin's concept of design, 167–68; Lamarck, critique of, 45–47, 112; law, concept of, 123; verification, theory of, 205 n. 22; will, critique of, 128
consciousness 57–58, 126–46
consensus 69, 80–85, 229 n. 1
continuity, of mental phenomena in man and simplest organisms 61, 127; of nature, 85; of vital and mental phenomena, 67
contrivance, Paley's account of 72
Crane, D. 188
culture 23; shift in context of Darwin's scientific theory, 193
cultural circle. See circle, cultural.
cultural criticism of science 168–71
cultural elite 188–89
cultural significance of Darwin's theory 58, 94, 208 n. 1
cultural tension 15, 27–33, 173; and emotional ambivalence concerning science, by Lyell and Darwin, 29
Cuvier, G. 53

Darwin, Charles: anthropomorphism, 213 n. 50, 217 n. 33; author, 3, 110–11, 130, 199 n. 4; chance, 3, 117, 118, 159, 170, 194; consciousness, theory of, 135–36; cultural circle (*see* circle, cultural); Darwin family, 17, 18, 88; ethics (*see* morality, this entry); expression, theory of, 136, 137; first drafts of theory, 151, 193; free will, 127, 128; influence by British ethical tradition, 145–46; influence by